TEACHING ECONOMIC AWARENESS

TEACHING ECONOMIC AWARENESS

Edited for the Economics Association
by Richard Dunnill and Steve Hodkinson

Heinemann Educational Books

Acknowledgements

Heinemann Educational Books Ltd
22 Bedford Square, London WC1B 3HH

LONDON   EDINBURGH   MELBOURNE   AUCKLAND
SINGAPORE   KUALA LUMPUR   NEW DELHI
IBADAN   NAIROBI   JOHANNESBURG
PORTSMOUTH (NH)   KINGSTON

© The Economics Association 1988

First published 1988

British Library Cataloguing in Publication Data

Teaching economic awareness
   1. Economics—Study and teaching
   (Secondary)—Great Britain
   I. Dunnill, Richard   II. Hodkinson, Steve
   III. Economics Association
   330'.07'1241   H62.5.G7

ISBN 0 435 33000 4

Designed and typeset by
Latimer Trend & Company Ltd, Plymouth

Illustrated by Gecko Ltd
Bicester, Oxon.

Printed and bound in Great Britain by
Thomson Litho Ltd, East Kilbride, Scotland.

The Publishers would like to thank the following for
permission to reproduce copyright material:
Economics Association, *Understanding Economics* series,
Economics Education 14–16 Project, 'Young Person as
a Producer', sponsored by the Economics Association,
Longman Publishers, 1985, for extracts 1–4 on p. 37
and for the graph on p. 40 (adapted); the *Financial
Times* for the three maps and extracts on p. 13, and for
the 'World Economic Indicators' tables on p. 14;
Michael Smith for the article on p. 157–8 which
appeared in the *Guardian* of 24 September 1984;
Staffordshire Education Committee, *Geography in the
School Curriculum Local Industries*, (Occasional Paper 2),
1983, for the diagrams on p. 81 (left).

Contents

List of contributors

Christopher Andrews — Teacher of Economics, Cheslyn Hay High School, Staffordshire

Paul Clarke — Lecturer in Education, EcATT, University of London Institute of Education

Peter S. Clarke — Head of General Studies, North Manchester High School for Girls

Jim Cockburn — Head of Sixth Form, Cramlington High School, Northumberland

Peter J. Davies — Lecturer in Education, EcATT, University of Manchester

Richard Dunnill — Lecturer in Education, EcATT, University of Manchester

Barry Finlayson — Lecturer, Jordanhill College of Education, Glasgow

Ken Hall — Head of Economics, King James's High School, Knaresborough

Irene Hewitt — Principal Teacher, Larbert High School, Stirlingshire

Steve Hodkinson — Lecturer in Education, EcATT, University of Manchester

Matthew Jones — Politics Association

Phil Jones — Department of Trade and Industry Fellow, EcATT, University of London Institute of Education

Joe Kellaway — Coordinator for Economics, Mansfield High School, Brierfield, Lancashire

Jan Kelly — Deputy Director, Geography Schools and Industry Project, Oxford University, Department of Educational Studies

Barry King — Her Majesty's Inspectorate

Peter Leech — Deputy Headteacher, Burnholme School, York

Steve Lepper — Coordinator for Economic and Political Awareness, Great Cornard Upper School, Suffolk

Jean Long — DES Fellow, University of Manchester and St Wilfrid's C. of E. High School, Lancashire

Stuart Lunn — Head of Social Studies Faculty, Connah's Quay High School, Clwyd and representative of The Association for the Teaching of the Social Sciences (ATSS)

Barry McClelland — Head of Economics, King David High School, Manchester

Paulette McLoughlin — Head of Economic Understanding, Droylsden High School for Girls, Tameside

Patricia McNally — Coordinator, Economics Education Project, Northern Ireland Council for Educational Development (NICED)

Jan Meadowcroft — Head of Humanities Levenshulme High School for Girls, Manchester

Joy Muir — Head of Economics, The Wallace High School, Northern Ireland

Elaine Owen — Advisory Teacher in Business Studies/Economic Understanding, Tameside

Ian Pearce — Deputy Director, Centre for the Study of Comprehensive Schools, University of York

Elizabeth Pollock — Head of Business Studies, Bangor Girls High School, Northern Ireland

Steve Rowe — Advisory Teacher, TVEI, Enfield

Mike Ryan — Assistant Principal Teacher, Economics and Modern Studies, Jordanhill College School, Glasgow

Brian Stevens — Manager, Banking Information Service

Allan Stewart — Deputy Director, Economics Association Economics Education 14–16 Project

Angus Taylor — Headteacher, Cramlington High School, Northumberland

Linda Thomas — Lecturer in Education, EcATT, University of London Institute of Education

Peter Thomas — Head of Economics, Business Studies and PSD, Ashington High School, Northumberland

Tony Turner — Senior Teacher, Glebelands School, Surrey

Sara Wall — Head of Economics, Southgate School, Enfield

Alan Walmsley — Her Majesty's Inspectorate

Margaret Walters — Senior Lecturer in Careers, Richmond-upon-Thames College

Sue Walton — Heinemann Educational Books

Sarah Wilkinson — Head of Economics, Politics and Sociology, West Hatch High School, Chigwell, Essex

Preface

The school case studies which form the heart of this publication result from a seminar which was organized by the Economics Association and held at the University of Manchester in February 1987. The seminar was funded by grants from our publisher, the Banking Information Service, BP plc, the Department of Trade and Industry, the Economics Association, the Northern Ireland Council for Educational Development and the School Curriculum Development Committee: without their support and encouragement the seminar could not have taken place.

The success of this first seminar on economic awareness was due mainly to the commitment of the participants both in preparing their papers in advance and in the discussions at the seminar. Special thanks are due to our publisher, Sue Walton of Heinemann Educational, and to Eileen Baines and Doreen Stoodley in the EcATT office at Manchester for their extraordinary work in preparing the papers and arranging the seminar.

The Economics Association's organizing group, which comprised the editors, Barry Finlayson and Linda Thomas, invited all members of the Economics Association to submit case study proposals. Hard choices had to be made, and we were unable to invite many teachers whose work is suitable. The editors are responsible for the inclusion of the papers published here, though the responsibility for the content of the papers rests with the authors and their schools.

Richard Dunnill
Steve Hodkinson

General introduction

Background

Interest in the development of economic aware-ness in the UK has never been higher. In England and Wales, successive government publications and statements have recognized the important potential role of economics education in citizen-ship and in adult working life. Major public com-panies and financial institutions have identified economic awareness as a major thrust for their involvement in education and the community. The work of the Economics Association's Economics Education 14–16 Project has been prolific and its influence seminal. DES, LEAs, industry and com-merce and higher education have come together as partners to form the Economic Awareness Teacher Training Programme (EcATT), based at the University of London Institute of Education and the University of Manchester. And, most recently, the School Curriculum Development Committee has launched its initiative 'Educating for Economic Awareness' to coordinate the economic awareness movement nationally. In Northern Ireland, econ-omic awareness has been identified as an import-ant focus for the Department of Education's secondary school curriculum review, and the Northern Ireland Council for Educational Develop-ment's (NICED) Economics Education Project is nearing the end of its third year of successful and growing activities. In Scotland, with its central impetus, recent curriculum reform has ensured that opportunities exist for all young people to receive an economics education at secondary school and pilot work is being carried out in the early years of secondary schooling.

These initiatives and others have helped to create a climate in which the long-term goal of achieving an economically literate population is realizable.

The seminar

The seminar was the fourth to be organized by the Economics Association. Seminars in 1973 and 1975 had focused on 'O' and 'A' level and debated the differing viewpoints within the UK on the desir-ability of extending the teaching of economics to younger and less academically able young people. The 1985 international research seminar attempted to draw together the global research and develop-ment activities of economics educators.*

The purpose of this seminar was to provide an opportunity for teachers of economic awareness in schools to share the problems and development issues they had experienced in implementing econ-omic awareness programmes in differing curricular contexts. It was intended to:

- make a practical contribution to economic awareness teaching
- encourage teachers to reflect on their work in school and to make it available to the edu-cational community at large
- reveal the areas of progress and common concern in a number of schools where the need for economic awareness has been recognized
- bring together subject associations and organiz-ations with an interest in economic awareness in schools

The scope of discussion at the seminar was not restricted to any particular issue although it was aimed primarily at the 11–16 age group. Suffice to say that three themes dominated:

1) the need to describe the nature and meaning of economic awareness
2) the implications of choices being made by schools over the curriculum context for economic awareness
3) the process of introducing economic awareness into schools

Different perspectives on each of these themes exist and are reflected in the teachers' work which follows. Some schools envisage the development of economic awareness as a truly cross-curricular experience, an ambitious and long-term task; whilst others see the process beginning with short modules of work in years four and five, or as an opportunity to enhance departmental status. In Scotland, work with 12–14 year old students appears to be seen as preparation for specialist economics courses, whilst most of the examples from England and Northern Ireland are not seen as 'economics' but as 'economic understanding'. The educational background and training of the economic awareness teacher is an issue raised in many of the case studies – some still see the specialist economics teacher as the key deliverer, but others see a different role for that specialism, one of encouraging and supporting the professional development of any teacher who might become involved.

Two things, however, are certain:

1) no one felt the need to argue the case for economic awareness – all agreed that the case had been made and accepted nationwide
2) everyone saw economic awareness experiences as being for *all* students and, in the long term, necessary throughout the 5–19 years continuum.

The participants are, moreover, anxious that their work be read in the spirit in which it is offered – not as examples of 'best' practice, but as attempts to portray things as they are and to reflect on and review progress. The case studies are here to challenge and to be challenged. All hope that as a result of sharing their experiences, successes and failures, the national movement for economic awareness of which they form only a small part will take a further step forward.

*The collections of papers from the seminars held in Manchester (June 1973), Worcester (September 1975) and London (July 1985) were published as follows:

Whitehead, D. J. ed. *Curriculum Development in Economics*, Heinemann Educational, 1974.

Robinson, T. K. and Wilson, R. D. eds. *Extending Economics within the Curriculum*, Routledge and Kegan Paul, 1977.

Hodkinson, Steve R. and Whitehead, David J. eds. *Economics Education: Research and Development Issues*, Longman, 1986.

So, what's it all about?

The papers in this book portray nineteen schools, their teachers and pupils. Nineteen schools of all types, sizes and locations. Teachers of many subjects, ranging from economics and business studies, through PSE, history, careers, geography, pre-vocational, mathematics and English, and including biology, home economics and music. Students of all ages, from those of 11 to sixth-formers of 18. Nineteen schools bound by a common thread, that of exploring ways of developing economic awareness for all young people in their charge.

This section of the book is intended to act as a guide. To this end it attempts three things. First, it investigates some of the general issues arising from the case studies and the seminar at which they were considered. Second, the issues raised by the differing curriculum contexts in which economic awareness is placed are explored. Third, the grouping of the case studies into five clusters is explained.

Three main questions are dominant and run throughout:

1) what is economic awareness?
2) why is it important?
3) how can schools enable all pupils to become economically aware?

The editors have resisted the temptation to give personal responses to these questions or to summarize received views. An economic awareness bibliography is provided for those who wish to discover more about particular issues. Our task is to share the experiences of a group of teachers, to voice their thoughts, and to help comprehend their journeys. You are warmly invited to join in the quest.

What is economic awareness?

Is it a definition?

In discussing this issue, one participant at the seminar suggested (only half) jokingly; 'Economic awareness is about being streetwise without the jargon!'

Meanwhile, the papers present a range of descriptions. Muir describes three aspects for students to be aware of.

1) that every action of an individual involves choices and that these choices may imply costs and benefits not just for the individual but for society as a whole
2) how (productive resources) can be organized and how new technology has had an impact on methods of production
3) that spending is constrained by income and influenced by many other factors such as advertising.

However, later, she adds another:

4) 'to make them question the way things are done in our society'.

McLoughlin, on the other hand, views economic awareness as 'a way of thinking ... a means for pupils to assess and evaluate situations'. This is a view shared by Kellaway, who expresses it vividly as 'the ability to assess situations, events and processes (human activity) through the illuminating beam of economics'.

However, for most contributors such descriptions do not appear to come easily. For them, questions remain:

- 'What is a basic economics education?' and ... 'are concepts vital?' (Jones)
- 'What economic awareness ought to be taught to all of our pupils?' (Peter Thomas)
- 'What constitutes worthwhile experiences in economic awareness?' (seminar participant)

Nevertheless, the papers do present some recurrent themes which address the issue.

Is it the course?

Some portray their notions of economic awareness through the ways their different courses are constructed. In Scotland, Hewitt and Ryan describe courses which have been built from lists of concepts and skills, organized into clusters headed: production, consumption and exchange. Kellaway goes further in detailing a number of 'key concepts' and then devising lessons to act as 'concept carrying vehicles'.

Others use themes such as money management (Pollock, Muir), or employment and unemployment (Andrews, Leech, Hall and McMahon) to provide a focus for their courses, and one uses themes which students have identified as being important (Long).

Is it a process?

Many perceive it as a process of exploration, for themselves and their fellow-teachers as much as for the students. Andrews, who is working with over 200 students, makes the point that 10 members of staff are also involved, and that experience shows that 'no assumptions could be made about the economic awareness of staff'.

What seems clear from the case studies, and certainly emerged from the seminar discussions, is that an economic awareness description must go further than constructing lists of aims and objectives, concepts and themes. Peter Thomas recalls a meeting at which all the core course modules were explained to the Head of English, who agreed that much of the information transmitted during the course was useful and probably valuable in its own right, but asked: 'What do the pupils *do* in their lessons?'

It is at this point that a consensus seems to emerge. Economic awareness is described as being about:

- investigating
- collecting, analysing and evaluating data
- asking questions
- involving life and the community
- more than description ... a process of enquiry

Davies writes of students being 'encouraged to ask the questions which would help them make sense of the processes underpinning the evidence in front of them'.

Economic awareness is presented as being a student-centred, collaborative, active process which enables students to develop the necessary skills and information to become economically aware. The natural links between active learning and other curriculum initiatives are acknowledged – the active economic awareness classroom will also involve numeracy, literacy, graphicacy, social skill development and take account of political, social, moral, race and gender issues. As Clarke and Lepper explain, these natural links across the curriculum can prove a positive advantage: 'Economic awareness aids colleagues rather than adding to their burden.'

In viewing economic awareness this way, many acknowledge a debt to the Economics Education 14–16 Project and its materials *Understanding Economics* (Longman, 1985). These materials may have played little part in the course, but their underlying philosophy and techniques have been influential.

The case studies refer to other sources of material and there is clear evidence that much work is being done on designing new activities. Thus, several contributors incorporate students' comments and examples of work into the papers. Indeed, this was seen as a way in which the whole question of what 'economic awareness' is might be considered in the future. By observing and describing our classrooms, and presenting our students' responses and ideas, perhaps the notion of economic awareness might be more clearly developed. Certainly, the students' comments and work deserve close scrutiny (see Walters for instance).

None of the contributors claims to have resolved the issue. All admit that they are only starting the journey to an unknown destination. All view themselves as being involved in continuous improvement which benefits teachers as well as students. All agree on the need for work to proceed towards a realistic description of economic awareness which is process-oriented and encourages development. Most would agree that, at best, economic awareness means *the ability to evaluate critically the use of resources, by individuals, groups and communities in local, national and global contexts.*

One thing is certain: the work of developing further ideas about economic awareness will continue in the nineteen schools, albeit in many different ways. As Andrews say, 'it is a constant process of review and further development'.

Why are these schools working in economic awareness?
Is it that important?

Which key factors have influenced the school's work?

Some papers illustrate the influence of factors outside the school. Several refer to DES, HMI and SCDC documents as being instrumental in encouraging economic awareness (see, for instance, Clarke and Lepper, Jones, Taylor, Wilkinson and Wall). In Scotland the impetus came from a central government initiative in the 'social subjects' (see Hewitt and Ryan). In Northern Ireland, the Northern Ireland Council for Educational Development (NICED) was establishing an economic awareness curriculum project which schools were invited to join (Muir, McMahon and Pollock). However, despite the favourable climate which national pressures helped to create, other and more immediate reasons seem to have carried just as much weight.

LEA initiatives feature in many papers. More than half the case studies taken from the English system report on the effects of LEA initiatives. Some worked with Advisers or Inspectors in devising their courses, while others responded to documents. Thus, a local initiative. 'The Suffolk Curriculum', gave further support to Great Cornard School (Clarke and Lepper).

In Manchester, a reorganization of secondary education produced this statement from the LEA:

'There are aspects of life skills and knowledge needed for life in society which are unlikely to be learned unless taught in schools, e.g. some of the concepts of economics.' (McClelland *et al.*)

In Tameside, a letter from the LEA Adviser called for courses for all pupils dealing with 'how the country earns its living ... and the structures and purposes of small business and commercial ventures' (McLoughlin).

Two further external factors are apparent. First, the Economics Education 14–16 Project and its materials and their dissemination is given as another reason for a school working on economic awareness (Walters and Kellaway, for instance). Second, the fact that 1986 was Industry Year helped schools to develop economic awareness courses with a careers and industrial slant (see McMahon, Clarke and Lepper). Again, however, for all the apparent importance of these external factors, almost all cite internal reasons as being just as important in facilitating the development of courses in economic awareness.

In two of the schools, economic awareness is being used as a focus for cross-curricular developments. Long explains how 12 staff were seen as providing a possible cross-curricular dimension to economic awareness. Clarke and Lepper describe a school that has adopted economic awareness as a key factor in its curriculum plan: 'Economic awareness was a good "link" between subjects and helped to place subject material in a "life skills" context.'

In three schools economic awareness is providing the focus to reinvigorate core courses. McMahon, for instance, writes disparagingly of his careers course: 'The materials used remained patchy and the course lacked coherent themes.'

Several papers describe the use of economic awareness as a way of encouraging more active teaching and learning strategies inside their schools and of promoting teacher development. Thus Leech and Hall maintain that 'emphasis was ... shifted away from the transmission of theory' towards, as Leech and Hall put it, 'learning strategies which involved pupils in doing things and studying real life situations, where possible at first hand'. (See also Clarke and Lepper, Andrews, Long, McClelland and others.)

Finally, in some schools, the flexibility of arrangements in parts of the curriculum enabled economic awareness courses to be developed because the curriculum was always changing to accommodate fresh ideas. The paper by Peter Thomas, for example, describes 10 years of continuous review and change.

Through a combination of some or all of these internal and external influences, the nineteen schools have been able to begin the development of programmes of economic awareness.

A justification?

As noted in the Preface, few of the contributors felt the need to justify economic awareness as an essential component of a youngster's education. To make the point, however, suffice to mention three papers and one statement made in the seminar.

Jones, Linda Thomas and Long all describe situations which are unashamedly idealistic. Jones writes of an institution proud to be a comprehensive school, Thomas of a course designed to present a world perspective, and Long of challenging the male image of economics education. Many of the others are aiming just as high in their hopes and their work. The economic awareness movement is built on such foundations. As one speaker at the seminar said: 'We are all affected by the economy – we all have a right to understand it!'

Perhaps this is the only justification that really matters.

How are the schools developing programmes of economic awareness?

Prior to addressing this issue, it is worth pausing to consider the wider context in which all the nineteen schools are operating.

All have been involved to varying degrees in a period of tension within the education system, with problems of morale and resource shortages afflicting the nineteen as they have many other schools. At the same time, all are participating in many, if not all, of the changes affecting schools across the UK, including GCSE, TVEI, Profiling and Records of Achievement as well as local changes such as reorganization. Given such circumstances, it is hardly surprising that discussions at the seminar produced a list of practical constraints that seem to have affected the introduction of economic awareness:

1) a crowded timetable
2) opportunities for teacher training
3) busy curriculum managers
4) many competing initiatives
5) resources
6) personalities
7) organizational models
8) LEA support
9) time, commitment, and parental and student expectations and attitudes to change.

It is therefore all the more remarkable that schools have been able to progress so far. A statement made at the seminar perhaps best reflects the spirit in which this has been achieved:

'We must be optimistic in believing that all teachers can take on board economic awareness and new ideas – not pessimistic, setting up bureaucracies which guard empires and inhibit dissemination.'

This optimism and belief in people's ability to take on change seems to be the key factor in most of the schools. Others, however, can be viewed as no more than a diverse collection of experiences. Each stands by itself and the groupings adopted are based largely on the curriculum contexts in which economic awareness is being developed. In many cases, this is the extent of a section's homogeneity.

The papers summarized

Section 1: the core module approach

This consists of eight papers which portray schools' developing economic awareness programmes in core course, often in a modular format.

Andrews describes the development of a three-week module, focusing on unemployment, for a fourth year Integrated Humanities course in a North Midlands comprehensive. The course is aimed at 200 students and involves 10 members of staff. Initially, trades unions and unemployment were examined, each for two weeks, and some of the *Understanding Economics* (Longman, 1985) material tried out. In the light of this, Andrews outlines the developments that led to a three week module on unemployment. In his view, four lessons were learned:

1) teachers can become more economically aware
2) an active approach is essential
3) including the perspectives of other disciplines helped teachers and students
4) race and sex bias can be exposed and tackled.

The course is still developing – time may well see it becoming less prescriptive and with new modes of assessment.

Jones describes an ambitious core programme in a West London comprehensive. 70% of student time is occupied by core courses which have evolved over 10 years. Following the introduction of Political Literacy, Economic Literacy was developed using both *Understanding Economics* units and some developed in the school. The course now forms part of an NEA Integrated Humanities GCSE. A favourable climate for change in the school, together with external support from teachers' meetings, allowed the course to be developed quickly and fairly successfully. However,

Jones is not completely satisfied. He planned and prepared the course but is openly self-critical about not involving more staff at the planning stage. He has produced a package which is student-centred, flexible and, in its third year, largely unchanged. Jones argues that, had he spent more time with his teachers, the course would be developing and moving on.

McClelland, Owen, Clarke and Meadowcroft present a picture of Manchester, with very little traditional economics education, reorganizing its schools and thereby encouraging modular developments in economic awareness. Three schools are described. Owen outlines how, in the first school, an economic awareness module was set up by non-specialists. She emphasizes the advantages of having committed staff but is worried about the effect of staff changes. Clarke describes a module in consumer education in the second school. He comments on the educational effectiveness of the work for him, as well as for the students. Meadowcroft presents a picture of a four week module, now being extended to six weeks, in the third school. The three schools are inner-city comprehensives, and the writers express common concerns over modular components of courses, particularly their limited time, evaluating their effectiveness and their reinforcement of subject barriers. All agree that their modules represent only the start of long-term development.

Linda Thomas describes the development of a module within a social studies core course involving 15–20 members of staff at a South London comprehensive. She sees external support through teacher meetings and visiting support teachers, and internal factors such as a clearly defined course philosophy and school-based INSET, as combining to assist the introduction of economic awareness. She also reflects that the course needs to continue its development, especially with staff changes and with other ideas about economic awareness emerging, but she worries that the necessary training and support will be difficult to facilitate at present.

Kellaway charts the development of a nine week economic awareness module within a PSE core. Never having taught any economics, Kellaway admits to a lack of confidence when first running the course. Therefore, although possessing a clear philosophy about education, he found it necessary to experiment for a year using a module borrowed from another school. This experience, together with the results of trials with some *Understanding Economics* units, enabled him to devise his own module based around a definitive list of high-order concepts and an active classroom process.

Like Kellaway, Long found the *Understanding Economics* units a valuable starting point. She depicts a traditional school that tries to use economic awareness as one means to create a more favourable climate for change. The students negotiated the key themes, and although she feels that some mistakes have been made, Long is able to see her module as being the start of a process of development.

Pollock describes how the Business Studies department has established a six week module in the fourth year, and reorganized its third year course with four periods per week. Again, she comments favourably on *Understanding Economics* and the effects of teacher meetings. For her, a big challenge has been encouraging members of the staff to develop their skills in active learning. She comments that 'the (positive) response of pupils to new styles of working has been one source of motivation for teachers', but concludes that much remains to be done if many of the staff are to feel at ease.

The final paper in this section provides something of a bridge into the other sections. Walters outlines a school in which the Head and the Adviser have become convinced of the need for economic awareness. As in several of the preceding papers, there are links through teacher meetings, with other schools engaged in similar work and the *Understanding Economics* units are used. Initially, materials and strategies were tried out across the curriculum, which eventually led to a module, plans for 20-minute slots in the pastoral programme and a TVEI Mini Company, as well as work in several subjects. Industrial action limited INSET to team teaching. Also included here are many comments from students, and a teacher reaction that seems to indicate some degree of success: 'They've (the students) never really talked to me before!'

Key points about the development of economic awareness in core courses and through modules are raised in these papers. Seminar participants added their concerns:

- 'Modules can reinforce subject barriers, restrict staff development and often have low status amongst staff and pupils.'

- 'If economic awareness occupies 10 hours out of a total school career lasting 15,000 hours, what do the pupils emerge with? What skills, concepts, insights and reflections?'

Nevertheless, modules do represent a starting point, a manageable focus from which to develop.

Section 2: Economic awareness through subjects

Five case studies approach economic awareness from the standpoint of an existing area of the curriculum. These schools are working on ways to allow economic awareness to be identified and delivered through existing courses, albeit with some development.

Davies takes geography as his focus. He portrays the development of an existing third year geography course and of efforts to bring out economic awareness in fourth and fifth year examination courses. Several reasons for adopting this approach are advanced, and his aims include 'trying to get teachers to learn from each other and therefore encourage them in "unfamiliar" territory' (that of economic awareness).

Despite redeveloping the third year course and starting work on years four and five, Davies is not satisfied. Like Jones, he regrets concentrating on lesson materials and the meaning of geography and economic awareness at the expense of time with his teachers. Thus, he feels the third year course to be over-prescriptive and the economic awareness as presenting serious challenges to the structure and assessment of fourth and fifth year courses.

Taylor presents business studies as one, although not the sole, vehicle for encouraging economic awareness. In view of its rising popularity and associations with TVEI and pre-vocational courses, Taylor argues that it presents a golden opportunity for development. He says it provides 'a panorama of experiences' that could help establish informal economic awareness. However, he is careful to view such a development in the context of recent national initiatives and as a continuum of economic awareness, carefully coordinated from the primary sector into secondary education.

McLoughlin explains how she was appointed as a geographer and yet is now coordinating economic awareness programmes in years two and three, GCSE Economics, and working on a module of PSE for fourth and fifth years. She describes the importance of her LEA's developing policy and the commitment of senior management.

Muir writes about developing economic awareness courses whilst being Head of Economics in a highly academic school in Northern Ireland. In the third year, an existing money-management course due for change has been replaced by a six week module in economic awareness. In the sixth form, economic awareness now contributes to the liberal studies programme. As with some previous papers, help was found in the *Understanding Economics* materials and in teacher meetings. Muir reports on the reaction of the Head of English to the lessons, and says 'The response of the pupils was marvellous!' but that many non-specialists were uncomfortable with the approach. Muir states that the course will soon be reviewed and changes introduced in the light of experience. In addition, some cross-curricular ideas may be floated.

McMahon describes the experiences of a teacher trained in English who is now in charge of a careers programme running in each year. He briefly reports on a second year optional course in economic awareness before concentrating on careers. He describes himself as being distinctly unhappy at the lack of realistic contexts in the programme. However, following trials with some *Understanding Economics* units and after attending a teachers' meeting, he has been able to construct an extended course involving literature, an investigation into the careers of two members of a family (one in a small firm, the other in a large firm), a visit and a role play situation. Economic awareness has helped to produce a more satisfying careers course. McMahon admits that the stituation is still experimental, but optimistically points to the development of third and sixth year courses.

Section 3: The Scottish experience

The two case studies from Scotland provide a different focus. The more tightly structured Scottish system is leaning towards the development of economic awareness with younger students and within the 'social subjects'. Hewitt and Ryan both describe 12 and 13 year olds following concept-based courses designed, partly at least, to act as tasters for future examination options.

Hewitt outlines her background in economics/business studies, while Ryan works more in economics and the humanities. Nevertheless, the emphasis is on specialists teaching courses designed to introduce a discipline. Both writers describe trying to make the courses topical and interesting, selecting suitable concepts, producing their own resources to make enough demands on pupils. In addition, Hewitt presents a very detailed course outline, while Ryan describes a multi-disciplinary module on the West Highland Railway Line.

Section 4: Economic awareness as a focus for change

This deals with two papers that see economic awareness as a means of promoting widespread change in the schools concerned, as well as providing an essential component of education.

Clarke and Lepper outline the strategy adopted by a Suffolk school in its move towards changing both the curriculum and teaching and learning styles. Curriculum coordinators have been appointed in six areas, including economic and political awareness, with a remit to:

- seek cross-curricular opportunities
- supply materials
- devise INSET for staff
- develop links with the coordinators and teachers

By spring/summer 1986, economic awareness had been identified as a strong linking agent across subject boundaries, and work was going on in such areas as mathematics (economaths!), music, home economics and history. The difficulties as well as the achievements of such a strategy are described. For Clarke and Lepper, a separate subject called economic awareness would be a retrograde step. They argue that, despite the costs in time and resources, the strategy being developed is remarkably cost-effective when balanced against creating a specialist department.

Leech and Hall develop a picture of how a department, consciously assessing and evaluating its work, gradually comes to affect much of the school's work. Economic awareness is described in a third year course, and the process of change is highlighted in fourth and fifth year provision. Over four years, a position has been reached in which nearly all pupils have an opportunity to develop economic awareness. The importance of using school-based INSET in a particular way is outlined, and they comment that active learning strategies have enabled these developments to 'enrich, not duplicate, the rest of the curriculum'.

Like Clarke and Lepper, the writers emphasize the importance of not building empires. Instead they advocate helping their colleagues to develop their own skills and thus to tackle their own issues, whilst at the same time developing economic awareness in pupils. Indeed, Leech and Hall advise the acceptance of less favourable timetable commitments, rooms and the like if this will gain the confidence of others.

Section 5: A school's history and a school's thinking

Finally, two detailed papers are presented on the work that has been carried out. Peter Thomas outlines the life history of a course, tracing its development over 13 years. He highlights the effects on the course of such changes as CSE Mode 3, a new Headteacher, work experience and, especially, active learning. This paper is notable for the way in which the course seems to have become more flexible and experimental, as if ever-increasing change has built up the confidence to try yet more change! Thomas concludes that the course will continue its evolution, but adds that important questions are appearing. For instance, just what should all students experience when completing a course in economic awareness?

Wilkinson and Wall conclude this section with some intriguing reflection and evaluation. Wilkinson established economic awareness courses in all years at a comprehensive school for 11–18 year olds in North London. She outlines her aims and strategies. On Wilkinson gaining a new job, Wall replaced her and inherited overall responsibility for these courses. Wall describes six issues concerning economic awareness, and how information was gathered from teachers and students in order to shed light on them.

The picture that emerges from this paper is perhaps so unique that it can only apply in detail to that school. However, a variety of more general issues are highlighted that can be seen as widely relevant. In addition, the writers identify six key questions and end by stressing the need for staff development:

'The success of such a curriculum development depends upon teachers making sense of what is happening and then being actively involved in implementation, evaluation and further development at all levels.'

Some final points remain to be made. If the case studies in Section 1 report a largely modular approach to the development of economic awareness, the remainder employ in various ways what could be called an 'infusion' strategy. Despite this, however, some common characteristics may be identified:

1) *Curriculum management*. Infusion appears to rely upon a degree of curriculum management, be it by the senior management, a department or a key individual. A key individual (two or more in some cases) is needed anyway as coordinator, often with access to training and support, and preferably with some experience in and enthusiasm for economic awareness. Through their work, coordinators build links between teachers and subjects, creating something of a team, either loosely or tightly knit. The team shares resources, writes and shares schemes of work and a degree of commitment emerges. A final but essential element appears to be INSET or support for the team with the coordinator/s networking developments inside and outside the school.

2) *Teaching and learning materials*. A large number of papers acknowledge the importance of ready-made resources, especially Longman's *Understanding Economics* units. However, virtually all the contributors warn against a preoccupation with materials. As Andrews comments:

'One of the problems of taking up new materials, whether they are created "in house" or produced externally, is the tendency to adopt such a package and leave it unaltered or underdeveloped'.

Instead, several papers advocate more staff development as a way of developing meaningful courses in economic awareness.

3) *A process of innovation.* Each of the 19 papers describes a process of innovation. This process appears to depend upon teachers sharing their experiences, training, planning and working; reflecting and even teaching together. A particular characteristic is an emphasis on the development of general expertise from this sharing process, rather than relying on 'experts' for a single 'right' approach. Obviously, advisers and coordinators would need to work *with* teachers during this process.

4) *Staff development and training.* This sharing could become the focus for training, be it school, LEA, or more widely organized. The training itself could develop the role of coordinator, the notion of economic awareness, its place in the curriculum and the skills of teachers in active learning strategies. Whatever the details, the contributors make it clear that such a process should be continuous, and allow those involved to feel part of the innovation.

A conclusion: some ideas to consider

Our starting point was to describe the schools and teachers as being on a journey. Already they had met and accepted one challenge, that of beginning the journey. To openly declare their intention to continue travelling, and thereby to develop,

change and improve their work, is to accept a second and perhaps more difficult challenge.

This in its turn challenges the reader to consider these issues:

1) To reflect on the nature and meaning of economic awareness. Should a precise definition be demanded and, if so, from whom? Or is a process of 'creative ambiguity' really a strength, encouraging teachers to think things through for themselves rather than relying on 'experts' for answers?

2) In what context should economic awareness be included in the curriculum? Each context described here has implications, strengths and weaknesses.

3) By what means should economic awareness be introduced into and developed in a school? In the papers, the teachers themselves point out the implications of their strategies.

This book is concerned with the teaching of economic awareness. Nevertheless, the issues raised are respresentative of educational innovation in general. A final challenge therefore faces the reader, irrespective of the curriculum area or the proposed innovation:

4) Will your educational institution be prepared to undergo the kinds of questioning and critical thinking employed by teachers in these nineteen very varied schools?

and

5) Furthermore, faced with the question: 'What do the pupils *do* in their lessons?' what would be your response?

It is upon this journey that the reader is now asked to embark. It may be long but, judging from the papers, it will be lively, ever-changing and often very enjoyable!

Section 1 *The Core Module Approach*

1 Developing an economics module for an integrated humanities core course

Christopher Andrews

Cheslyn Hay High School, Staffordshire

Background

This paper describes the development of a three-week module on unemployment for a fourth year integrated humanities course. Initial discussions were between the county's Advisory Teacher, the Head of Humanities and the teacher in charge of economics. It is written from the perspective of the economics teacher and outlines the principal issues involved in communicating the economics message not only to more than 200 pupils, but also to 10 members of staff.

Cheslyn Hay High School is situated between Cannock and Wolverhampton with a catchment area comprising mainly small villages. However, the population is employed in the nearby urban centres and pupils come from predominantly working- and lower-middle-class backgrounds. In 1985–6 there were 985 pupils on roll, including a sixth form of 88 pupils.

Other than a successful 'A' level course, the selective use of the Economics Association's Economics Education 14–16 Project materials[1] in integrated humanities is the main course of economics education in the school. (There is a broadly defined economics content in the careers programme and also in commerce teaching.) The use of 14–16 material dates from 1984 when Cheslyn Hay became one of Staffordshire's pilot schools, and of the 10 members of staff currently teaching humanities, five were involved from the beginning.

In 1984–5 the materials used were presented more or less consecutively over the autumn and summer terms of year four (see Appendix 1). A module entitled 'People and Work' prepared pupils for one week's work experience at the end of the summer term and this preparation included two-week/six-hour units on both unemployment and trades unions.

Developing the module

Four major aspects relating to the understanding and promotion of economic awareness were identified in preliminary discussions and yielded the following four aims for the module as a whole:

1) The experience gained from September 1985 indicated that no assumptions could be made about the economic awareness of staff. Redesigning and extending the Unemployment module would attempt to raise staff conciousness about both the methods and content of economics.

2) There was a desire to promote a more pupil-centred/questioning and skills-based approach than had hitherto been the case. To an extent, therefore, the definition of economic literacy changed, as did (by implication) the methods best suited to teaching this topic.

3) Given that the module was part of a humanities course there was an obvious requirement to consider the geographic, historic, social and moral dimensions of unemployment.

4) Pupils typically expressed extreme forms of

both race and sex bias when discussing the cause of unemployment and it was felt the module should attempt to expose this.

Once these four broad aims had been identified the question of economic content and skills was addressed in the light of the dual constraints of teaching time and access to resources (i.e. VCR, computer facilities, reprographics). In reality access to resources and availability of relevant information was not a problem in 1985. The time allowed was increased to give three weeks/nine hours of lessons at the expense of part of the trades unions unit which is now introduced in the closing stages of this work.

Bearing in mind the time available and the emphasis placed upon developing pupil skills, the format of the module evolved in such a way that it focused on the issue of new technology, although the various other 'causes' of unemployment were also included (the teacher notes caution against encouraging a monocausal explanation). There were a number of additional reasons for this decision; for example, the Wapping newspaper dispute provided a living example, there being several conflicting attitudes and opinions expressed about the effects of new technology (e.g. more employment?). Furthermore the questions are 'concept rich' in relation to economic theory (e.g. market forces, opportunity cost, time horizons). It is not clear whether the module uses any concepts not already present in other *Understanding Economics* units, but it does reinforce the application of most of them and increases the perceived relevance of economic methods and concepts. An interesting historical case study based on the Luddite Movement raises questions about the reaction to 'new' technology and provides an introduction to the role of trades unions. Finally, considerable material from a wide variety of sources is available in relation to new technology, its uses and possible consquences.

Prescriptive or flexible?

The brief description of the content of the module given above can be elaborated by reference to Appendix 2 (teacher notes) and Appendix 3 (pupil

notes) which contain examples of the material used.

One of the principal concerns of the economics teacher as a new appointee to the school, in developing work for use by a wide variety of 'non-specialist' teachers, was the question of teacher notes.

Given the desire to develop a skills-based approach in the pupils' work, guidance for staff in this area, as well as economic content, was an important issue. Events during 1985 effectively circumscribed the usual process of staff meetings, but it is pleasing to be able to review the extent of the progress that was achieved despite this.

As already noted, the approach taken was to provide for variety in the core material by using not only economic content and method but also geographical, historical and simple mathematical skills. The ability and willingness of all staff to participate in the teaching of the subject matter was aided by this approach. Similarly, all staff were able to add their own specialist background material where appropriate and to emphasize points they felt to be relevant elsewhere in the humanities course, or indeed in the wider curriculum (e.g. cross-references to studies in the history of the Luddite movement).

The emphasis placed on economic literacy which is illustrated in the pupil tasks and resources is to an extent mirrored in the teacher notes. For example, the early lessons are more obviously of a data analysis type and have specific given answers, i.e. they are highly prescriptive. Commentary for later lessons is deliberately less formalized except where specific economic content is required (e.g. avoidance of a monocausal view of unemployment). The aim here was to strike a balance between structured support for teachers and flexibility for individuals to interpret and act upon the materials in their own way.

Anecdotal evidence from the staff provides the most reasonable appraisal of success in relation to these objectives. The short duration of the module and its setting in a wider economic literacy context would render attempts at a more rigorous analysis somewhat unjustified and certainly more complex. Comments from the staff in informal debriefing sessions do not provide wholly satisfactory responses to some of the issues raised earlier, but they do indicate a measure of improved understanding and awareness of data analysis techniques.

Staff confidence in approaching the heavily modified content and skills required for the module was undoubtedly affected by a decision at faculty level to retain the previous assessment questions. This did mean that it was to some extent possible to teach to the assessment items and thus to avoid some of the main aims of the new material. However, this could be viewed as a short-term cost of introducing such a considerable revision. The target now is evidently the design and implementation of new assessment items to complete the development.

Conclusions

Any concluding remarks must be seen in terms of the processes of both course and staff development which are ongoing in the school, as well as more general interests. As noted in the introduction, one of the problems of taking up new materials, whether they are created 'in-house' or produced externally, is the tendency to adopt such a package and leave it unaltered or undeveloped. In relation to developing a meaningful economic awareness, this type of treatment is in fact counter-productive, as economics then becomes defined as the didactic content of specific units or modules.

Interviews with staff have brought forward two groups of comments about the module on unemployment and about general economic awareness. The positive points of the module are:

1) It is 'user friendly' − staff and pupils gain access to a topic which previously they may have perceived as being too difficult.
2) Pupils are highly motivated by the content and the methods used, which is reflected in improved performance in their assessment.
3) It stimulates discussion of issues such as pupil-centred learning, skills-based understanding and GCSE in general.
4) It introduces computers to the humanities course.
5) It makes use of interactive video techniques.
6) Pupils appreciate the relevance of the topic and demonstrate some positive attitude modification.

7) It reinforces the economics units used elsewhere and emphasizes the appropriate skills.

Observations about the effectiveness and implementation of economic awareness in the integrated humanities course fell into two related groups:

1) Continued stimulus is required to provoke staff (and ultimately pupils) to consider what economics is about and what it might offer them.
2) The 'pool' of teaching staff is not at all constant and new material within units and new units themselves help to bring all members of the faculty to the same starting point. This version of course development may also have many advantages in fostering a measure of 'teamwork' for particular groups of teachers.

Considering the promotion of economic awareness as a constant process of review and of further development permits the most optimistic interpretation of progress. The active involvement of other members of the faculty is encouraged by such an approach, which in turn leads to better understanding of the aims and methods of economics teaching.

Reference

1 Economics Association, *Understanding Economics*, Longman, 1985.

Appendix 1: 'People and Work' theme outline

All the economics units have teacher notes which include skills, and these can be readily related to assessment objectives. The underlying themes are the cultivation of all aspects of oral communication, and the development of sociological, economic, historical, and political perspectives. Objectives are to be constantly made explicit.

Autumn term

Week 1
Allocation of sets; course outline distributed and discussed
Family tree and sociological symbols; Royal Family to my family

Week 2
Nuclear families and extended families; development of the nuclear family
Film – The Industrial Revolution: This emphasizes essay technique – spend a lesson going through material and a lesson in controlled conditions writing it up (thorough marking essential)

Week 3
An investigation (introduced in class, four one-week H/Ws: emphasis on skills of research)
Probably some overlap from previous week
The Family in the 1980s
Roles (short homework) and discussion

Week 4
The functions and dysfunctions of the family; socialization

Week 5
The generation gap (role-play); the family and the state

Week 6
Assessment – combination of Bethnal Green and marriage and divorce statistics
Finishing off work and revision technique for next assessment

Week 7
Assessment – functions of family and state
Introduction to second part of course, emphasizing themes of Young Person as a Consumer and Citizen.
(Family History assessment handed in)

Week 8
Talk from CAB; consumer protection

Week 9
What determines the price a consumer pays, using E14–16 units – 'Prices' and 'Price of Pop' and new videos

Week 10
Overlap from previous week

'The Accident' (E14–16)
Preparation for 'Community Expenditure' (E14–16)

Week 11
'Community Expenditure' (E14–16)
'Local Authority Rates' (E14–16)
Classroom simulation video

Summer term

Week 1
'What is work?' (E14–16), Video input, in three classrooms
'Two Workers' (E14–16), Who does what? worksheet

Week 2
'Andy's Car' (E14–16) slides in lecture theatre; follow-up worksheet in class; division of labour, specialization, interdependence – worksheet

Week 3
STRIFFIDS – group production exercise. Explanation (and practice) in lecture theatre in lesson 1 and simulation in following lesson; third lesson debriefing and worksheet on the division of labour

Weeks 4, 5 and 6
Unemployment module. This is being prepared by An and Ca after consultation with the Economics Adviser in Staffordshire. Format will be: (1) unemployment and you; (2) & (3) unemployment – local, national, international context; (4) & (5) causes of unemployment, especially technological; (6) historical case study on technological unemployment; (7) unemployment – so what? costs to the individual and nation; (8) policy strategies

Week 7
'Price of a Perm' (E14–16), functions of management worksheet. If there are problems with unemployment module coming on stream this week's work can go into week 4

Weeks 8 and 9
Trade union module. This is being prepared by An and Ca and revising previous work. Probable format: use of trade union officials on work of trade union; historical perspective types and function follow-up; trade unions and wages/collective bargaining, probably using an E14–16 project module

Week 10
Assessments

Week 11

½ pupils on work experience. Also many pupils out on Art and Duke of Edinburgh field trips. Relevant preparation work for those on work experience next week

Week 12

½ on work experience. Pupils returning from work experience – debriefing, oral exercise, writing up booklet

Week 13

Completion of work experience booklets

Note the links of work experience with the pastoral system and English Department

Appendix 2: Unemployment module – teacher's notes

1) Unemployment and you (Lesson 1)

Introduction

This is the first of 7/8 hour lessons on the topic of unemployment. The basic idea is to make use of pupils' existing knowledge to create a context in which (a) they are made more aware of the implications of the present situation in the labour market on *them*, (b) they begin to weigh the pros and cons of the various pathways open to *them* at 16 +, (c) they begin to ask fundamental questions about the nature of unemployment – past, present and future.

Objectives

1) use of small group and class discussion (skill)
2) ability to consider wider implications of a course of action (skill)
3) ability to weigh and discern pros and cons (skill)
4) way in which unemployment statistics are arrived at (idea)
5) how an individual can enhance his/her market-ability (idea)

Organization

The lesson utilizes statistics on CHHS fifth year leavers over past 5 years, and an information sheet on 16 + pathways and some pros and cons of each one.

The style of the lesson should be based on group discussion work to make use of pupils' knowledge to build up a network of key ideas on the board.

The amount of guidance given (e.g. use of information sheet as a summary or as a stimulus) will depend on your working knowledge of the class.

Suggested format

1) Opening format: 'Where do you think last year's fifth year ended up?'; 'What percentage of them went into the various ways?'; 'How do you think this has changed over the last 3 years?' The response to each of these can be summarized and supplemented by key statistics. (Use 250 pupils per year as a base for percentages.) 'What changes have taken place and why?'
2) In groups think of advantages and disadvantages of each option using key ideas such as finance, qualifications, personal skills and maturity, your attitudes at 15/16 etc.
3) Report back; one group takes the option and other groups add or detract as circumstances dictate.
4) Issue summary sheet for pupil to keep in his book.
5) A piece of written homework which can form basis for start of next lesson (i.e. what have they learnt, what had they not considered before, etc.).

Key statistics

See pupil notes (Appendix 3)

Unemployment

Introduction

I have taken note of the content and ideas contained in NEA Integrated Humanities proposals and GCSE Economics proposals. In particular, four guiding questions seem relevant:

1) What do we want *all* pupils to understand?

2) How do we want ideas and themes to develop?

3) How can *all* pupils gain a positive experience?

4) How can assessment be developed?

Economic literacy can be interpreted as a methodology (of analysis of information, presentation of data, evaluation of implications) which is to be achieved through the study of key economic ideas (e.g. demand, supply, opportunity, cost, etc.).

The exercises and information in this booklet are based on a mixture of skills — *numeracy* and *literacy* are to the fore, but considerable weight is given to *graphicacy*.

Minimum level of understanding should include the following points:

1) Appreciation of the variable pattern of unemployment in time and in space

2) Following from (1), the complexity of the causes of unemployment. They should use this data to *reinforce* the definitions of types of unemployment (cyclical, structural, technological, etc.). However, it is important to stress that *all these types of unemployment can and do exist at any given time.* Furthermore it is exceptionally difficult to discover a major or dominant cause.

3) Just because we have focused in the rest of this 'module' upon technological unemployment does not mean that this is necessarily the only or major cause of present or future unemployment.

2) The history of unemployment in Britain (Lesson 2)

1) Based on graphs to show percentage unemployed 1861–86.

2) Gives information.

3) Skills — how to read graphs (axes, range of data values; time scale; percentage versus absolute values; calculations of per cent).

Part A

Practise skills with teachers/individual back-up as required. Unemployed people are those who are seeking work/would accept a job if one was offered. A proxy variable is used to gain official data (i.e. the numbers registering as unemployed at benefit offices).

Part B

Uses skills developed in part A. 'Fourth paragraph': now we have a more detailed critical description of the unemployed, and in particular we can see how there can be large divergencies from a trend pattern (i.e. part A is an *oversimplification* in terms of highest and lowest rates of unemployment).

Part C

Answers should follow the analysis/style of parts A/B, but require knowledge of events (e.g. W.W.1 & W.W.2) and recognition of the implications *vis-à-vis* unemployment.

3) Unemployment in Britain today (Lesson 3)

Part A

Question 1 reinforces the various implications of using average figures: (i) what do pupils understand about the meaning of the word? (ii) what's an advantage of using an average figure? (iii) what's a disadvantage? (iv) how is an (arithmetic) average worked out (formula).

Question 2 briefly shows regional divisions of UK.

Question 3 raises issues: is the government to blame? how bad is unemployment? why?

Part B

Action 1: skills of 'transference'.

Action 2: use of average.

Action 3: analysis of own work; demonstration of the UK north/south divide.

Part C

Question 1: unemployment means to people in our region? how would people in other regions view our position?

Question 2: can you expect empathy with our region from people in the south?

Question 3: introduce political ideas/dimension.

Each pupil to illustrate own map, and of course give a title and key.

4) Unemployment in other countries (Lesson 3)

Part A

Action 1 presents data/ranking exercises to show how presentation can distort.

Part B

Action 1: demonstration of above ideas.

Action 2: relation between absolute quantity and percentage.

Part C

Use a key to colour appropriate countries. Write accurate answers/quantities.

Each pupil to illustrate own copy of map and give title and key.

5) Causes of unemployment, especially technological (Lesson 3)

Introduction

This follows on from unemployment: personal, local, national and international context. The main aims are to (a) acquaint pupils with different types of unemployment; (b) focus on technological unemployment using a case study to throw up complex issues such as job creation, job destruction, services, occupational and geographical mobility; (c) demonstrate that technological unemployment is not a new idea by preparing the ground for the Luddite case study in next unit; (d) show how the economic issues are complex and help move pupils away from the simple notion that machines automatically destroy jobs, by developing a network of economic ideas and relationships.

Objectives

1) use of small group and class discussion (skill)
2) ability to consider complexity of issues (skill)
3) ability to develop generalizations from a specific case study (skill)
4) identification of different types of unemployment (idea)
5) a consideration of the nature of technological unemployment and key economic concepts associated with it (idea).

Organization

1) Follow up last lesson and identify key points by posing questions such as 'Was unemployment particularly high at certain times?'; 'Was unemployment particularly high in certain areas/regions?'

   Introduce new ideas: 'Can you think of some jobs that only exist at certain times of the year?'; 'Can you think of some jobs which *appear* to be going because of work being done by computers/robots?'
2) Introduce worksheet on 'Types of Unemployment'. This will have some working definitions of unemployment types and a number of situations where pupils have to match them up. Use this as a basis for small group work and class discussion.
3) Focus in on *technological unemployment* and say that we are going to investigate the effect of computers on jobs and answer the question: 'Do machines automatically destroy jobs?'

   Pupils split into small groups and issued with *office case study*. Teacher then acts out situation and directs pupils to discuss the use of computers in the office by using key stimulus questions. Teacher encourages groups which may need it.
4) Following lesson: *EITHER* teacher gets groups to report back and a network of economic relationships is built up. Group goes to H5 *to see an example of what computers can do in this situation; OR* as above but other way around (but with video input as well).

   Information sheet is issued and key ideas focused upon. Pupils answer questions for homework. Question and answer sessions on these, forms opening session to next lesson on The Luddites, an historical case study.

6) New technology and unemployment (Lesson 4)

Introduction

This follows on from the new technology case study. In essence it attempts to place technological unemployment into some kind of long-term historical perspective (i.e. 'men' v machines is not just a 1980s phenomenon). The Luddites issue (simplified) is contrasted and compared with the print-workers' dispute to bring out their perspective, to focus on two different industries and help pupils make contrasts and comparisons from two different time spans.

Objectives

1) use of evidence interpreptation (skill)
2) ability to extract key issues from individual examples (skill)
3) ability to compare and contrast from two different examples in two different time periods
4) understanding of on-going nature of technology on employment (idea)
5) understanding of wider implications of 'men' v machine issue.

Organization

This will depend on the ability level of the group as to how much guidance needs to be given (e.g. with average and below-average pupils a key point framework on board might help – with top sets they could approach it with minimum of guidance but an emphasis on discussion afterwards).

Some kind of debriefing will be essential afterwards to demonstrate conflict of interests (i.e. unemployment? greater efficiency and lower prices to consumer? greater profitability for employers? occupational and geographical unemployment problems for those laid off?).

A follow-up essay would be very appropriate.

Appendix 3: Unemployment module – examples of pupil notes

1) What will I do at the end of the fifth year?

Introduction

Previous Cheslyn Hay High School fifth form (figures are approximate percentage):

	1980	1983	1985
Stay at school	32	24	29
Employed	23	17	6
College	7	8	8
YTS (WEEP)	11	38	42
Unemployed	23	11	5
Unknown	4	2	8

Certain trends over time should be apparent

1) Employed↓ Unemployed↓ YTS↑
2) From last year's fifth year, 4 in 10 started YTS, 3 in 10 stayed at school, 1 in 20 were unemployed.

What about you?

We have looked at the options open to you at 16 and tried to put together points for (PROS) and points against (CONS). Remember these points are *generalizations*.

YTS

Starting this year, the Youth Training Scheme is being extended to two years (16–18). (Pupils who do a year elsewhere, e.g. school or college, can do one year starting at 17.) This scheme also emphasizes the idea of *training* for skills.

PROS

Year one – £27.30; year two – £30 (one-year YTS, £27.30 for 3 months, £35 for 9 months) and help with travelling expenses (you only pay first £3 per week).

May be entitled to free prescriptions.

Work experience, training and some form of qualification. Quality of schemes are improving. Some are excellent.

Can lead to full-time (e.g. some areas retailing and hairdressing tend to use YTS as a 'long interview' before appointing someone).

Variety of training available, many do not need qualifications.

After two years you will have gained in confidence maturity and independence.

CONS

Child Benefit £7. (£7.10p) is lost.

Cheap labour?

Training and qualifications may be better at school or colleges.

No job guaranteed – You may train in an area which interests you but may not be in demand.

May only be a few places in certain interests e.g. Art, Sports Centres.

You may become despondent at 18 if there is no prospect of employment.

Stay at school

Students stay at school for three types of courses –

'A' levels for two years or retake exams for one year or special one-year courses. Some students study a mixture.

PROS

Child Benefit £7 (£7.10) remains. Travelling expenses remain low. Books and other equipment provided. Possibly a means-tested low-maintenance grant for those in real need.

May do better as you are familiar with other pupils and staff. School will be more caring as we have known you from your younger days.

Improved qualifications give you a better chance in labour market.

'A' levels are the way to higher education. Qualification demands for employment are rising all the time.

Work experience (probably) and other qualifications (community work and sport) to broaden your outlook and help you mature.

CONS

No wages.

Some people may prefer a change of environment. Qualifications do not *guarantee* a job.

Some pupils may prefer a more vocational YTS course.

Less work experience than YTS.

College

Students go to college for two types of course, general ('A' levels or 'O' levels CPVE) or vocational (engineering, hairdressing, business studies, secretarial, building technician, caring, scientific, catering).

PROS

Child Benefit £7 (£7.10) remains. Some travelling expenses, small equipment grant, possibly a means-tested low-maintenance grant for those in real need.

New place and therefore a new environment and new people to meet.

Maybe further to travel.

Vocational qualifications are recognized by employers.

Can do 'O' and 'A' levels.

Work experience for those on vocational courses.

CONS

No wages.

Some people prefer a place where they are known.

Will it be less caring as you are there only for a short time?

School is probably the best place for 'O' and 'A' level courses. School does not offer so many vocational qualifications.

Maybe no work experience for those on 'A' level courses. Probably less provided in terms of sport and community involvement.

Employment

In 1985 about 15 pupils out of 250 started employment. The jobs were mainly general jobs and temporary or part-time and a few were apprenticeships.

PROS

In apprenticeships a skill or trade is bound over a long period of time.

Some skills are in short supply in country.

Probably a job at end in firm.

General jobs will probably pay higher than YTS and provide real working experience.

Being in work helps build confidence, maturity, independence and self-esteem.

CONS

Wages are relatively low (some are slightly higher than YTS).

Very few are available.

Child Benefit goes.

There may be no chance for extra training or gaining qualifications.

Person may be sacked after a trial period. Young people are often first to go if firm is not doing so well.

Unemployment

In 1985 about 15 pupils out of 250 were registered as unemployed.

PROS

£18.20 supplementary benefit per week. Possibly other benefits depending on circumstances.

Time is your own to do what you like.

Possibly part-time study at college depending on the hours you do.

CONS

Child benefits go. Boredom, may lose contact with friends who are doing something else, loss of confidence, people may think you are lazy.

2) The history of unemployment in Britain

This exercise is designed to show you what has happened to unemployment in Britain since 1861.

It will also develop your analytic skills — show you how to look at graphs.

It should also suggest questions to you such as 'Can unemployment be reduced?'

Part A

These questions ask you to describe as fully as you can the appearance of the graph. The first thing to do is to study the accompanying graph. Then answer the questions in sentences.

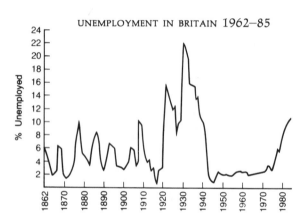

UNEMPLOYMENT IN BRITAIN 1962–85

1) What is the lowest rate of unemployment shown by the graph?
2) What is the highest rate of unemployment shown by the graph?
3) What is the range of unemployment on the graph?
4) What percentage of the working population were unemployed in 1885?
5) What percentage of the working population were unemployed in 1985?
6) What percentage of the working population were unemployed ten years ago?
7) Give three years when the rate of unemployment was falling?
8) In 1868 approximately 6% of people were unemployed, one hundred years later the percentage figure was approximately 3%. Does this tell us anything about how many people were unemployed in 1968 compared

with 1868? Explain your answer carefully and give a numerical example to show what you mean.

Part B

Your answers to part A give a description of the general shape of the graph, but do not tell us the whole story. Using the same techniques and methods, describe what happened to the numbers of people unemployed during these three periods:
1861 to 1914
1948 to 1970
1970 to 1986
You should be able to write a paragraph of at least three sentences for each period.

Write a *fourth* paragraph to say how your description of unemployment between 1861 and 1986 is different now from the description you gave in part A.

Part C

Using your general knowledge or by carrying out research at home, you should be able to add major events to the graph which might explain some of its rises and falls. Say what these are and how they affected the number of people unemployed.

3) Unemployment in Britain today

This exercise will show you where unemployment is highest (and lowest) in Britain today. It shows how the government divides up the country when it collects this data.

You will further develop your skills and find yourself thinking up more questions, which again may not have simple answers!

Part A

Study the data for September 1985. Then answer these questions in sentences:

1) How many areas or regions is Britain divided into?
2) Calculate the average rate of unemployment for September 1985.
3) Who is the Labour Party spokesman for employment and how did he describe the figures?

Part B

Use the data for January 1986 and the outline map of Britain for these questions:

1) Copy the map and its key for the regions A to K (do *not* include the figures for each region).

2) Shade those regions on your map which have a higher than average (13.2%) rate of unemployment.

3) Using your map, describe in your own words where the regions least affected by unemployment are.

Part C

1) Which region in Britain has the lowest rate of unemployment?

2) Which region has the greatest rate of unemployment?

3) How does our own region compare with the average rate and with the lowest and highest rates of unemployment?

UNEMPLOYMENT IN THE UK

a)

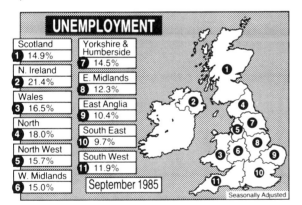

MR JOHN PRESCOTT, the Labour employment spokesman, interrupted the debate on public ownership at the party conference in Bournemouth yesterday to denounce yesterday's unemployment figures.

He described the figures as "a tragic indication of the Government's economic policies and a continuing scandalous waste of human resources."

Labour Party conference, Page 10

b)

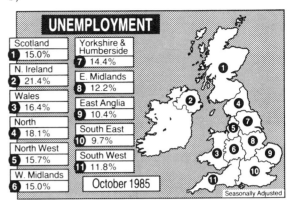

The seasonally-adjusted unemployment total fell 4,000 to 3,174,800 last month, equal to 13.1 per cent of the working population. The unadjusted total, which includes school-leavers, fell 69,000 to 3,276,861 or 13.5 per cent, writes Philip Stephens.

Over the past three months the sharpest rise in unemployment has been in Northern Ireland, where it has increased 0.5 per cent. There were rises of 0.1 per cent in the south-west, Yorkshire and Humberside and in Wales.

In the south-east, west Midlands, east Midlands and the north there was no change in the unemployment rate over the past three months.

The highest concentration of unemployment is in Northern Ireland where the rate last month stood at 21.4 per cent. In the north of England it stands at 18.1 per cent and in Wales at 16.4 per cent.

c)

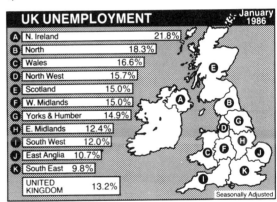

THE seasonally-adjusted unemployment total rose by 20,600 this month to reach a record 3,205m, representing 13.2 per cent of the working population.

The unadjusted total, which includes school-leavers, also reached record levels, rising by 134,600 to 3,408 m, or 14.1 per cent.

Over the past three months the adjusted jobless total has risen by an average of 10,500 a month, compared with a fall of 800 per month to the three months to November.

In the year to January the average unemployment rate for the UK has risen by 0.3 percentage points. In

Northern Ireland, however, the increase was 1.4 points and in Yorkshire and Humberside 0.7 points. East Anglia, Scotland, the southwest and Wales have also shown increases above the national average.

The most favourable trend in the West Midlands, where there was no change in the unemployment rate over the same period, while the increase in the north-west was 0.1 points.

The number of vacancies at jobcentres fell by 2,400 on a seasonally-adjusted basis to 139,700 in January, the lowest for a year.

4) Unemployment in other countries

The tables show data for unemployment in eight countries, including the UK. It gives percentages of the working population unemployed and the number of people unemployed.

For example, in February 1986, 14.0% of the UK working population was unemployed; put another way, 3,382,000 people who wanted to work could not find a job.

This exercise examines the way in which numbers such as these can give two different stories about how much or how bad unemployment is in Britain.

Part A

1) To *rank* a set of figures means to put them in order of size, largest first smallest last. Rank this list of countries using the numbers of people unemployed in each country in February. The USA is first, so write the others in a column underneath like this:

   USA   8,527,000

   Belgium   541,400

2) Now rank the countries again but use the percentage figures this time.

Part B

1) Notice that nearly all the countries change their positions in the 'league tables' when using different measurements of unemployment.

   Give an example of a country which is at the top of one list and then the bottom of the other list. Include the figures for numbers of people unemployed and percentage rate of unemployment.

2) Explain why a country which has a great many unemployed people (such as W. Germany, 2,590,300) can have one of the smallest percentage rates of unemployment. (A clue: if a country has 100 people in it and 5% are unemployed, this would give 5 unemployed people.)

Part C

Using the data and base map provided, illustrate Britain's position in the unemployment league for Europe.

Can you think of an alternative way of presenting the data?

Comment on the usefulness of these methods.

UNEMPLOYMENT IN OTHER COUNTRIES

World Economic Indicators

UNEMPLOYMENT

		Feb '86	Jan '86	Dec '85	Feb '85
UK	000s	3,382	3,408	3,273	3,324
	%	14.0	14.1	13.5	13.7
USA	000s	8,527	7,831	8,023	8,395
	%	7.3	6.7	6.9	7.3
		Jan '86	Dec '85	Nov '85	Jan '85
W Germany	000s	2,590.3	2,347.1	2,210.7	2,619.4
	%	9.6	8.7	8.2	9.7
France	000s	2,493.9	2,436.3	2,495.1	2,541.9
	%	10.7	10.5	10.8	11.0
Italy	000s	3,133.2	3,076.1	3,062.4	2,954.6
	%	13.7	13.6	13.5	13.1
Netherlands	000s	760.8	749.5	741.8	804.2
	%	13.6	13.4	13.2	14.3
Belgium	000s	540.4	542.4	541.1	619.4
	%	13.1	13.2	13.1	15.0
		Dec '85	Nov '85	Oct '85	Dec '84
Japan	000s	1,540.0	1,590.0	1,590.0	1,420.0
	%	2.9	2.9	2.8	2.6

World Economic Indicators

UNEMPLOYMENT

		Dec. '85	Nov. '85	Oct. '85	Dec '84
UK	000s	3,270.0	3,259.0	3,277.0	3,219.0
	%	13.5	13.5	13.5	13.3
		Nov. 85	Oct. 85	Sept. 85	Nov. 84
US	000s	8,140.0	8,291.0	8,274.0	8,142.0
	%	7.0	7.1	7.1	7.1
W Germany	000s	2,210.7	2,148.8	2,151.6	2,189.2
	%	8.2	8.0	8.0	8.1
France	000s	2,495.1	2,504.9	2,436.2	2,524.9
	%	10.7	10.8	10.5	10.9
Italy	000s	3,078.6	3,023.5	2,938.4	2,812.1
	%	13.5	13.3	12.8	12.3
Netherlands	000s	741.8	743.4	757.6	797.5
	%	13.0	13.1	13.3	14.0
Belgium	000s	541.1	552.8	564.0	617.8
	%	13.1	13.4	13.7	15.0
		Sept. 85	Aug. 85	July 85	Sept. 84
Japan	000s	1,500.0	1,480.0	1,450.0	1,590.0
	%	2.72	2.59	2.56	2.75

5) Types of unemployment

Cyclical

This describes the idea of cycles in the economy. At times the economy in this country and the world booms, and spending, investment and production go up and unemployment comes down. At other times the economy in the world and at home slumps, and the reverse happens (e.g. unemployment goes up):

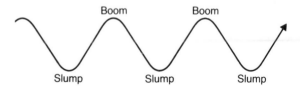

In the 1930s in this country and the world there was a long and large slump and cyclical unemployment was high.

Structural

When demand in a country and from abroad for a good is high, many factories will be producing that good. Production will be high and employment will be high. If demand for the good produced in this country falls because (a) there is foreign competition or (b) the good is no longer needed because there is an alternative on the market, then production falls, factories close and unemployment rises. Once people leave those factories they are unlikely to be employed making that good again. This is called *structural* unemployment because the structure of demand has changed.

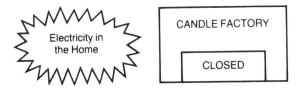

Seasonal

When a good or service is only demanded at certain times of the year, then that good or service will only be produced at certain times and so people will only be employed at certain times. They will employed at certain seasons and *unemployed* at certain *seasons* (e.g. Father Christmases are seasonally unemployed between Christmases):

24 December   27 December

Regional

If the country is divided into certain areas or regions, it can be seen that some areas have higher levels of unemployment (e.g. structural) than others (e.g. West Midlands has a high level of regional unemployment and London and the South East a low level).

Technological

If a person loses his job as a direct result of the introduction of a labour-saving machine, he is said to be technologically unemployed:

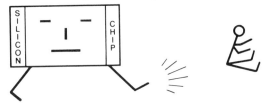

Voluntary

If a person chooses not to work and not to register as unemployed, he or she is an example of voluntary unemployment.

Match the examples to the type of unemployment

1) Bradford Council reduced its staff in one section from 44 to 22 with the introduction of nine word processors resulting in an increased productivity of 19% and an estimated annual saving of £59,000. . . .

2) 'I can remember when there were six cotton factories down this street working all day and night. Now look at it, all closed down. People just want these cheap imports or man-made fibres – I don't understand it.' . . .

3) 'I get myself off to Blackpool in May for five months, always casual work in the season. Probably go over to Germany in the autumn for some grape picking. Then back here to sign on.' . . .

4) 'I'm off down south – no prospects here for youngsters. I know kids of 21 not had a proper job since they left school.' . . .

5) 'Well they reckon things are beginning to pick up. It's been bad these last three years but better times are coming.' . . .

6) 'You know what you can do with your jobs and your government schemes!!' . . .

2 *Economic awareness in an extended fourth and fifth year core curriculum*

Phil Jones

Hounslow Manor School

The school

Hounslow Manor School is a multi-racial co-educational comprehensive with some 1,250 pupils on roll. It is currently suffering from the general effects of falling rolls and under-subscription. The main effect of this has been a contraction in the number of the staff. However, the 'curriculum' remains the school's main strength and in recent years considerable change has taken place in an attempt to offer a basic curriculum entitlement to all pupils:

'We are a comprehensive school. Above all else this influences our aims. We believe strongly in equality of opportunity for all pupils no matter what ability, race, colour or creed ... at Hounslow Manor we have two (aims): ... to create conditions in which every pupil can achieve the highest possible standards of intellectual, physical and moral development (and) ... to assist each pupil to take his/her place in society with confidence by preparing each pupil for self-knowledge, life and parenthood, useful citizenship, a successful career and the worthwhile use of leisure.'[1]

The introduction of an economic awareness component for all fourth and fifth year pupils should be viewed in the light of these aims, and should also recognize the considerable curriculum change that has been occurring.

The humanities context

All fourth and fifth year pupils follow an integrated humanities course as part of an extended core curriculum which accounts for some 70% of curriculum time (see Appendix 1). This evolved over 10 years as a result of individual initiatives rather than a grand plan, but the influence of the Curriculum Deputy cannot be underestimated in encouraging and responding to such initiatives. The opportunity to introduce economic awareness came in 1983 when it was proposed to extend the core programme. Social education and careers had formed part of the core since the early 1970s with a focus on religious and health education and careers guidance. With the retirement of the Head of Social and Religious Education, and the creation of a new post of Head of Social Education, the emphasis within social education changed to include aspects of adolescence and personal relationships, crime and punishment, the media, local history and sex education. A new Head of Careers widened the scope of the careers programme to look generally at the world of work and prepare pupils for work experience.

Social education provided a different learning situation from some other subjects in that pupils were encouraged to contribute their ideas through group discussion usually following an initial stimulus in the form of film, video, speaker or similar input. The emphasis was, therefore, on pupils' contributions rather than on teachers as providers of information.

The availability of extra teaching periods gained

from mathematics and English allowed the 'social education team' (as it had now become) to develop a new course structure. Careers was absorbed into social education and a life studies programme established. Individual members of the 'team' were able to construct modules in areas they felt appropriate. Social education also came under the umbrella of the humanities faculty, and the Head of Faculty and Head of Economics worked together to develop a political literacy course in 1983 and an economic literacy course in 1984. Social education became a continuous experience for pupils throughout the fourth and fifth years in contrast to other areas of the core which operated usually on a termly basis.

Integrated humanities has now been introduced to replace these areas of work. The decision came from a desire to build end-of-course certification into a programme that was highly regarded by the staff and involved a degree of pupil and parent credibility. A number of options were examined, but the syllabus that appeared to allow the course to remain in its existing form was the NEA Integrated Humanities scheme which provides for 100% coursework assessment, gives a wide choice of option modules and a 'free option' which allows economic literacy to be included.

The economic literacy module

In November 1983 the school's 'Board of Studies' agreed to include economic literacy as part of life studies. Whilst the decision was something of a formality it gave the Head of Economics an opportunity to think more clearly about the purposes which such a module would serve. In doing this, reference was made to two key documents of the late 1970s – the DES's Curriculum 11–16,[2] especially the section concerned with Economic Understanding, and the Economics Association's The Contribution of Economics to General Education.[3]

There appeared to be two constraints. First, there would only be a relatively short time available; and second, staff outside of the committed 'team' would very likely be responsible for its presentation to pupils. Some of these admitted to

being reluctant to become involved and frightened of the subject.

One term was allocated for fourth year work and nine weeks for fifth year. These time constraints clearly affected the content of the module and, in the case of the fifth year module, prompted the writer to consider how materials should be presented and what support staff involved could expect (Appendix 2 illustrates the time allocation and structure of the module). A major factor in both of these decisions was the involvement of the school in the University of London Institute of Education's dissemination network for the Economics Education 14–16 Project from April 1984.

Owing to the lack of continuity between fourth and fifth year work, two separate themes for modules were decided upon. The fourth year programme would focus on 'the individual' and the fifth year on 'issues'. The availability of pre-publication versions of Understanding Economics[4] enabled relevant materials to be selected for the two themes. It was, however, necessary for these to be supplemented with units developed by the Head of Economics.

The 14–16 Project units seemed to ease staff fears about the subject content. Each unit was a complete package of pupil materials, teacher's notes and follow-up activities. The units designed by the Head of Economics followed the same format even down to suggested answers to worksheet questions. However, the Head of Economics was relatively inexperienced with the units at this stage and not aware of their full potential. Moreover, in practice, some of the staff merely collected the units and asked pupils to complete the worksheets without any kind of development.

With the adoption of Integrated Humanities and Economic Literacy as the 'free option' it was necessary to submit a syllabus to the NEA. The module was to be one term in duration, and the submitted syllabus was written to contain the existing teaching programme rather than the syllabus which had determined the teaching programme.

The letter from the Joint Matriculation Board approving the syllabus recognized that an important emphasis was on 'the role of the individual within the economy' but stressed that the module should also further 'an understanding of some of the social and moral aspects of the modern world which concerned the likes of individuals and the communities of which they are a part'.

It is interesting to note that the choice of themes and units were solely those of the Head of Economics. Other team members, and the members of staff who would be teaching the module, were not involved in the planning. A strength of the political literacy course was that it had been planned by those responsible for teaching it. It had, moreover, been team taught, flexible and constantly under review.

Economic literacy in practice

But what was the experience of pupils in lessons? The following represents the writer's observations on his own lessons, comments from discussions with colleagues, and work generated by pupils.

It soon became clear that if pupils were to make sense of their experiences, then far greater time would need to be spent on the individual units than had been envisaged. For example, if pupil contributions were to be viewed as important and valuable (a course aim) then time had to be allowed for developments in addition to those suggested in the teacher's notes. One implication of this was that not all the units would be experienced by pupils, but this was not considered a disadvantage since teachers were encouraged to 'mix and match'.

The 'survival' simulation (Appendix 3, Fourth Year, Lessons 1 and 2) generated considerable student activity.[5] During debriefing, pupils were asked to consider the task they had undertaken, the nature of resources, problems encountered, and the methods of organization. Within my own lesson, few (if any) pupils recognized the nature of the individual's own resources, concentrating more on the physical resources available. This activity enabled pupils to complete a piece of written work on resources and different ways of using them.

The activity based on contrasting photographs (Fourth Year, Lessons 3 and 4) was one enjoyed not only by pupils but also by a number of the teachers who used it. One teacher developed the ideas generated by pupils to focus on 'diet and health' for the remainder of the module, adapting the other units to this end. For example, Lessons 5

and 6 (Fourth Year) were adapted to examine some of the choices involved in what we eat. Pupils investigated their own diets, food advertising, sales promotion and packaging, and completed survey work concerning the eating habits of pupils at lunchtimes and the effects of the rapid development of numerous 'fast food' outlets in the locality. The income/spending diary (Lessons 7 and 8) was similarly adapted to examine spending patterns on food and the links with income. A significant factor here was that the teacher was able to take some of the ideas generated for use in his lower school 'home economics' lesson. My own group became interested in 'The Eskimo' and smaller groups investigated aspects of eskimo lifestyle in greater detail, especially the impact of 'developed' nations on the eskimo in the form of the costs incurred/benefits received.

Lessons 5 and 6 (Fourth Year) allowed pupils to consider the nature of advertising and carry out investigations of their own. Pupils also referred back to the previous units as well as to work done in their third year geography course on development and the nature of wants and needs. This was very fruitful with one particular group as it coincided with the 'Ethiopian Famine Appeal' and provided a forum for many of the pupils' questions.

The income and spending diary activity (Fourth Year, Lessons 7 and 8) enabled pupils to collect and analyse their own data. A large number of questions was raised about the nature of income (Was the person with the highest weekly income necessarily better off? What about non-monetary benefits enjoyed or those provided by others?) and spending patterns (Does the amount of money we have determine how it is spent? Some pupils may have to buy their own clothes or pay for necessities like transport, others may have them provided and therefore have 'freedom' to spend on frivolous goods . . .). A number of statistical questions also emerged particularly concerning the relevance of 'averages'. The range of income levels within the group often rendered the average figures meaningless and pupils were quick to recognize this. This allowed other statistics (e.g. the national unemployment rate) to be introduced and questioned.

These units tended to fill all the time available for fourth year work in the original Life Studies programme. However, the introduction of the one term economic literacy module as part of Integrated Humanities gave teachers an opportunity to remain faithful to the original idea of two themes, but using some of the later units which focused more on issues (see Appendix 2).

The data provided for 'Community Expenditure' (*Understanding Economics*) was modified to include direct reference to Hounslow and the locality. Thus reference to road maintenance was to a particularly notorious road in the centre of Hounslow; Hounslow Manor School was one of the suggested school closures for the Education Committee; reference was made to a specific children's home in Hounslow for the Social Services Committee, and so on.

Pupils enjoyed this activity and were encouraged as a follow-up to bring in local newspaper articles or to share their own experiences relating to local spending. Significant questions about local priorities were raised:

- who makes spending decisions?
- what are the costs and benefits of certain spending decisions?
- could more services be provided?

It transpired that quite a high proportion of pupils in one particular group lived in council housing. They had specific questions about their own areas in terms of the facilities and services provided, and especially about a controversial plan to build a new leisure centre in one of the more affluent areas of the borough. This seemed to fit closest to the philosophy of the original Social Education programme – that pupils' own contributions were to be valued and encouraged – something that was perhaps in danger of being lost among the pre-defined programme of units.

The idea behind the Inflation and Unemployment stimulus was that pupils would consider issues that receive considerable prominence in the media (see Appendix 4). The inflation unit started with pupils viewing a slide of a supermarket window from the early 1970s. Prices are prominently displayed and a brainstorming session followed. Pupils were asked to compare the prices displayed with current prices. Questions raised included:

- why have prices risen?
- does it matter that prices have risen?
- who determines/controls prices?

The unemployment data was intended to divert attention away from unemployment statistics towards the implications of unemployment for the individual, the immediate locality and the economy as a whole. The second data sheet stating the 'apparent' causes of unemployment was generated by one particular group of pupils with no guidance from the teacher. These were then thrown back at the group for a fuller discussion. Overall the units perhaps encouraged a recognition that there might be many and conflicting causes and therefore no simple solution.

Assessment

The adoption of the NEA Integrated Humanities scheme, in sharp contrast to the non-examinable nature of the previous course, necessitated serious thinking about assessment. However, as candidates would not be entered until the 1987 joint 'O' level/CSE examination, the Board did not require notification of formal assessments until early 1987.

It was decided to base the assessment on what pupils had done to avoid the constraints that would be imposed by setting formal assessment tasks prior to the module. The scheme of assessment in the NEA's syllabus allows for this:

'The flexibility of the scheme enables centres . . . to vary the basis of assessment for individual candidates according to both their particular ability, and the degree of freedom offered to the course.'[6]

What seems an important consideration here is the purpose of such assessment. Invariably it will be for the purpose of the examination, but will this guarantee that pupils' development in terms of economic awareness will be assessed? This is a problem for the current Head of Department to grapple with.

Reflections

Writing this case study from a 'safe distance' has allowed me to review a number of aspects of the economic literacy programme as it currently operates in the fourth/fifth year of the school.[7]

1) A favourable climate for change already existed in the school and the ease with which the 'package' was adopted perhaps encouraged complacency on the part of the author. Neither the aims nor the content was challenged. The relative isolation of the Head of Department as a 'one person' department reinforced this. Other perspectives were needed.

2) With hindsight the aims of both the original programme and that submitted as a syllabus for the Integrated Humanities module raise a number of questions:

   - Was sufficient attention devoted to the aims *prior* to the content planning?
   - What is meant by the notion of 'some basic economics education'? What could reasonably be achieved in such a limited time?
   - How should the 'key concepts' be chosen? What are (or should be) 'key concepts'? Was the choice merely random, justified by some vague reference to those 'which are likely to be within the sphere of their own (the pupils') experience'? Is it vitally important that the concepts be identified so clearly?

3) The issue of staff development looms large. No other staff were involved in the planning of the module. Despite being encouraged to experiment with the units, the majority felt uncertain about material with which they were unfamiliar. Only one of the 'team' developed the course beyond the suggestions in the teachers' notes. Consultation and reviews with other staff about their experiences only took place on an *ad hoc* basis.

   Is it realistic to expect non-specialist staff to evaluate the experience of the pupils from an economic perspective without the benefit of in-service training? Can we also assume that specialists will automatically recognize the nature of economic awareness?

   In retrospect, far too much attention was devoted to content and materials with little heed paid to other staff members involved, in terms of their development in appreciating what economic awareness might be and adapting to alternative teaching/learning strategies with which they may have been unfamiliar. Providing them with the package of materials and teacher's notes is clearly not sufficient.

4) I had envisaged that the course would change in the light of experience. In practice the 'package' remains unchanged. Is this a strength or a weakness? As a result have the staff become more competent at handling familiar materials or is it an indicator that little thought is being given to evaluating the module?

5) The school provides a relatively short timeslot for economic literacy. Is this the best way to develop economic awareness? Might not a better approach be through a broader curriculum involvement so that there is a degree of continuous experience for pupils? Moreover, should there be a clear link with the lower school curriculum so that coherence and progression are encouraged?

Notes and references

1   Hounslow Manor School Prospectus.
2   *Curriculum 11–16: Working Papers by Her Majesty's Inspectorate, a contribution to the current debate*, DES, 1977.
3   *The Contribution of Economics to General Education*, Report of an *ad hoc* Committee of the Economics Association, 1977.
4   Economics Association, *Understanding Economics*, Longman, 1985.
5   'SURVIVAL, a simulation to introduce students to the study of economics', W. E. Jennings, in *Handbook for Economics Teachers*, ed. D. Whitehead (Heinemann, 1979).
6   NEA – Integrated Humanities Syllabus, Scheme of Assessment, paragraph (K).
7   At the time of writing Phil Jones was seconded to a post of Department of Trade and Industry Fellow at the University of London Institute of Education.

Appendix 1: Fourth year curriculum, 1986–7

Extended core

English (7 periods)
NEA, GCSE English Language and Literature

Humanities (5 periods)
NEA, GCSE Integrated Humanities:
  The family
  Law
  Pollution
  Conservation
  Economic literacy
  Politics and beliefs
  Careers
  Health education

Modular maths, science and technology (13 periods)
Lead to:

1) Single Certification in the NEA Mode-III GCSE (KMP) – approximately 50% course-work
2) Double Certification in the NEA, GCSE Modular Science and Technology

Pupils take four core modules plus 10 option modules over the two-year course (one module = four periods for 8 weeks)

Games (3 periods)

Constrained options
Aesthetic (4 periods)
One from: Art; Pottery; Music; Drama

Open options
One from: Art; Music; Drama; Pottery; CDT; French; German; Spanish; Business Studies; Home Economics; History; Geography; Religious Studies; **Economics**; Typing

Appendix 2: Economic literacy in life studies

Hounslow Manor School: Economic Literacy

Aim
Quite simply to provide some basic economics education for all pupils across the ability range.

The course
Fourth year: A one term unit consisting of approximately 12 lessons (12 × 35 mins).

Fifth year: A 9 week unit (9 × 35 mins).

(As from September 1985 the time allocation is likely to be increased when economic literacy becomes one of the components of 'Integrated Humanities' which will be followed by *all* fourth/fifth year pupils.)

The course is divided clearly between the fourth and fifth years. The fourth year programme concentrates on introducing pupils to economic concepts which are likely to be within the sphere of their own experience – scarcity, choice, opportunity cost, limits to spending, and so on.

The fifth year programme takes a broader view and considers the macro-economy and major issues of problems.

Appendix 3: Proposed integrated humanities module

'Economic Literacy' (free option)

The main aim of the content of this component is to introduce students of all abilities to *some* economic concepts with an emphasis on the role of the individual within the economy. This should enable students:

● to make judgements about economic issues and recognize and understand economic terminology

● to develop skills relevant to these judgements,

i.e. distinguish between statements of fact and expression of opinion, present arguments and points of view, evaluate data, and so on.

● to recognize the importance of values, the conflicts that arise from differing value judgements and to examine their own values.

Proposed syllabus

1) Nature of human 'economic' wants – factors that determine individual wants, including age, taste, status, etc.
Relationship between infinite wants and finite resources – satisfaction of wants through consumption of goods and services.
Relationship of satisfaction of wants to personal purchasing power and level of state provision.
Extent to which individual wants to be satisfied within economies and between economies.
Demand and price – market demand.

2) Production – the chain of processes involved – interdependence between each link – the interdependence of workers in different industries and the different sectors of industry.
Impact of technical change – extension of range and quality of goods available to satisfy consumer wants – substitute goods.
Role of advertising as an information link between producer and consumer – means of persuasion.
Interdependence of producers and consumers.

3) Income – creation of income – the distribution of income wages – supply of and demand for, labour – derived demand. Relationship between personal spending and level of personal income – personal budgeting – opportunity cost.
Means of affecting the distribution of income. Relationship between employment and consumer expenditure.

4) Provision of goods and services through international trade – interdependence of trading nations – international payments and exchange rates.

5) Unemployment and inflation – with emphasis on the effects on the individual in terms of satisfying wants.

6) State provision of goods and services – public

goods and merit goods – economic welfare considerations.
Constraints on provision by the state – taxation – budgeting. The costs and benefits associated with state provision – distinction between private and social costs/benefits.

Teaching units

● SURVIVAL – simulation to introduce some basic economic concepts concerned with the 'economic problem': scarcity, choice, production, distribution, specialization of labour, etc.
(Fourth year: Lesson 1; Lesson 2 follow-up)

● 14–16 Project – Young Person as Consumer – 'Consumers'
Based on contrasting photographs designed to stimulate discussion about human wants, satisfaction of wants, level of purchasing power, etc.
(Fourth year: Lesson 3; Lesson 4 follow-up)

● 14–16 Project – Young Person as Consumer – 'Wanting'
A simple analysis of the influences on individual demand and highlighting the interdependence of consumers and producers.
(Fourth year: Lesson 5; Lesson 6 follow-up)

● 14–16 project – Young Person as Consumer – 'Paying'
By surveying pupils' own income and spending, the idea of income distribution and the relationship between levels of income and spending is introduced.
(Fourth year: Lesson 7; Lesson 8 follow-up)

● 14–16 Project – Young Person as Consumer – The Price of Pop
An audio tape recording is used to develop understanding of factors influencing demand for a product, especially the relationship between demand and price, and the effects of a change in demand on sales.
(Fourth year: Lesson 9; Lesson 10 follow-up)

● 14–16 Project – Young Person as Producer – Andy's Car
Illustrates the idea of 'interdependence' between producers and consumers, workers in different industries, derived demand, consumer spending and employment, and the idea of production as a chain of processes.
(Fourth year: Lesson 11; Lesson 12 follow-up)

● 14–16 Project – Young Person as Producer

– The Rate for the Job
Introduces the idea that wages are influenced by factors on both the demand and supply sides of the labour market.
(Fifth year: Lessons 1 and 2)

- INFLATION/UNEMPLOYMENT
A look at two major economic problems where the effects on the individual are highlighted, especially the effects on choice and the social costs involved.
(Fifth year: Lessons 3 and 4)

- INTERNATIONAL TRADE
Britain's trading position with the rest of the world – interdependence and links with Third World – increased provision of goods/services through trade.
(Fifth year: Lessons 5 and 6)

- STATE PROVISION OF GOODS AND SERVICES
  — 14–16 Project – Young Person as Consumer
    – Budgeting
    Introduce idea of simple individual budget – notion of 'opportunity cost' and develop this to central/local government expenditure/income.
  — 14–16 Project – Young Person as Citizen
    – Who Pays?
    Introduce idea of State provision of goods/services.
  — 14–16 Project – Young Person as Citizen
    – Community Expenditure
    Role play exercise in which pupils consider economic criteria in making environmental social and political judgements on implementing a series of local government spending cuts.

Appendix 4: Illustrative material

Inflation

Look carefully at the slide.

1) Make a list of five of the products advertised in the supermarket window along with their prices.
   ....

2) Estimate what you think the prices of these products might be today.
   ....

3) Try to explain why the prices are now different?
   ....

4) What do you think has happened to wages during this time?
   ....

5) When you are talking about i_____n we usually mean that both *prices* and *wages* are
   ....

6) (a) Look at the selection of newspaper cuttings. Make a list of all the inflation rates you can see.
   ....

   (b) Which country has the lowest rate of inflation?
   .... What is the rate? ....

   (c) which country has the highest rate of inflation?
   ....What is the rate? ....

   (d) Imagine the United Kingdom had the same rate of inflation as the country with the highest rate. You buy something today for one pound. How much do you think it would cost in a year's time?
   ....

   (e) If you were working, what would you want to happen to your wages if prices were increasing by this amount?
   ....

   Can you explain why you would want this to happen?
   ....

   (f) Which groups of people do you think would suffer most from such a dramatic increase in prices?
   ....

Spending in shops shows sharp rise in February

Average pay rise is 6% says CBI

Annual rise in earnings stays 7¾% in January

Fuel and material costs up by 9.5%

By Max Wilkman Economic Correspondent

INFLATIONARY

Bank lending rise forces up money supply

Industry materials costs up 8.6%

Rate of inflation stays at 5.2 pc

RETAIL PRICES (1975 : 00)

	Apr 84	% change over previous year
W. Germany	143.4	3.2
France	242.1	7.8
Italy	376.0	11.5
Netherlands	161.5	3.5
Belgium	181.1	7.5
UK	259.4	5.2
US	191.5	4.5
Japan	153.4	2.3

A 50 Mark note, worth about £195 sterling when issued in June 1919 would then have bought two dozen eggs available at 7 pfennigs each in 1914 A 10,000,000,000 Mark note was worth £1 sterling when issued on 1 October 1923 Three weeks later it would have bought one-seventh of an egg

Inflation in Brazil heads for 224 pc

Argentina : Inflation 688%!

Zero inflation by 1988 predicted

Unemployment – Study sheet 1

Look at the unemployment stimulus. Discuss the cases within your groups, then answer the following questions.

1) List any words or phrases which describe the feelings of the unemployed workers in the extracts shown here (e.g. 'it makes you feel a failure').

2) Why do you think they feel like this?

....

3) Has lack of money had a major effect on these people? Support your views by referring to the extracts.

....

4) How do members of the family suffer economically when the major wage earner becomes unemployed?

....

5) Can you think of any ways in which shops, pubs, clubs, businesses and so on could be affected if there was a large number of unemployed people in their area?

....

6) Can you think of two effects that growing unemployment has on the Government's spending plans?

....

'People say to me: Oh your life is one long holiday ... I've not had a job for two years, and with a police record, I'm not likely to get one very easily. I stay in bed most days till about one o'clock; there's nothing to get up for. You'd be surprised how much you can sleep if you try. When I wake up and think of all the hours I've got to fill I think "Oh Christ", you find yourself looking forward to when the kids' programmes come on telly. That's when you realize just how far you've started to rot. The estate where I live is a bit posher than some of them, a lot of people are going to buy their houses. You feel conspicuous if they see you laying around in the daytime, they look at you as if you were something the cat sicked up on the new carpet.'
(Man, 30s)

'My wife has known nothing but debt and poverty ever since we've been married ... I ought to feel glad being able to spend so much time with my kids while they're young. But I just feel shame that I can't provide them with the things they need. We have no life together, I've even stopped looking for work. Some days I feel like topping myself ... if there's no hope for me, what chance will there be for them?'
(Unemployed man, Sunderland, 20s)

Photograph of Job Centre

'I worked for 25 years in the pit, and I never had a day off work; but then I got arthritis of the spine – I get £40 invalidity benefit. I give £14 to my wife and children; we're separated ... I can't eat starchy food because of my diabetes. I'm supposed to eat meat and fruit, but how can I on £26 a week. I can't buy clothes, when things wear out I can't replace them. I feel shabby. My only outings are to the hospital ... I can't go to the club to buy a drink for anyone; I can't even afford one for myself ... I get very depressed and lonely. I've no hope ever of working again ... It makes you feel useless, you feel you've no right to exist.' (Man, 50s)

'If you've got no work, everything seems to mock you. It might be me, but you feel it. The television, the adverts, everything, the papers are full of the lives of millionaires, the shops are full of things you can't afford ... it makes you feel humiliated ... it destroys your self-respect ... your kids can't have what others do, it makes you feel a failure.' (Man, 40s)

UNEMPLOYMENT STIMULUS 1

'The trade unions have resisted the introduction of new machinery which would have allowed firms to compete with countries like Japan. They can produce similar products much more cheaply and efficiently than we can. Look at the Sunday Times – it was shut down for a year because the unions didn't like the new computerized equipment.'

'I used to sell most of the tractors I produced abroad. But then because my production costs increased I was forced to put up my price, and orders fell. I had no option but to make some of my employees redundant.'

'It's the government's fault. They have concentrated so hard on curing inflation they have allowed unemployment to rise and forced people to accept lower rates of pay. You can't have low inflation and full employment.'

Photograph of
People's March for Jobs

'The Government is too soft with the unemployed. Benefits are far too high – no one will work if they are paid to do nothing. Cut unemployment benefit and social security – that's the answer?'

'It's all the workers' fault, especially the trade unions. They have gained large increases in pay without working any harder. Why, even the number of hours most people work in a week have fallen. Firms just can't afford to employ as many people.'

'Look around in the shops and you will find that most stainless steel cutlery is made in the Far East. They can produce it much more cheaply than firms in Britain. Workers are prepared to work for much lower wages. A city like Sheffield has suffered a tremendous blow as a result.'

'I used to work for a washing machine manufacturer in the paint shop, then the firm installed a robot-controlled paint sprayer which could work faster and eventually more cheaply than humans. Twenty of us were made redundant.'

UNEMPLOYMENT STIMULUS 2

3 Economic awareness in a developing modular structure – the experience of three Manchester schools

Barry McClelland with Peter Clarke, Elaine Owen and Ian Meadowcroft

'Economics education, in some form, is desirable for the whole ability range 14–16, and its extension for this age group should therefore be encouraged.'

Economics Education 14–16, NFER 1980

When Holley and Skelton wrote these words[1] there was very little evidence of economic awareness being taught in Manchester schools. A small number of schools (6 out of 29) offered economics as an option to 'O' level and CSE. Approximately 50% of schools offered commerce, and others felt that they offered elements of economic awareness to pupils through personal and social education.

The shortcomings in this provision were evident. The availability of economics and commerce as 'options' meant that they were not open to the whole ability range. Economics, especially, was the preserve of the more academic pupil. On the other hand, it is questionable as to how much economic awareness was being provided through commerce. A survey of schools in Manchester carried out by one of the writers in 1985 showed that teachers of commerce themselves held widely differing views concerning the economic awareness content within their courses. PSE programmes posed a similar problem in that teaching was largely being carried out by members of staff who were not trained as economics teachers.

Manchester schools therefore faced two problems:

1) could the curriculum be modified to allow economic awareness to be provided for the entire ability range?
2) how could resources be developed for use in the classroom by non-economists?

School reorganization in Manchester in 1982 created the opportunity for the curriculum to be modified. In *A Curriculum for Today and Tomorrow* (1982) the local authority stated:

'There are aspects of life-skills and knowledge needed for life in society which are unlikely to be learned unless taught in schools, e.g. . . . some of the concepts of economics.'[2]

The LEA also suggested the methodology for the implementation of economic awareness: a modular course under the contemporary studies umbrella. Contemporary studies was to be allocated four periods per week (10% of the timetable) with modules varying in length from two or three weeks to a whole term. The involvement of Manchester schools in the dissemination phase of the Economics Education 14–16 Project in September 1984 provided resources which could be used in the classroom by non-economists, thus creating the opportunity for Manchester schools to expand their provision. This process was encouraged by the active involvement of the LEA, both financially and developmentally, in meeting the costs of providing the Project materials to all participating schools and by supporting a coordinator and an INSET programme.

The introduction of modules of work in economic awareness has proved popular in the Manchester schools. Of the 18 schools involved in the LEA's programme of work in July 1986, nine had already introduced a module of economic awareness into the curriculum, two teaching the module to third year pupils. Outlined below are the modules of work introduced into three of the schools.

Trinity Church of England High School

Trinity is an 11–16 coeducational school which has recently moved to a single site close to the city centre. Economic awareness was introduced into the school in September 1984, when Manchester LEA became involved in the dissemination phase of the Economics Education 14–16 Project. The Head of Humanities and Contemporary Studies commented:

'This Project offered the answers to some questions regarding the introduction of a basic economics programme into the curriculum which I'd had on my mind for some time.'

Pre-publication versions of units from *Understanding Economics*[3] were tried out with pupils in CSE commerce to gauge their reactions to them. The appointment of the commerce teacher to the position of Head of Humanities and Contemporary Studies facilitated the introduction of an economic awareness module, which would use the Project materials in fifth year contemporary studies (see Appendix 1). She was optimistic: 'I felt very comfortable about the materials and what we could achieve using them.' The economic awareness module is spread over 10 weeks, with one hour per week.

In 1985–6 sets of pupils circulated round a team of three teachers, but this was reduced to two teachers in September 1986. The staff members involved are not trained in economics, but feel they have benefited from the support of the LEA coordinator, both via INSET and in their classrooms. They feel that the modular structure has permitted them to gain confidence and to develop more quickly because they have been able to use the same materials with different groups throughout the year.

Teething problems were bound to occur as the staff grappled with pupil-centred activities for the first time. However, practice and help from the LEA coordinator facilitated the transition from more traditional approaches.

Course assessment consists of a simple question sheet at the end of each unit which attempts to ascertain whether or not the pupils have understood the basic objectives of the unit. The pupils are also involved in evaluating the course at the end of the fourth and fifth years by means of question sheets, in which they are asked to state their views on the value of the various modules.

One effect of including new areas of experience into 'core' courses of this type can be to reduce its status in the eyes of both staff and students. The Head of Humanities and Contemporary Studies feels that status was not a problem in this case because she 'so firmly believes in the course and gets the Head's backing'.

She feels that the Head of Department plays a crucial role in the process. She has now left the school with no guarantee that her successor would have the same priorities. Two further developments were intended:

'The impact on the curriculum could have been far-reaching had it developed in the way I'd intended. It would have supported the Manchester Modular Humanities GCSE I wanted to adopt which was to have included an economics module.'

and

'As Head of Humanities and with a team with similar views to my own, it was readily agreed that we should introduce economics lower down the school as a basis of support for possible future courses at 14–16 as well as being an essential part of any general education programme.'

In this case both these developments have been continued, but teacher mobility between schools can still be a major factor in the long-term development of a curriculum.

North Manchester High School for Girls

North Manchester is an 11–16 girls' comprehensive school in a residential area to the north of the city centre. It draws in pupils from local council estates and from a wide range of socio-economic backgrounds.

Economics education was introduced into the curriculum in 1982 in response to local authority guidelines. Initially this took the form of a consumer education module as part of the general studies course for all fourth and fifth year pupils and was introduced by a teacher with previous experience of teaching economics. Manchester's involvement in the dissemination phase of the Economics Education 14–16 Project in September 1984 created the opportunity for an economic awareness module to be introduced for fifth year pupils.

An eight-week module with four lessons per week is now in operation (see Appendix 2). Topics taught in 1985–6 included standards of living, interdependence of wants, advertising, budgeting and starting in business. Student activities included role-playing, problem-solving and simulations. Stimulus material in the form of computer programs, photographs, cartoon strips and television were employed.

The module is taught by one teacher, the Head of General Studies. He has found INSET arrangements very supportive because they 'allowed teachers to meet and benefit from shared experiences'. To him these informed discussions with colleagues were important because he 'felt competent to use the materials but was very aware that (he) was the sole teacher of the course'.

He faced two main problems, the organization of computer facilities and course organization:

'Perhaps the most serious problem is the time it takes to develop a well-structured and meaningful course and undoubtedly the need for effective course planning/preparation should be a high priority when devising in-service training sessions.'

He feels that the course has made an impact on both pupil and teacher. For the pupil:

'As a result of this and other modular courses the curriculum is much broader and more relevant to the needs of the young pupil.'

For the teacher:

'I have found teaching this course stimulating and rewarding – I have re-thought my ideas about the ways in which pupils learn and changed my teaching methods accordingly. There is far more pupil participation in the lesson.'

The school intends that the module will eventually be validated by the Northern Partnership for Records of Achievement (NPRA). The validated unit would then form part of a Letter of Credit issued to the pupil by the Northern Examining Association (NEA).

Levenshulme High School for Girls

Levenshulme is an 11–16 girls' comprehensive which caters for pupils from a densely populated area about four miles from the city centre. There is a large Asian ethnic community in the school.

Economic awareness has been developed as part of a two-year course in life skills which has a modular structure. In 1985–6 the economic awareness module was one of 10 modules in the fourth year, each being given four afternoons within the timetable.

Two reasons are put forward for the inclusion of economic awareness as part of the life skills course:

'Economic awareness, at the very least, was important for all pupils.'

and

'There was nowhere else in the existing curriculum that economic awareness could be put. In addition, the fourth and fifth year curriculum had been revised only a year earlier so there seemed little chance of introducing a major course in the immediate future.'

The approach adopted was constrained to a large extent by the situation. The teacher in charge commented:

'I was writing a life skills module, although the content might be economic. I wished to include if possible elements of consumption, production and macro-economics.'

'I wished to use the Economics 14–16 materials

as I felt that the approach was not only correct from an economics point of view, but also fitted in well in a life skills course.'

Activities for week one were devoted to computers. The teacher hoped to use three units from *Understanding Economics* – the set of colour slides showing different methods of payment from 'Alternatives', the 'Bank Loan', role-plays and the spending diary from 'Paying'. In the event only two of these activities proved to be possible in the time.

Activities for week two were devoted to production. The teacher hoped to use elements from 'Production Record Sheets', 'Ice Cream Factory' and 'Tiny Atom Radio'. However, he found again that the discussion and interest aspects resulting from the use of 'Production Record Sheets' was so great that one of the units had to be omitted.

Activities for week three investigated the 'citizen'. It was proposed to use 'Community Expenditure', 'Who Pays' and 'The Accident' but the whole afternoon was taken up by 'Community Expenditure'.

Week four was used to pull things together and to assess the pupils. The circular flow of income was introduced via discussion.

In September 1986 the time allocation for the module was increased from four to six weeks, giving grounds for optimism. The teacher hoped that this would allow some of the activities planned for in 1985–6, but not used, to be included in the programme.

Conclusions

Modular development has, then, facilitated the incorporation of economic awareness into some schools. The three schools described above were not in · a position, prior to the introduction of modular structures, to offer economic awareness either as part of the core curriculum, or as an option. The pressures on curriculum time for separate subjects were enormous.

But how effective is the modular approach in allowing economic awareness to be developed in the classroom? Clearly any meaningful response requires some consensus on the meaning of econ-

omic awareness, a consensus which has not been available to teachers.

However, some insights into the question might be gained by considering the materials used, the confidence and competence of teachers in using them and the curriculum time available.

Units from *Understanding Economics* formed the basis for the materials used. Teachers in the three schools expressed satisfaction with the materials, feeling that they met the objectives of the courses established. With regard to the teachers themselves, differences emerged between those who were experienced in teaching economics, and those who were not.

In two of the schools the modules were taught by experienced teachers of economics who were able to develop courses for themselves and to transfer their hopes into the classroom with relative ease. In the third school, outside help was needed to give confidence to the teaching staff. Confidence and expertise developed relatively quickly, because the staff was able to teach the same modules a number of times in the year, and so become familiar with them.

With regard to the time available for economic awareness to be developed, in one school a four-week module clearly gave little or no opportunity. The teacher coordinator in the school was outspoken (but not optimistic) in giving this view: 'Ideally, the only way to make sure that pupils receive a thorough grounding in economic awareness could be to provide a two year module!'

Staff in a second school were less concerned, feeling that it was more important to develop their own experience and to build on from that.

The Head of General Studies in the third school regarded the introduction of a module as only a beginning.

'It would be nice to have more time ... this would facilitate the investigation of other areas of economic awareness in greater detail. However, the main thing is that the modular approach has created the opportunity for economic awareness to become part of the core curriculum ... otherwise there would have been nothing available for the pupils.'

This last point does perhaps summarize the importance of the situation. Modular structures have facilitated the introduction of economic awareness as part of the core curriculum in a number of schools, but if coherence and progression are to be achieved, the introduction of a single module with a severe time restriction can only be seen as the starting point of long-term development.

References

1 Holley, B. and Skelton, V. *Economics Education 14–16*, NFER, 1980, p. 186.
2 Manchester Education Committee, *A Curriculum for Today and Tomorrow*, 1982.
3 Economics Association, *Understanding Economics*, Longman, 1985.

Appendix 1: Contemporary studies module in economic awareness (Trinity Church of England High School)

The course was designed in the following way because it was felt to be important for pupils to be able to view themselves as consumers and citizens in economic terms and these seemed to be major areas of neglect in the fourth and fifth year curriculum.

The course was set up to allow pupils to become aware of their position in an 'economic' society and to enable them to realize that choices exist and that their decisions can influence behaviour. We also wanted pupils to be aware of the part played by society in our economic system and how individual actions and decisions as well as collective/political decisions are economically important (illustrated).

The following units from *Understanding Economics* were used:

YOUNG PERSON AS A CONSUMER

A 'Consumers'
B 'Wanting'
F 'Budgeting'
I 'Price of Pop'

OUTLINE OF CONCEPTS FOR ECONOMIC AWARENESS COURSE USING 14–16 PROJECT MATERIALS

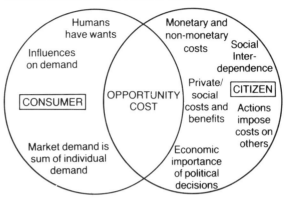

YOUNG PERSON AS A CITIZEN

A 'The Accident'
B Vandalism (unpublished unit)
D 'Costs and Benefits'
C 'Community Expenditure'
G 'Who Pays?'
H 'Public Spending'

The course was designed to run for ten one-hour lessons in *one year only*, with both fourth and fifth year pupils, who up until this time had no economic awareness courses of any kind.

Assessment was not entirely satisfactory. A checklist sheet was used containing the main economics terms and ideas being sought out of each lesson. Pupils were asked to comment on whether or not they felt they understood certain words/phrases. Differences between pupil and teacher's views provided a basis for discussion!

We also included 'Consumers' as part of the second year humanities course in the theme 'A Look into the Future – a Consumer Society'.

Appendix 2: Economic awareness module outline (North Manchester High School for Girls)

The economic awareness module is taught to groups of 25 fifth year pupils as part of the general studies course. General studies is part of the core curriculum for all fourth and fifth year pupils.

The course runs for 7/8 weeks for two hours a week and the groups rotate between the teachers involved in general studies.

Week 1

The aim of the first lesson is to introduce the ideas of scarcity, choice and opportunity cost using the two photographs from 'Consumers' (*Understanding Economics*) as stimulus material. The class 'brainstorm' and produce a list of words/phrases and then divide into groups to discuss the ideas which arise. The differences between wants and needs, necessities and luxuries are established. The second lesson reinforces the first by considering the interdependence of wants. Here a car/holiday/house or other major purchase is used as stimulus and pupils work in pairs or groups to discuss how one purchase necessitates another.

Week 2

Follow-up work on 'Opportunity Cost' – each pupil has an imaginary £50/100 to spend and prioritizes her wants/needs. Reasons for choices are given and shared with others in the group. Time is available to introduce further stimulus material concerned with comparative living standards and differences of living standards within countries.

Week 3

The above leads on to a wider budgeting exercise – 'Budgeting' (*Understanding Economics*). Pupils act out Maya's budget and work in groups on the worksheets provided. The pressures on Maya are identified and, in the following lesson, pupils are encouraged to prepare their own weekly budget and to give reasons for the choice they make.

Week 4

A computer program, 'Estate Agent' (Longman, 1985)*, is used to identify the factors which affect the demand for and the price of houses. There are considerable practical difficulties here if the com-

puter room is not available, but it is possible to use one computer and a large TV screen in the lecture theatre where the TV is clearly visible. Pupils make decisions about the house prices after working through part of the program – the teacher simply operates the computer according to the girls' instructions. Data are recorded on the worksheets which accompany the program.

A follow-up lesson entails the girls visiting an estate agent and bringing to school leaflets, brochures, etc., showing housing details and prices. In pairs or groups the girls identify the factors influencing the actual prices of houses in their own area.

Week 5

The notion of advertising is developed by working through the unit 'Wanting' (*Understanding Economics*) and through a TV programme, 'To Buy or Not to Buy' (BBC, 1986)†, which acts as a stimulus for the worksheet or as an aid to group discussion about how consumer choices are made.

Week 6

The production process and the part played by individuals in it is introduced.

The photographs 'Two Workers' (*Understanding Economics*) are shown and pupil responses are recorded individually. Groups of pupils arrive at an agreed statement about each person's role in the production process.

In the follow-up lesson four or five groups discuss issues/ideas which have emerged from the initial lesson, such as working conditions/pay and bargaining/qualifications/training/skills etc.

Week 7

A more intensive study of a small business is carried out by using the case study 'Price of a Perm' (*Understanding Economics*). The aim is to examine the concepts of cost, revenue and profit and the task involves decision-making and problem-solving skills as pupils identify with Jackie and her situation.

The worksheets are completed in lesson one and

*Computers in the Curriculum, Longman, 1985.

†Economics: A Question of Choice, BBC, 1986.

the problems faced by Jackie are considered in lesson two.

Week 8

The final lessons utilize the CAL program 'Workers or Machines' (Longman, 1985). Pupils, in pairs, make decisions about the labour input at various stages in the production process and attempt to evaluate their results. Some of the problems of resource allocation facing the management of larger firms are explained. Ideally pupils require one computer/monitor between two but the program can be run successfully using one computer in the manner outlined above.

4 An admission-year economics module for a 13–18 comprehensive school

Linda M. Thomas

Tamworth Manor School, Merton

Tamworth Manor is a coeducational comprehensive school in a London suburb. Two other secondary schools are situated within half a mile of Tamworth School, a girls' ex-grammar school and a boys' ex-grammar school. Comprehensive reorganization in 1970 brought Tamworth Manor School, an ex-secondary modern coeducational school, into competition with these two schools which retained their single-sex status. During the early 1970s it struggled to survive as parents consistently chose the other schools. Its transformation into an over-subscribed school, providing stability and continuity in a community which has its share of deprivation and racial tensions, is the result of inspired management, a committed teaching staff, an imaginative and flexible curriculum and a pastoral care policy which permeates the whole school and extends into the community.

In 1983 a new Head of Social Studies was appointed to lead a crucial department in the school. Social studies is given the same prominence as English, mathematics, science and games, as part of the core curriculum for all years, and is taught by a team of between 15 and 20 specialists in geography, history, sociology, economics, RE, English and PE. Such principles as mixed-ability teaching, community involvement and concern for worldwide issues are part of its fabric. The following is a list of the core topics studied in the third, fourth and fifth years:

- *Third year*
  Human Origins
  Human Needs and Personality
  Non-Industrial and Industrial Societies
  Economics of Industrial Societies
  Man – Environment
- *Fourth year*
  World at War
  Mankind Divided: Rich World – Poor World
  Prejudice, Racism and Minorities
  Urban Growth and Problems
- *Fifth year*
  Personal Relations and the Family
  The State and Welfare Provision
  Law and Order
  Conclusion – Future for Man

In 1983 the new Head of Department reinforced the position of social studies in the school by developing an overall philosophy and structure for the course and by making module development a group responsibility. It was in this context that, in 1984, the school was invited by the Economics Research and Curriculum Unit (ERCU) at the Institute of Education to join the London network of the Economics Association's Economics Education 14–16 Project.

The introduction of an economics element

During the 1984 summer term, social studies staff used some of the project teaching units (*Understanding Economics*[1]) in a variety of curricular contexts to gain familiarity with the economic ideas and with the implications for classroom work. 'Budgeting' from the *Young Person as Consumer* and

'Community Expenditure' and 'Vandalism' from the *Young Person as Citizen* modules were used in fifth year lessons. Staff concerns were expressed by the Head of Department at a network meeting. He drew attention to the nature of the social studies course and, in particular, to the contents of the fourth year module 'Mankind Divided: Rich World – Poor World':

1) meaning of rich-world/poor-world
2) historical background to global inequality; residuals of colonization
3) perpetuation of poverty:
    core – periphery economic model
    trade – aid system
4) breaking away from under-development; rural development, intermediate technology, etc.
5) conclusions:
    global interdependence
    Keynesian Brandt v. radical new economic order.

He then outlined five key problems for the introduction of an economics module based on project materials into the social studies core curriculum:

1) project emphasis on personal economic literacy and its relevance to national/international issues
2) individualized as opposed to group activities
3) limited aims of project when set against the aims of humanities core
4) multi-cultural emphasis in humanities (+ opposition to prejudice)
5) staff knowledge and competence.

Two possible solutions emerged from the meeting and further discussion – the adaptation and extension of the Economics Education 14–16 Project materials and the provision of some assistance for school-based in-service training of the social studies team.

A module of work was designed to incorporate the department's perspective (see Appendix 1). Arrangements for teacher support included the preparation of detailed notes (see Appendix 2). In addition, informal meetings with staff from the University of London Institute of Education and teachers seconded during 1984 under a BP fellowship scheme gave support within the classrooms.

The module was taught to third year classes during the winter terms 1984–5. At the end of the year the social studies examination included an economics unit.

The position in 1986–7

The economics module is now a half-term module with individual teachers free to use any of the original units. The original end-of-year examination unit is administered at the end of the half term as a class test.

The course coordinator for the third year course reports that there is an urgent need to change the module to take account of developments in thinking about economic awareness and in teaching and learning strategies but she recognizes that this will only be feasible when circumstances permit the necessary in-service training.

The process

The picture painted above is of a dynamic department in which teachers are actively engaged in a process of evaluation and development. Two questions remain unanswered:

1) why did this particular development occur?
2) what is its effect on the curriculum, teachers and students?

In responding to the first question, the effect of one or more factors may be easily exaggerated. However, it is important to record the intervention of external agencies and interesting to speculate about their influence.

In 1983–4 the Humanities Adviser for Merton in collaboration with Advisers from the London boroughs of Hounslow and Waltham Forest opened the discussion about economic awareness with members of staff at the Institute of Education. Eventually, seven LEAs in London formed a partnership with the Economics Research and Curriculum Unit at the University of London Institute of Education to establish a London network for the Economics Association's 14–16 Project based at Manchester University. Tamworth Manor became one of the 30 network schools when it was launched in April 1984.

Each school undertook to use some of the project's materials during the summer term and to consider ways of introducing economic awareness programmes into its curriculum. Support was provided by ERCU staff and by teachers seconded under the BP fellowship scheme. Teachers were freed on seven days from April 1984 to July 1985 to attend network meetings at the Institute, and local twilight meetings were also arranged.

An additional resource was made available to Tamworth Manor. The writer, a member of the Institute's staff, was also a part-time teacher at the school, and was able to assist the Head of Economics to prepare the module, to introduce the materials to other staff and to provide assistance and advice for the team of teachers both informally and at meetings. There is no doubt that the presence and active involvement in 1984 of the writer and the BP fellow, both at the planning and implementation stages and inside the classroom, together with the link in 1984–5 with a national curriculum development project, had a considerable effect during the first year. But all external support was withdrawn at the end of 1985 and since then major changes in staffing have occurred. (The Head of Department, for example, has been seconded for 1986–7, and the present course coordinator was not a member of Tamworth Manor staff when the module was first introduced in 1984.) Despite these changes, the module survives as an integral part of the third year course and an economic awareness programme is firmly established in the core curriculum.

The current course coordinator supports the module because of the relevance and accessibility of its content and the quality of its activities in which students are involved. But at the same time it is possible that opportunities for group work and for the kind of critical reflection where students could share their perceptions of the experiences provided are less fully exploited than opportunities for transmitting the knowledge which is necessary to pass examinations. Members of staff are aware of this and recognize that a further stage in the process of development will require them to work together to examine and evaluate the validity of the experiences provided in terms of a wider range of learning outcomes.

References

1 Economics Association, *Understanding Economics*, Longman, 1985.

Appendix 1: The module

The economics module was given the title *Producers and Workers* and was sub-divided into four units of work: 'Introduction', 'Enterprise', 'What about the Workers?' and 'Megatronics'.

1 Introduction

The introductory unit establishes the idea of an economic system which exists to transform scarce resources into the goods and services which people want.

'Consumers', a unit from the Young Person as Consumer module of *Understanding Economics*, illustrates by means of two photographs some of the characteristics of industrialized and less developed countries. The photographs are adapted to provide more information and to link with previous work on eskimos. In the first activity students compare certain features of the two economic systems.

The remainder of the introductory unit concentrates in depth on one aspect of industrialized societies – interdependence. 'Andy's Car', a unit in the Young Person as Producer module of *Understanding Economics*, contains a tape and slides. The worksheet format employed in the unit is changed slightly to facilitate group analysis of complex questions about the car industry, its decline, the effects of that decline and possible solutions. For example, the car-production graph is adapted; one group of pupils is placed in the position of an unemployed ex-British Leyland worker and prepares the case for putting a tax on foreign cars, while another group argues against the idea of a tax on foreign cars from the standpoint of a person looking for a new car.

2 Enterprise

The enterprise unit explores some of the choices made by small and large businesses. It is based on case study material. The hairdresser in the first case study, Jackie, has decided to set up in business on her own. Figures for both costs and benefits are provided in 'Price of a Perm', a unit in the Young Person as Producer module of *Understanding Economics*. Students work in groups to obtain the necessary data about costs and revenue to allow them to carry out an evaluation of the various choices made by Jackie. The large city centre hairdressers, Scissors, where Jackie's brother John works, is relatively secure and prosperous. Students are given data for Scissors and, as a home-work task, prepare the graph of total costs and account for the difference in costs between Jackie's business and Scissors. The second case study – the 'Ice Cream Factory', another unit from the Young Person as Producer module – allows further exam-ination of the apparent and real costs and benefits of large scale enterprises. Students are to be introduced to the case study by means of a matching exercise. To facilitate this the unit is adapted by cutting up the cartoon scenes depicting the production of ice cream and the textual de-scriptions of the process which accompany them. Students work in small groups to sequence the cartoons and to match them with appropriate captions. The effects on redundancies of introduc-ing machines, the boredom of some jobs, the need to advertise to sell increased output, and the effects of mass production on prices are considered, first by the groups and then in a class discussion session. Homework tasks are based on textbook information about the ownership and control of various types of business and on a collage of newspaper cuttings on various business ventures – for example, local cooperatives.

3 What about the workers?

The third unit examines the meaning of work. 'Two Workers' is a unit in the Young Person as Producer module of *Understanding Economics*. Two photographs, one of a potter, the other of a supermarket assistant, provide a stimulus for dis-cussion of similarities and differences between different jobs. The concept of work is explored further by means of 'What is Work?', another unit from the same module which uses extracts from a Schools Television programme in which a number of teenagers describe their working conditions.

- Extract 1 is the case of a youth who cannot get a job and decides to set up a window-cleaning round. It illustrates the types of costs involved in setting up such a small business and the characteristics of this particular business.
- Extract 2 extracts the ideas of working condi-tions by showing how a young woman left her job to set up a small scale secretarial agency.
- Extract 3 shows a wind surfing instructor whose job is indistinguishable from his leisure pursuit.
- Extract 4 is concerned with a group of unem-ployed teenagers in Hartlepool who do volun-tary work for a 'pound a day'. Their 'wages' are to cover travelling expenses and to maintain a telephone as a contact point for people who want jobs done.

A set of questions helps to introduce the idea that people 'work' and produce goods or services which are of worth to other people without actually being employed or paid for doing a job.

4 Megatronics

This unit, which is due to be published by Long-man in 1987, is centred on a small Welsh village in which Megatronics, the main employer in the area, is fighting to stay in business. It provides a context in which students can apply their developing skills and concepts and a means to integrate and assess the work covered in the other three units. Students are given information on the state of the firm and, in groups, simulate the discussions arising from a management announcement to reorganize the firm. The unit ends with students being encouraged to consider all the costs, benefits and value judge-ments involved.

Appendix 2: Teacher guidance and assistance

Many of the staff who were expected to teach the four units had no formal training in economics. Assistance took the form of detailed teachers' notes and informal meetings at which the teachers were introduced to the units.

The teachers' notes for each unit contain a description of the economics content and purpose and suggestions for organizing the lessons. These are based on suggestions given in the teacher guidance sections of *Understanding Economics* and *Economics: A Question of Choice*, a BBC Schools Television series.

1 Introduction

Description*

This introduction forms a bridge between previous and future work. It establishes the idea of an economic system which exists to transform scarce resources into the goods and services people want. Two case studies from different systems illustrate how individual choice is constrained and influenced not only by personal circumstances but also by the nature and effects of the economic system itself.

In some countries (illustrated by the first photograph and word picture) industrialization and economic development have given families access to fast transport and communication systems, to a wide range of consumer goods and services, and to a legal system which tries to safeguard their rights and to make their responsibilities clear as consumers and workers. And yet the implications of the choices made about the use of resources in these countries are the threat of pollution and environmental damage, unemployed labour resources and disparities between those families with access to employment, higher education and purchasing power and those without such access. In addition, the choices made by these countries have had an effect on other parts of the world.

In other countries (illustrated by the second photograph and word picture) resources remain largely under-utilized in the Western sense and a traditional way of life is undisturbed. Individual families and communities are often self-sufficient. The pattern of world trade condemns many communities to rely on agriculture. The vicissitudes of climate may then leave families prone to famine and starvation. Here, for all but a few, there is no access to fast transport and consumer products or to an infrastructure of public health and educational services.

*Adapted from *Economics: A Question of Choice*, BBC, 1986.

Thus, in all economies choices have to be made about the use of resources – choices by individuals, families, firms, villages, local councils and by government, and the freedom to choose is constrained by personal circumstances, by the national and international economic systems in which we live, by the choices made by everyone else, but above all, simply because resources are scarce.

Throughout this unit, pupils will be encouraged to ask questions about the choices they and other people make when using scarce resources. To help them to do so they will be introduced to and allowed to practice the simple framework of questions which economists have developed to investigate choice behaviour and the way in which economic systems work:

1) What benefits are provided by using scarce resources in a particular way?
2) What are the costs of using scarce resources (in terms of money, time, effort, etc.)?
3) Do the costs exceed the benefits for the particular choice?
4) Are any other costs involved? Would an alternative use of the resources yield more benefit? Are other people affected by the choice?
5) Are any scarce resources being used in the best way? What is best?

One way to organize the three lessons

1) Resources used: two photographs and the features exercise (illustrated). *Content*: the questions which are to be the focus of the lesson – which ones are free to choose? how are choices restricted in each case? *Student activities*: (a) brief initial discussion by whole class; (b) work in pairs or threes on the activity; (c) two groups to form a larger group to compare responses and to record on a larger sheet.

2) Resources used: slides, tape, worksheet. *Content*: interdependence and some of its effects. *Student activities*: (a) class viewing/listening and discussion of worksheet questions; (b) work in pairs to complete worksheet.

3) Resource used: car production graph (illustrated). *Student activities*: (a) small groups to prepare the case against taxing foreign cars *or* the case for a car; (b) class presentation by each group, and debate.

The boys in the photograph live in Cape Dorset, off the coast of Canada. They live in a cold and harsh environment. When they grow up they and their families will depend on their hunting skills for survival. The eskimos' traditional way of hunting is complicated. However, it does not damage the environment in any way.

The boys live in an Eskimo tent made from canvas strong enough to withstand the terrible Arctic winds. Inside there are few possessions; nevertheless everything essential is to hand. Their mother made their clothes, including the sealskin boots which were sewn by hand.

Photograph of Eskimo children hunting

The man in the photograph suffers with a bad chest because he worked for an asbestos company. He finds living in an eighth floor council flat difficult but the council have not yet found him something else.

His weight doesn't help. His doctor has told him to give up smoking because he's got high blood pressure, and to go on a high protein diet. But if he stops smoking he eats more, and in any case he's unemployed and can't afford the diet. He's over fifty and unlikely to get a job now. It's a relief to get into the pub and have a laugh with his mates.

Photograph of middle-aged man eating meal

Look at the following list.

Put a tick in column 1 if you think the description fits the person in the first photograph. Tick column 2 if it fits the person in the second photograph. [Have two blank columns on the right of the page, clearly labelled 'Column 1: first photograph' and 'Column 2: second photograph'.]

Then *add three other things* to the list and put ticks in the columns.

—Can buy a newspaper
—Can grow or catch most of the food he/she needs
—Can be looked after when ill
—Can learn the history of his or her village or town and the people living there
—Can be independent
—Can learn to play a musical instrument
—Can buy food and clothes
—Can teach younger people how to survive when they grow up because he or she has been taught to do so
—Can go and watch sport
—Can breathe pure fresh air
—Can make his or her own clothes
—Can never be unemployed
—Can be looked after when old
—Can travel very cheaply
—Can avoid heart attacks, lung cancer, diabetes
—Can own his or her own house

CAR PRODUCTION GRAPH

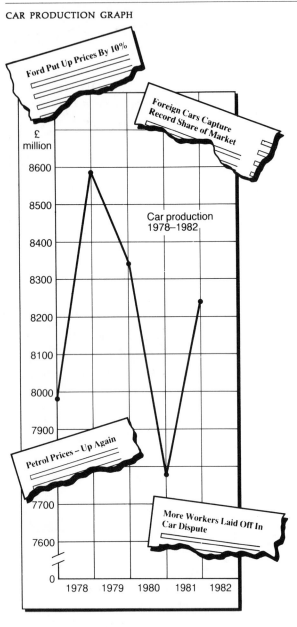

asked to conduct an objective evaluation rather than a straightforward description.

The hairdresser in the first case study, Jackie, has decided to set up on her own. Figures for both costs and benefits are provided, and even at this stage it is possible to note the effect of a value judgement on her part. When she was working in a large establishment she was paid £51 per week. Now she allows herself only £30 per week. Despite this fact, her future is not guaranteed. If she decided to continue with her business she may have to advertise, raise prices, take a further cut in salary or reduce the hours of her part-time assistant. Each one of these alternatives represents a real cost to her, to her customers or to society. On the other hand, the large city centre hairdressers, Scissors, is relatively secure and prosperous.

The second case study – the Ice Cream Factory – provides the means to examine the apparent and real costs and benefits of large scale enterprises; for example, lower prices, the effect on redundancies of introducing machines, the boredom of some jobs, and the need to advertise to sell any increased output.

One way to organize the three lessons

1) Resources used: case study of Jackie's hairdressing business; case study of Scissors. *Content*: different concepts of costs and returns for a small business. *Student activities*: (a) work in pairs to complete the worksheet; (b) class discussions of suggestions made in response to the last question – what should Jackie do if she fails to break-even? (c) homework task – Scissors.

2) Resources used: case study of the ice cream factory. *Content*: focus issues: (i) what is the difference between home-made and factory-made? (ii) why are machines used to make ice-cream? (iii) what is the difference between the manager's job and the computer operator's? Which one could be done by machine? *Student activities*: (a) small group matching exercise and discussion of the focus issues; (b) report back and class discussions.

3) Resources used: textbook accounts of various kinds of businesses; newspaper reports. *Content*: ownership and control of business organization. *Student activity*: homework tasks.

2 Enterprise

Description

Work on enterprise continues the practice established in the Introduction. It investigates the use of a framework of questions which allows pupils to investigate the way in which the economic system works. In particular, it explores some of the choices made by small and large businesses. Pupils are

3 What about the workers?

Description

Work is often defined and discussed in conventional terms – for instance by making a comparison between employment and unemployment, by concentrating on trade union activity and with reference only to paid employment. Discussion of such crucial matters rarely encourages reassessment of the concept itself or a recognition of the contribution made to the welfare of the community by activities which are not conventionally classified as work. This unit addresses these issues.

One way to organize the lesson

Resources used: two photographs (What is work?); video. *Content*: different concepts of the nature of work. *Student activities*: (a) comparison of the two photographs in pairs; (b) small group work on the issues raised in the video, each group to concentrate on one extract; (c) class presentation by each group, and discussion.

4 Megatronics

Discussion*

Ours is an age of innovation, one in which the outcomes of human ingenuity and invention are available to those engaged in the productive process. Decisions by firms about the use of workers, machines, entire factories and locations are of major significance in an economic system which can no longer guarantee alternative employment for unused labour resources, and which openly competes with trading neighbours for customers, both at home and abroad.

Weighing the costs and benefits of different combinations of factor inputs and of substituting capital for labour, one factory for another, etc., is not new. It was as important to the architects of the industrial revolution as it is to the captains of commerce and industry today.

However, vivid pictures of the early mechanized factories seem to pale when compared with the roboticized assembly lines of today and the metal and plastic domestics of tomorrow. It is the speed

*Adapted from *Economics: A Question of Choice*, BBC, 1986.

of current technological change which has shattered the traditional view of the worker and the workplace. Mass-employment assembly lines are a thing of the past.

The benefits to larger firms are evident. Increased productivity rates mean greater output potential, increasing returns to capital and labour and the prospect of lower prices. Workers are freed from the monotony of the production line. Moreover, investment in the 'new' manufactures like telecommunications can create the wealth to allow health, education and leisure facilities to be provided for future generations.

Yet, real constraints on change do exist. Trades unionists accept the benefits from new technology, but are naturally wary of mass, and enduring unemployment. They call for sensitive leadership by the Government and a just division of the costs and benefits of change. Small firms' choices are also constrained. Unable to generate a sufficient surplus or to obtain the loan capital required to keep abreast of change, their competitive edge is dulled and many fail. And all too often, whole communities find themselves caught in the middle of all this, depending upon a mass media with its own interests to provide information and a platform for local views to be made public.

The questions raised here are the essence of economics. The contribution which technological change can make to economic development is not in question. However, can its implementation be managed in the best interest of all citizens?

One way to organize the four lessons

1) Resources used: information sheets – the village, the company, newspaper stories of international pressures on the company. *Content*: basic information about location, costs, the multinational aspects, etc. *Student activities*: comprehension tasks; (b) complete the 'Get it Right' worksheet in pairs.

2) Resources used: briefing and agenda sheets for four groups – managers, unions, community, reporters. *Content*: effects of business decisions on different groups of people, and their responses. *Student activities*: (a) in groups, hold meetings to examine the situation and to formulate policy in preparation for the main meeting; (b) one reporter for each group to issue a press release agreed by the group, to cover the main decisions.

3) Resources used: notes produced by students themselves, plus the press releases. *Content*: the development of criteria for evaluating alternative strategies. *Student activities*: the main meeting — whole-class discussion; students in their roles attempt to research a compromise.

4) Resources used: a score sheet for recording the results of the various meetings and activities; a set of questions evaluating the final decision. *Content*: recording of decisions. *Student activities*: (a) individuals to record the decisions taken, with reasons at each stage of the exercise; (b) pairs, then small groups, and finally the whole class, to evaluate the final decision 'out of role'.

5 Economic awareness in a 'core' PSE carousel course

Joe Kellaway

Mansfield High School, Brierfield, Lancashire

Mansfield High School is situated amongst the solid terraced housing of a nineteenth century industrial village between the towns of Burnley and Nelson in north-east Lancashire. Here the textile industry still employs one in four workers. The school's intake – once 1,000 and now 700 – is mainly working class, but includes pupils from more prosperous outlying postwar housing and has a 20% Pakistan ethnic community. Economics is taught neither as a separate exam subject nor in any humanities/social science course. The school's provision of economics education is via a nine-week 'Economic Awareness' module which is a component of the personal and social education (PSE) course taken by all but the 'brightest' 10% of fourth and fifth year pupils. There is, however, some input of economic concepts through such upper school option subjects as commerce, business studies, economic and social history, geography, home economics and RE.

The school's PSE course

The PSE course was set up in 1980. Until 1986–7 it was taught in mixed-ability groups, but the introduction of a City and Guilds '365' course in which pupils stay together for PSE has led to change. Groups vary in size from 18 to 26 pupils. Each pupil receives a total of 99 seventy-minutes lessons of PSE in the two-year course. The modules, each of which lasts nine weeks, are:

- *Fourth year*
  Traffic Education
  Health Education
  Community Service
  World of Work
  Law and Community
  Keyboard Skills
- *Fifth year*
  Political Education
  Computer Appreciation
  World of Work
  Moral Education
  Economic Awareness

The economic awareness module replaced a leisure education module two years ago.

The course is not externally accredited, but the school is currently looking at the Northern Record of Achievement (NPRA) accreditation scheme for the modules. In the PSE scheme pupils move from one module to another, with the teachers remaining with individual modules throughout the academic year. In this way the teacher uses the same material with four different classes in one year. The obvious disadvantages of this approach – such as not knowing individuals too well or the lack of development of the 'relationship' with the group – have been weighed against the considerable advantage that each teacher becomes skilled in using the material and can thus more effectively ensure that the material meets desired aims.

Until two years ago a combination of factors led to the PSE course being described as 'boring', 'irrelevant' or a 'waste of time' by some staff and pupils in the school. It had low status. An absent (seconded) Head of Department for two out of three years, the use of dining rooms as PSE classrooms, the opting out of the course by the 'top' 10% of pupils to follow additional 'O' level lessons, and the staffing of PSE sometimes with fill-in staff at the end of the timetabling exercise, did not help. Many of these problems have now been tackled. A 'team' of teachers has been established and the Headteacher and Deputy Headteacher are personally involved in the teaching.

The teacher and his rationale for PSE

I took economics at 'A' level and continued study-ing it for the first four terms of a social science degree course. From that date in 1973 when I specialized in economic and social history and politics, my contact with economics has been through the other social sciences. I studied public policy in a Masters Degree and sociology and history for PGCE. Until I began the school's PSE module on economic awareness, I had not taught economics in school, but I had constructed various modules for PSE over the previous six years: computer awareness, industrial relations, world of work, political literacy, and advertising.

Certain guidelines structure what I hope to achieve in a PSE module, each lesson being 'built up' from the perceived need to:

- introduce key concepts relevant to the subject
- promote skills learning and practice
- use examples within the pupils' frame of refer-ence
- introduce 'significant' factual knowledge where relevant
- motivate and interest pupils

Central to this is a belief that every concept is teachable and that one must find the appropriate concept-carrying vehicle. An attempt is made to identify the key concepts pertaining to a module and to find appropriate learning materials. The material is usually based on information already possessed by pupils, and then attempts to build outwards towards new knowledge which is con-sidered useful to know as well as being usable in reinforcing the particular concept being learnt. It is also useful to link lessons by referring backwards and forwards to the other lessons in the module so that pupils gain confidence and understanding.

At the same time I seek to help pupils develop and practise useful skills. In most PSE lessons this means

- participating in group/class discussion
- participating in non-friendship groups to achieve a group aim in the allotted time
- forming/following/criticizing a line of argu-ment
- participating in one-to-one simulations involv-ing interviews, discussions or negotiations
- comprehending, translating and analysing sti-mulus material to produce either a synthesis or extrapolation

Given that the PSE course is compulsory and has been held in low esteem in the school in past years, I see it as my job to make PSE lessons particularly enjoyable and interesting. My own criterion for the success of a lesson is whether or not pupils walk out discussing it.

The module in economic awareness

Despite these high ideals the practice has been more mundane. When the economics module was set up two years ago, both the lack of time and confidence in what economic understanding was all about led to the use of a scheme from a colleague in another school. This was a mixture of money management and consumer education. It was based around saving for, choosing, buying, insuring and complaining about a 'stereo'. It had some plus points: it was thematic, it involved a consumer article close to pupils' hearts and minds, and it got the teacher through the ten-week course. However, I was to teach it eight times that year. The negative points were obvious and I began to experiment. The first lesson on saving pocket money turned into a lesson dealing with the idea that 'Economics is partly about analysing a budget, so that the allocation of scarce resources needs careful scrutiny, as does the extent to which any individual can be an active agent in his or her economic situation.' The lesson on consumer rights became a role-play about taking back a faulty item, again set in the context of not wasting limited personal resources. The lesson on insuring the stereo turned into a role-playing exercise about the implications of a motor accident.

I also began to dip my toe in the water with regard to teaching other economic concepts, such as supply and demand, price theory and specialization. The 'stereo' theme was dropped and into its position came a much more functional Mars Bar! I tried to explain economic terms that youngsters would hear on the TV news or read in a newspaper (inflation, the Chancellor's Budget, the balance of payments). There was even a stab at monetarism. Money management was disappearing fast, but consumer education remained. This is because I feel that it is important to let pupils practise skills so that they not only understand but can also use their understanding. It is no use knowing that personal resources are limited and that the Government intervenes in the market-place to ensure 'fairness' if you do not have the competence to complain to a shop manager that a new record or pair of shoes is faulty.

So one year on, although I felt happier with the economic awareness module, I still needed to find appropriate concept-carrying vehicles. I wanted to ensure that I covered 'the main economic concepts', whatever they proved to be. I had worked out some ideas (the usefulness of cost–benefit analysis and the advantages of specialization), but I felt that there must be more which I did not know about. I also wanted to develop more active processes to get away from talk, chalk and note-making.

Introduction to the Economics Association's Economics Education 14–16 Project

It was at this stage that Lancashire LEA decided to resource 12 schools with the Economics Association's 14–16 Project materials (*Understanding Economics*[1]) and Mansfield High was one of the chosen schools. The package was impressive. After struggling around with money management material and my own ideas, and finding little of relevance in inspected commerce books, I thought this was a godsend! The Head of PSE and I participated in eight valuable in-service days during which we used and discussed about one-third of the units and reported back on others tried in the classroom.

That year's (1985–6) lessons were devoted to experimenting with as much of this 'exemplar' material as possible. Some units were instant 'hits'. For example, 'Tiny Atom Radio', 'Price of a Perm' and 'Land Use Planning' stand out as units which are active in process, whose settings are readily understood by pupils, which have interesting activities, and which also carry important economic related concepts. Other units misfired, and some worked better the second time around. Some were altered. Several of the units have so much work in them that the possibility of using them in a 10-lesson course is limited.

After three terms of using the material and attending the Lancashire LEA/Economics Education 14–16 Project's in-service days, I felt in a position to sort out my own module. Central to this module was the writing up of a definitive list of key 'high-order' concepts which I believed together made an 'economic perspective'.

An 'economic perspective'

Having an economic perspective must mean the ability to assess situations, events, processes (i.e. human activity) through the illuminating beam of economics. An economic perspective can thus give pupils a new and useful way of looking at activity in the various 'worlds' pupils live in – be this the creation of a monetary value for a Mars Bar or attempts by the West to help relieve a famine in Africa. An economic awareness course should show pupils that an analysis of the use of resources by humans is helpful and productive, that an economic understanding is possible, that resource decisions by individuals and communities are necessary and have calculable but multi-faceted consequences (which can be categorized into 'costs' and 'benefits') and, perhaps most importantly, that options for the future use of resources exist.

I believe that the best possibility of 'delivering' an economic perspective in a PSE course is to concentrate on providing pupils with an understanding of the following ideas:

1) humans identify, transform and use up resources
2) resources are generally scarce
3) obtaining and transforming resources involves costs
4) demands upon resources by individuals/collectivities are extensive
5) usage of resources involves opportunity costs for the individual and others
6) allocation and usage is affected by price, by government prescription, by advertising and personal judgement
7) cost–benefit analysis aids decision-making
8) economic activity is interdependent: as well as personal and family-based economies there are societal and world economics
9) economic decisions by some affect others, e.g. firms' decisions have implications for those who work, live nearby, use the product, etc.

This abstract list of ideas had, of course, to be translated into material which would demonstrate its usefulness. First, the material had to be focused so that pupils could learn concepts at their concrete level. Thus, I introduced concepts whilst discussing pocket-money, typical young people's jobs, youth club decisions, Mars Bars and complaining about a faulty stereo. However, I also wanted to place the concepts in what could be described as significant areas of knowledge for an economically literate person. These were consumer economics and governmental economic policy-making. By consumer economics I mean the ability to

- make rational market place decisions
- see the purposes and dangers of advertising
- understand the need for and operation of consumer law.

As regards macro-economic policy, I wanted pupils to apply their learnt economic concepts to aspects of government policy-making so that they could participate, as citizens, in an informed manner. The themes I chose were inflation, the balance of payments, the budget and job creation schemes.

Module outline lesson by lesson

The above discussion on key concepts and experiential and significant knowledge areas were translated into the 10-lesson framework shown below. The numbers in parentheses refer to the foregoing concept list:

Lesson 1: wanting – basic human needs; their extension into 'wants' and resource usage (1, 2, 4)

Lesson 2: pupils' budgets – a look at pocket-money, paid work and a cost-benefit analysis of jobs such as paper rounds and shopwork

Lesson 3: price – the cost of a product's production; supply and demand; theory of a Mars Bar (1, 3, 4, 5, 9)

Lesson 4: interest rates – the supply and demand for control over money; inflation (3)

Lessons 5–7 on consumer economics

Lesson 5: consumer choice – allocating personal scarce resources (1, 3, 4); creating demand (advertising) (5, 6); group allocation of resources (Youth Club) (6)

Lesson 6: consumer protection – of their scarce resources; role-play involving consumer law (3)

Lesson 7: insurance – spreading the risk of resource loss (3); costs/benefits of insurance (7); why premiums differ

Lessons 8–10 on macro-policy

Lesson 8: budgets/taxes – why the Government reallocates resources between citizens (6, 8, 9); why the Government provides collective goods (8, 9); how the Government affects consumer demand (6, 9)

Lesson 9: the cost of a job – a comparative analysis of the costs and benefits of job creation schemes (3, 7, 9)

Lesson 10: international trade – the balance of payments (3, 4, 9); exchange rates – the supply and demand of goods and currencies across borders

This shows that the course has strayed far from the project's materials. The concept-led approach has involved difficult decisions – some excellent units such as 'Tiny Atom Radio' and 'Land Use Planning' are not used. These units did not bring about the key ideas I sought. Other units which did concentrate on the concepts I was interested in were not concrete enough in their setting. They expected pupils to discuss material when most lacked pre-requisite background knowledge. For example, the 'Community Expenditure' unit involved Local Authority subcommittees deciding on marginal expenditure. I transferred the theme to that of expenditure on a school Youth Club. Moreover, some key concepts, skills and areas of knowledge are not covered by the project's materials and these had to be built from scratch.

Thus my search for a module which delivered an 'economic perspective' received its impetus from the Economics Education 14–16 Project material. However, because of the constraints of the 10-lesson format and the underlying methodology involved in the construction of the module, very little of the project material is used for this economic awareness course.

It is perhaps interesting to note that the school uses several *Understanding Economics* units in other PSE modules. In the Political Literacy course the simulated planning committee unit 'Land Use Planning in the Local Community' is used to convey the idea of the need for politicians to summate a community's values where there are competing ideas of costs and benefits. Other units are used in the World of Work module. The pictorial stimuli of 'Two Workers' is used to focus discussion of what we expect from work, while the oil rig/petrol station sequence from that unit shows the interdependence of work in society today. 'Ice Cream Factory' is used to discuss the process of production and the disadvantages and advantages of the factory system over craft production. 'Tiny Atom Radio' delivers the idea that firms are under pressure from the market-place and that working for such a firm might involve individuals in the need to change and adapt.

Reference

1 Economics Association, *Understanding Economics*, Longman, 1985.

6 Introducing an economic awareness module into a fourth year core course

Jean Long

St Wilfrid's C. of E. High School, Lancashire

St Wilfrid's is a Voluntary Aided Church of England 11–18 Comprehensive with 1,500 students. Students are drawn from a wide catchment area and from a largely middle-class background. Although the intake reflects a wide ability mix, the high level of parental support means that the school is geared to, and achieves, examination success.

In early 1984, Lancashire Headteachers and Deputy Headteachers were invited to the launch of Lancashire's involvement in the Economics Education 14–16 Project on a pilot basis. The Curriculum Deputy quickly realized the potential of this to the school, and became an enthusiastic supporter. The school applied to be one of the pilot schools – 12 out of 120 secondary schools in the Authority – and was delighted to be accepted.

The 14–16 Project materials were being published and on a two-day Induction Course in September 1985, duplicated copies were distributed both for training and for use in schools. The delay in receiving the published units caused some anxiety to those schools which had been given curriculum space. However, the duplicated copies served their purpose and by the end of term the schools were able to report their use in a variety of situations.

In St Wilfrid's, units were tried out with students in the 14–18 age range, on a number of courses ranging from fourth year mixed-ability Commerce GCE/CSE to sixth form Economics 'A' level and Integrated Humanities with continuous assessment. Encouraged by the students' increased motivation, improved social skills and higher standards of work, it was decided to devise a short module for the Christian Living course, initially only for fourth year students.

Background to the Christian Living course

A PSE course, replacing compulsory RE for fourth, fifth and sixth years, has existed for a number of years. The course occupies one hour per week. Many topics are covered from family life, alcohol and drug abuse to comparative religion and careers. Teachers work either on their own or in a team to produce teaching materials (usually in the form of a worksheet or a questionnaire) for their colleagues.

By 1984 the course had become stale and teaching strategies repetitive. Its status was low in the eyes of both students and staff and the quality of the students' written work was poor.

Desired outcomes

The Curriculum Deputy saw the units from *Understanding Economics*[1] being used:

- to raise the status of pastoral education within the school as a preparation for extending it across the whole age range from 11–18 years
- to attempt to extend classroom practices to include more active learning approaches

- to facilitate some cross-curricular work relating to economic awareness, since the 12 members of staff teaching the Christian Living course were from different subject areas
- to use well-prepared materials to enable students to compile a portfolio of work which could be a focus for discussion at an interview for work or further education

Only two of the 12 teachers involved in the Christian Living course (the Curriculum Deputy and the teacher in charge of economics) had training in economics. Therefore, a bid for TRIST financing for a school-focused INSET programme to train the other members of the team, plus up to 10 other members of staff, was submitted in January 1986 (see Appendix 1). This was rejected in favour of a consortium approach for all the 12 pilot schools in Lancashire. However, given that the TRIST course was not scheduled to run until late in the 1986 summer term, and that teachers' industrial action made other training problematic, it was decided to begin work without staff training.

Approach

In order to devise a scheme of work for the course, a negotiated learning exercise was tried. The device used for this exercise – a questionnaire – was familiar to both students and staff, but the process of negotiating with students over curriculum content was new (see Appendix 2). The students voted four items as their 'key areas', with the first item well ahead of the others. Their choices were:

1) a roof over your head
2) starting and running your business
3) work and wages (but not trades unions)
4) using a bank account.

It would have been possible to tailor the course to meet the perceived needs of each individual teaching group, but this would have taken too much time between the negotiations and the lessons. Accordingly, it was thought best to take the four topics and compile materials which could be used by the whole year.

A six-week module was devised using role-play, group work, picture stimulus and debriefing ses-

sions (see Appendices 3 and 4 for two illustrations from the module). The intention was to shift the role of the teacher to enable her or him to become facilitator, chair and supporter.

Each week's work was packaged with 30 copies of stimulus material, record sheets, file paper and teachers' instructions (suggestions). Resources such as a glossary of terms were sometimes included to help non-specialists feel more assured with the work. Teachers' instructions were deliberately common in format to ease familiarization, and were kept simple so that teachers could develop their own style with the units. Most of the units were adaptations designed to 'lead into' the use of *Understanding Economics* the following year. This also avoided problems of duplication in cases where students had used the published units on other courses. Each week's work was 'free standing' and could be used in any order. With six groups in each half-year, and 12 members of staff involved, work packs had to be passed on promptly (there was only one pack per topic, to reduce photocopying costs). Circulation lists were attached to the packs, and each member of staff had their own copy of these to chase up dilatory colleagues. The bottom of the circulation list on the pack was left blank, and comments were invited.

Outcomes

Amazingly, everyone got their pack on time! Teachers' comments were positive, especially those made orally to other teachers. It was felt that students had responded well, and many teachers were pleased to have taken part in the pilot scheme. As for the students, comments ranged from an acknowledgement by some that the material had allowed some development of social skills, to one student's question: 'But what has this got to do with Christian Living?'

Developments

The TRIST follow-up course allowed the school to send another four members of staff for some training. Those selected were part of a team running a course for third year low-ability students which would lead into a prevocational course in year four; a teacher of mathematics nearing the end of her probationary year, who also taught on the sixth form Christian Living course, and a colleague who was soon to be teaching economics at examination level. The course allowed basic familiarization with the paper-based materials (*Understanding Economics*), some hands-on experience with the CAL units[2] and an opportunity for colleagues to discuss how best to coordinate their efforts towards providing a series of experiences to enhance students' economic awareness. The two-day course was organized by the 14–16 Project team, but led by teachers from the Lancashire network. Perhaps one indicator of the success of the course was the speed with which the four teachers requested keys to the filing cabinet which held the teaching resources.

The economic awareness module has now also been extended to both third and fifth years. In addition, a sixth form course which includes work experience, links with local industry and modules leading to NEA's Integrated Humanities scheme will build on work in years three to five.

With hindsight . . .

Inevitably, in introducing economic awareness into a core course, mistakes were made. The main drawback of the course is that it is 'money management' in style. This was a result of having to compile an agenda for negotiation which would convey meaning to students unfamiliar with economic jargon and concepts. Perhaps negotiating the course with students was inappropriate although some useful findings emerged. On the other hand, perhaps the course should have been tailored to meet the expressed wishes of each group of students in order to respond to their part in the negotiations. The time constraints were felt to be too great for this, although the necessary data were available.

Formal evaluation of the course by students and staff did not take place – the module was the last one of the year and time ran out. This is an issue which will be considered in the future, but a preliminary review suggests that the module has been fairly successful in achieving the aims outlined above. Only the third aim of facilitating some cross-curricular work relating to economic awareness appears to have been met less fully than hoped.

The process

A number of factors contributed to the success of the work in the school, one which does not have a culture of innovation.

- a Deputy Headteacher who gave curricular space, and supported the initiative fully
- a teacher who was willing and able to do the work at 'ground level'
- carefully planned implementation, with a package for circulation which was new to staff, but with sufficient familiar support to reassure
- units which were easy to use, with clear (but not prescriptive) guidelines
- a mechanism whereby staff and students were encouraged to give feedback to the Curriculum Deputy or to the Coordinator

However, it is important to recognize that the school has only initiated a process of development in one area of the curriculum. Much remains to be done if the innovation is to be nurtured and its beneficial effects extended to other parts of the curriculum.

References

1 Economics Association, *Understanding Economics*, Longman, 1985.
2 *Computers in the Curriculum*, Longman, 1985.

Appendix 1: Application for support under TRIST budget for follow-up activity

The accompanying proposal (abridged) originated from the two teacher coordinators at St Wilfrid's CE High School who responded to the initial training days and identified training requirements.

The process of this project was to induct two school coordinators into the use of economic awareness units developed by the Economics Education 14–16 Project to act as a catalyst for change. The two-day INSET in September 1985 introduced the paper-based materials and the computer-assisted learning materials. The two-day INSET was based on experiential learning methods. Individual schools and groups were asked to identify immediate objectives for the Autumn term. The subsequent INSET in November reviewed work to date and concentrated on adaptation of materials to meet the needs of individual schools. Schools were given the task of identifying objectives to implement economic awareness for all students of all abilities in each school. The economics coordinator supported the network of school coordinators by direct observation of classroom practice, and by offering guidance, and disseminating good practice. The coordinator met senior school management to review prospects for curriculum change and implementation of the strategy.

The school coordinators at St Wilfrid's CE High School included a Deputy Head with curriculum responsibility. They identified additional training requirements to implement their objective of an economic and industrial awareness core course for all pupils. The need was to train colleagues in the skills of activity-based learning and economic awareness. These TRIST-trained coordinators would act as tutors. The outcome would be a nucleus of staff to coordinate the economic and industrial awareness objectives in the Christian Living core in the fourth and fifth years. This was to be essentially a personal and social development core. There would also be elements in the third year active tutorial programme.

The training course and follow-up in the school was to be monitored by the economics coordinator and the Economics Education 14–16 Project for the authority. There would be some measurement of these outcomes and it could form a model for further diffusion in other project schools.

The submission (abridged)

Objectives

1) To establish a substantial body of staff (at present non-specialist) who are aware of, and

in sympathy with, the aims and scope of the Economics Education 14–16 Project, for which Saint Wilfrid's is a pilot school.

2) To establish a body of staff who are familiar with the use of Project exemplar materials. Such staff should also, therefore, have the opportunity to develop, expand and modify Project materials to meet the needs of the pupils and students of Saint Wilfrid's.

3) To provide staff with an opportunity for experiential learning and thus equip them more fully for the anticipated teacher/learner relationships embodied in the ethos of the Project.

4) To provide staff with the opportunity for 'hands on' experience of new technologies and innovatory teaching strategies, e.g. computer software materials.

5) To provide a vehicle for the future establishment of an interdisciplinary working party of staff to plan and coordinate the development and dissemination of Project themes and materials across the curriculum.

Relationship to existing programme within the curriculum

- Years 6–7

  Students follow a general-interest course, Christian Living, which occupies a 35-minute per week timetable slot. In the course, suitable themes are negotiated between students and tutor within the context of the Christian perspective and current issues and debates. Use has been made of Lancashire Industrial Mission personnel and materials, but this has been the only source of vocationally based themes. A logical and much needed development of this activity would be to include aspects of the Economics Education 14–16 Project.

- Years 4–5

  Students undertake a 70-minutes-per-week course, again entitled 'Christian Living'. Themes in this course reflect, wherever appropriate, the Christian perspective and include:

  the individual
  the family
  the community
  drugs, smoking and alcohol
  the world of work

  It is a personal and social development course

which would naturally lend itself to, and benefit from, a substantial input of Project materials. For example, themes on:

poverty

discrimination

the role of industry

the role of individuals in the economy

would clearly fit into such a course.

- Year 3
Pupils of average and below average ability in modern languages follow a course in social and technical studies (STS). Within this is a unit of work laying the foundations for future development of themes on:

wealth creation

careers education

Some Project themes (e.g. Young Person as Producer) would suitably extend this work.

- All pupils will ultimately follow a course, currently at a pilot stage, to enhance and develop the school's Tutorial Programme. The teaching styles and strategies are in sympathy with those of the Project.

Examination courses

Some units of Project materials are likely to be appropriate for inclusion in the following examination courses − all of which are presently undertaken in the school:

- 'A' level
British Government & Politics
Economics
General Studies
- 'O' Level/CSE
British Government & Politics
Commerce
General Studies
Government, Economics & Commerce
Home Economics
Integrated Humanities
Mathematics
Sociology

Relationship to existing provision of in-service work

Saint Wilfrid's is a pilot school for the Economics Education 14–16 Project and, as such, Mr P. Crook (Deputy Head) and Ms J. Long (Head of Economics) attend the appropriate in-service courses.

Miss J. Bentley (Director of Sixth Form Studies) is undertaking a NWRAC extended part-time course on CPVE development, which is currently under discussion as a curricular extension to the school.

Mr K. Hall (Head of School) and Mrs M. Hunt (Deputy Head of School), both with wide experience of Upper School teaching at St Wilfrid's, are about to embark on a TRIST course entitled 'Active Learning Strategies'. From September 1986, they will coordinate the Tutorial Programme throughout the school.

It is anticipated that this team of staff will form the nucleus of the coordinating working party to be established following the proposed in-service course.

Background to provision of in-service work

Until recently, St Wilfrid's staff have had little opportunity to familiarize themselves with the type of teaching strategies embodied in the approach inherent in the project. Practical difficulties may be experienced in gaining the acceptance of this style by pupils, parents and other staff. There is, therefore, both a psychological and practical need for appropriate in-service work aimed towards building the confidence of participating staff.

Course programme: draft proposal

- Day 1
Introductory session
Group discussion − economic literacy entitlement of a school leaver within the curriculum
Report back and results of pupil-based survey − an exercise in negotiated learning
Project materials in action
Plenary session

- Day 2
Computer assisted teaching − sample lessons
Computer assisted learning − hands-on experience, small group activity
Project materials in action − themes, teaching styles and activities
The way ahead at St Wilfrid's − curricular organization and design

Appendix 2: Questionnaire for negotiated learning exercise

The school is piloting (testing) the 14–16 Economics Education Project. For the first time, St Wilfrid's students will have a section of work (module) in the Christian living course on economic literacy.

However, before deciding what units to have in the module, we would like to know *your* views on what should be taught. Would you please, therefore, complete the following questionnaire carefully – remember that the final module will take into account the results that you give.

We think that this is the first time that 'negotiated learning' has been tried across a whole year at St Wilfrid's and we rely on *you* to make it successful. You will certainly be helping the project team and we hope that the project will help you and that it will be enjoyable.

(Respondents were asked to encircle a number 1, 2, 3 or 4 printed on the right side of the questions.)

The questionnaire

Please circle the appropriate number:

1 means you think *everyone should learn* about this in the school
2 means you think it might be *helpful to learn* about this in school
3 means you think it is *not really worth learning* about this in school
4 means that you *already do this work* as part of another course and do not need to study it further

Making the most of your money
Budgeting
Good buy or goodbye money?
Complaining about faulty goods
Using a bank account
Buying on credit

The world of work
Wages – time rate, piece-rate and commission
Deductions – tax, National Insurance
Trades unions

Your own business
Setting it up and running it
Where to go for advice

Advertising
Types of advertising
Consumer protection
Who pays? Who benefits?

The cost of living
Why are some people poor?
How are prices set?
The Welfare State

A roof over your head
Buying or renting – pros and cons
Estate agents, building societies and mortgages

Impact of technology
New technology results in unemployment?
Effect on life styles

How does the Council spend your money?
Where does the Council's money come from?
How do Councils decide how to spend the money?

THANK YOU FOR YOUR HELP

Appendix 3: Module D (Work and Wages)

Work in groups of four to six people.

Section 1 ('Two Workers', *Understanding Economics*). Make a list of similarities and differences between the two workers shown in the picture. Then try to group ideas under headings; e.g. working conditions – clean/dirty; hot/cold; cramped/spacious. Discuss your ideas with another group.

Section 2 ('Rate for the job', *Understanding Economics*)   Match up the jobs advertised with the pay given. Give reasons for your choice. Discuss your ideas with another group.

Section 3   Work through the Payday sheet. Discuss your ideas with another group.

Payday

Imagine you have £2,000 to pay in wages for one week. How will you share out this money among the following?

Coal miner
Doctor
Police officer
Someone unemployed
School teacher
Nurse
Street sweeper
Airline pilot
Managing Director of British Oxygen
Member of Parliament
Footballer
Fire officer
Disc jockey

Arrange the list with the highest paid person at the top, going down to the person you think should get the lowest pay. Give reasons for your order of priorities. Compare your list with the lists of others. What differences are there?

Comments

Teachers were free to choose how to tackle this unit. Some used only one section; others tried to work through more than one.

It could have been organized so that each class was split into six groups, with two groups tackling each unit, followed by class presentation and discussion.

The Payday sheet is simple, but can reveal some important ideas and attitudes.

There is little 'activity work' in this unit, but group work is stressed.

Appendix 4: Module E (The Business Challenge)

Work in groups of four to six people.

Brainstorm
Shortlist – using criteria
Select
Research
Consult
Produce a proposal
Possible problems and sources of help

The Business Challenge

In this module we're going to look at ideas for starting up your own business. This may not be something you've considered before, but you may be surprised by what you can contribute to your group.

1 Think of a business idea

2 Write a list of your ideas

In your group of about four people, think of as many ideas as you can for setting up on your own.

Have you a hobby that could grow into a business?

Do you have any special skills (sewing, gardening, using computers) that others would pay you to use?

Is there a gap in the market – have you ever had difficulty in buying something you needed?

Have you any work experience which might be useful?

BRAINSTORM during this activity – do not discuss or comment on any idea, just let the ideas come and everyone write them down.

3 Select your most promising idea

Look at each idea and select a 'shortlist' of about six. Then think about each one in more detail. Write a brief summary of 'The Idea – the Market' (who would buy the goods or service produced). 'Setting-Up and Funding' (what would be needed, how much of your own money would go into the business, whether friends and relatives would help with finance, how you would present your case to the bank when asking for a loan). 'The Future' (possible areas you could expand into if successful, taking on staff, buying new premises).

4 Do some research

Are you the *right kind* of person to set up in business? Do you get on well with others? Are you well organized? Do others rely on you? Can you put across your viewpoint without being aggressive? Do you listen to others' advice and ideas? Do you give up easily?

What *training and experience* will you need? Where will you find it? How long will it take? Can you do anything *now* to help you attain your goal?

5 Consult the experts

As a beginner, you need to get as much advice as you can. This will mean talking to local retailers and business people, bank managers, accountants, advertisers, local press, Chambers of Trade & Commerce. Make out a list of people you would consult, and how you would find their addresses or telephone numbers. You would also need to look at the competition. How would you find out about that?

Market research can help you to decide on the quantity of goods you would need to supply, and on the price you can charge.

6 Produce your proposal

Now you will be in a position to select from your 'shortlist' of ideas the one you think is best. The next step is to prepare a proposal which would help to get the backing of a bank, or anyone else considering lending money to support your venture. You will need to include:

A clear description of your idea
Some details about your experience and ability
Evidence of market research
Staffing requirements
Estimated costs and income for the first year
The amount you require, repayment details, and any valuables you could offer as security against the loan (e.g. deeds, insurance, stocks and shares)

7 I don't think I can make it on my own!

Neither can anyone else! Advice and help are available – if you know where to go. The Careers Library is a good start. Also consult the Careers staff in school and in the Careers Office.

You may feel that you don't want to carry all that responsibility yourself. Have you thought of a cooperative venture with family and friends? Again help is at hand. Who would you approach to see if they would like to form a cooperative? What sort of job would need to be done? Which ones could you learn to do?

Life as your own boss is not without its problems. Can you think of any?

Comments

This is taken from the 'Business Challenge' (CRAC) and is a thought-provoking exercise.

On reflection, this would have been more suitable as the theme for several weeks' work to give students the opportunity to investigate and consult fully.

The 'brainstorming' technique was new to many students and staff, and the results were surprisingly good. Despite the shortage of time, many students and staff felt that the module had raised student (and staff) awareness of options open to them.

The original version of this employed a number of humorous cartoons from a National Westminster Bank publication, *Get up and Go with NatWest*.

7 Economic awareness and business studies

Elizabeth Pollock

Bangor Girls' High School, Northern Ireland

The school

Bangor Girls' High School is situated in a well-populated town and seaside resort, Bangor, Co. Down. Some 1,100 pupils are currently enrolled with a staff of 72 teachers. It is the only girls' high school in the district with a catchment distance extending to about 30 miles. The school offers a broad general curriculum with pupils studying up to seven or eight subjects.

Economic awareness through the Business Studies Department

The Business Studies Department has five full-time teachers and is involved with pupils from the third to the sixth form. The range of subjects offered is GCE 'A' level Accounts, GCSE Accounts, Economics, Business Studies and Typewriting (involving word-processing). In the third year, pupils are timetabled for four periods of a school-based business studies course which involves some basic ideas of economic awareness. In addition, since September 1986 a modular approach has been adopted for a fourth year course with all pupils being given the opportunity to take part in a six week module on economic awareness. It is hoped that future developments will lead to the extension of this course into the fifth and sixth years so that pupils can be better prepared for the transition to life outside school.

A programme of change

In 1983, an Inspector from the Department of Education in Northern Ireland suggested that the Business Studies Department should become involved in pilot work associated with the Economics Education 14–16 Project which was being carried out by the Northern Ireland Council for Educational Development (NICED). At this stage the school was asked to try out exemplar resource materials. Initially this was done with a fourth year Commerce class by one teacher from the Business Studies Department. After this pilot period, units were distributed to all teachers in the Business Studies Department to encourage them to use them as appropriate in the subject syllabuses and with any class. However, by the end of the school year it had become clear that the use of the resource materials needed to be more structured.

Economic awareness in the third year

In June 1985, teachers in the department met to prepare a new course for third year business studies. As a result of these discussions and the classroom experiments, they became both aware and convinced of the need for change. As Head of the Business Studies Department, the writer felt that the existing third year course content lacked relevance to the pupils, since it covered topics remote from their experience. (Part of the course, for example, included the study of business documents, how to construct them, and the role of the wholesaler and retailer – see Appendix 1.) Moreover, the teachers were convinced that any change should involve the inclusion of both individual and group work. The third year was chosen for review for a number of reasons:

1) there was a need to establish a course which would be more enjoyable and beneficial for the students than that on offer at the time
2) since it was a non-examination course the school was free to amend it as necessary
3) there was a need to provide a good introduction for both students and teachers to the likely requirements of the new GCSE syllabuses.

Great care was taken to provide a course which pupils could relate to. *Understanding Economics*[1] was seen to be very useful and, because of the flexibility of the resources, could be adapted and extension work implemented easily. An outline of the new course is included in Appendices 2 and 3.

At first some teachers were reluctant to try the new scheme of work because they had not been involved in the introduction of the materials in 1983. They felt insecure, not so much with the content of the course, but with the methods of teaching which were very different from those they usually employed. To overcome this, opportunities had to be provided for members of the Department to meet and discuss the problems, and to plan the scheme together. The department was joined at these meetings by NICED's Field Officer who helped in the vital early stages of planning. The scheme could not have progressed without the help and encouragement that the school received through NICED. Within the school the department received very positive support from the Principal, who provided opportunities for school-based in-service courses and encouraged staff to attend courses held outside school. Since September 1986 the implementation of the course has been easier with the arrival of two new teachers familiar with the methods of teaching involved and able to add elements of their own to some areas of the course. At the same time, other members of the department have become more comfortable with the new ideas, and exchanges of help and advice are developing.

Economic awareness in the fourth year

The modular work in the fourth form consists of six study areas, one of which is Economic Awareness. The other modules are First Aid, Computer Awareness, Study Skills, Grooming and Posture, and Communications. The pupils enjoy the short concentrated course and it is hoped that these modules will be carried through into fifth and sixth forms (see Appendices 4 and 5).

Assessment

The revised course required new methods of assessment since pupils were being encouraged to demonstrate new skills in addition to the basic recall of knowledge. In the initial stages this meant there was additional pressure, as the writer was required to formulate new methods of assessment as well as overseeing and planning the scheme. Regular school-based assignments were introduced, with guidance being drawn from GCSE assessment procedures. While progress in this area has been made, it continues to present the writer with a challenge.

Conclusions

Interest in the development of economic awareness has not been confined to the Business Studies Department. For example, the teacher responsible for working with lower attaining pupils has been enquiring about topics on money management and basic economic awareness. She feels that her classes would benefit from activities in these areas. In addition, in Home Economics, activities concerned with consumer aspects of life in the world outside the classroom are being developed.

In September 1986 the school became involved in the 11–16 programme of Curriculum Review and Development (in time all post-primary schools in Northern Ireland will be required to be involved in this programme). While still in its early stages, association with this programme has resulted in a general atmosphere of support and encouragement from school management for developmental work relating to economic awareness within the school.

The response of pupils to the new styles of working has been one source of motivation for teachers. The following are some of their comments:

'I have enjoyed the course ... I have learnt how to make money last, and how people with money problems have to budget carefully.'

'I did not like "Wanting" because it made us see how selfish we are ... we felt guilty for people less fortunate than us.'

The courses have now been running for one full year. Problems have occurred in persuading colleagues to adopt new approaches and to review their aims. It is clear, however, that there will be no turning back. At the same time much has yet to be done before teachers feel totally at ease in what for them is a new and challenging situation.

Reference

1 Economics Association, *Understanding Economics*, Longman, 1985.

Appendix 1: The original third year Commerce scheme

To introduce pupils to the world of commerce, in its most suitable form. Two periods a week.

SEPTEMBER

1   What is commerce?

A basic introduction – commerce concerned with the change of ownership of goods or services; buying and selling of goods at any stage, from raw materials to the finished product; commerce is situated between producers (who make the goods) and consumers (who buy the goods).

Commerce is divided into *Trade* (buying and selling of goods in order to change the ownership) and *services* (to assist buying and selling).

Trade – what it is (home and foreign); services or aids to trade; explain wholesaler, retailer, and manufacturer; and their roles.

2   The position of the retailer

A trader who provides goods and services to the consumer; positioned either between the manufacturers and the consumer or the wholesalers and the consumer; buys in large quantities from the wholesaler and sells in small, convenient quantities to the consumer.

3   Types of retailers

Independent retailers – tend to be small businesses owned by one man or by a small number of people.

Types of independent retailers – Door-to-door salesmen; market traders (study could refer to Wednesday's market, pupils could draw plan of market).

OCTOBER

4   Independent shops

Small corner shop – look at advantages and disadvantages.

5   Multiples or chain stores

Main points – part of a large concern; usually run from a central point; shops all have the same name and situated in many towns; all owned by the same concern; some chains specialize in only one class of goods.
Explain variety chain stores.
Discuss advantages and disadvantages.

6   Self-service stores and supermarkets

Main points – customers serve themselves, paying at a cash point; saves staff.
Discuss advantages and disadvantages.

NOVEMBER

7   Department stores

Main points – seen in most large towns; usually occupies a central position; sells a wide variety of goods; store is divided into separate departments.
Discuss advantages and disadvantages.

8   Hypermarkets

Main points – large forms of supermarkets situated outside towns.
Discuss advantages and disadvantages.

9   Vending machines

Main points – positioned in busy places offering goods for sale automatically; problem of vandalism.

DECEMBER

10   Banking

Early primitive man – Robinson Crusoe – how this process worked.

Barter – exchange of one good for another without the use of money. To succeed there needed to be – a double coincidence of wants; an exchange rate; divisibility of goods (some rates of exchange did not make it possible to trade); storage of wealth.

Lead on to the need for money – things used instead of money (shells, dog's teeth, beads, grain, spearheads, hides, arrowheads, etc.).

Qualities of money – must be durable; must be acceptable; must be divisible; must be portable.

Use of money meant that man could sell his surplus of goods in exchange for money and use the money to buy things he needed.

Metals used because – lasts longer; able to be divided into smaller units and sizes; scarce.

The functions of money – explain each in detail: a medium of exchange; a standard of value; a store of value; a standard for postponed payments.

The use of goldsmiths to start the first bank.

11   Deposit accounts

Who uses them (individuals and associations); people who do not need to use their money immediately;
the need for credit slips and withdrawal slips;
no cheque book;
seven days of notice needed to withdraw money for large amounts;
interest is paid;
cannot overdraw on money.

JANUARY

12   Current accounts

Paying-in book to pay money in;
cheque book used to transfer money;
statements sent from time to time;
no interest paid;
possible bank charges;
can overdraw with permission;
how to make money into a cheque book account.

13   Cheque system

What a cheque is;
the parts of a cheque;
the three parties to a cheque;
types of cheque (post-dated, stale, blank, dishonoured);
what an open cheque is;
what a crossed cheque indicates;
pupils have practice in drawing cheques.

FEBRUARY

14   Further work on cheques

Special cheque crossings – account payee only;
account payee only Barclays Bank;
not negotiable.

The use of a cheque card.

15   Further work on cheques

Counterfoil of a cheque;
stop payments of a cheque;
the bank statement;
how to clear a cheque (the simplest treatment).

MARCH

16   Other bank services

Looking at each one in detail – night safe;
cash dispenser machine;
budget account;
use of the foreign department;
standing order payment.

APRIL

17   Insurance

How insurance started;
the purpose of insurance;
pooling of risks;
the prospectus;
the insurance proposal;
the premium;
the policy;
the claim's form.

18   Principles of insurance

Insurable interest;
utmost good faith;
indemnity.

19   Why a businessman insures

Buildings;
vehicles;
employees;
the public;
money.

MAY

20   Advertising

How advertising is used in commerce;
why advertising is used;
types of advertising (informative, persuasive).

21   Ways in which to advertise

Television and radio;
newspapers;
magazines;
posters and hoardings.

JUNE

22   Advertising's 'hidden persuaders'

Discuss the following in detail – romance;
ambition;
personality appeal;
social acceptability;
work simplification (makes a task easier to perform).

TEXTBOOKS
Practical Business Studies
Modern Commerce
Comprehensive Commerce

Appendix 2: The revised third year Business Studies scheme

To give pupils a broad introduction to business studies; to enable them to make a more informed choice for future study; to enable pupils to relate to economic and commercial phenomena in their local environment; to provide an introduction to consumer protection, and develop economic literacy; to include some personal budgeting into their lives and prepare them to be young citizens. Work is based on the local area. Four 35-minute periods a week.

Needs and wants ('Consumers')

Human beings have certain wants; wants satisfied by consumption of goods in some ways; extent to which individual wants can be satisfied depends upon personal purchasing power; extent to which individual wants can be satisfied varies both within an economy and between economies.

Leading on to private budgeting ('Budgeting')

Pupils to look at their attitudes and to discuss other factors which influence their spending habits;
to introduce the notion that the purchase of one good or service involves forgoing others (*key points*: level of personal income is a constraint on spending; consumer spending influenced by a number of factors, pressures of peers, fashion, advertising, etc.).

Case studies of how the following are affected: unemployed; high income family; someone single.

Their spending affects local community

Existence of choice in retail markets – using Main Street and High Street (work could be based on slides); price differences of products in various shops – 'Local Shopping'.

How competition is used between retailers.

Consumer preference in respect of choice of shop and product for a variety of reasons such as price, taste, convenience – new shops starting up and why others have closed.

Leading to advertising ('Tiny Atom Radio')

Market research; costing; advertising campaigns.

Consumer awareness ('Alternatives')

Banking; types of accounts; current accounts; deposit accounts; borrowing money from a bank; bank giro; building societies; hire purchase; budget accounts; looking at a bank statement.

Consumer protection

Jobs people do ('Two Workers' and 'The Ice Cream Factory')

Why work?; division of labour; job satisfaction; pay; trade unions; specialization.

Local industry

Transport (road, ports, rail).

New technology

Computers, forms of transport, etc.

Resources

Understanding Economics, Longman, 1985.

Appendix 3: A closer look at the third year scheme

Term One

Needs and wants

'Consumers', and magazines	PICTORIAL STIMULUS – Class compares and discusses similarities and differences. Questioning on why different standards of living. Leading on to looking at needs and wants. Class lists 'needs' that Third World child has as opposed to Western child. Teacher explains term 'purchasing power'. Class given a list of items and distinguishes between necessities and luxuries. Class discusses the interdependence of wants through the purchase of a motor car or computer.

'Wanting', and advertisements from local newspapers	Class given a notional amount of money to spend and a list of advertisements. Class given three situations: single girl; a new baby brother's arrival; a couple of newlyweds. Discussion on how each of the above situations represent different sets of needs. Group discusses how needs change with age. Teacher explains the difference between informative and persuasive advertising. Class completes student worksheet. Individual pupils write a paragraph to say whether or not they agree with the statement 'Different people have different wants'. Class discusses whether or not their needs will ever be satisfied.

Personal budgeting

'Budgeting'	Through ROLE-PLAY pupils identify with the situation and the existence of limited resources and appreciate the implications of budgeting. Pairs of students complete the worksheet. Class makes judgements about their own spending by listing the items they spend their money on and identifying if these items would be luxuries or necessities. Class discusses what a budget is and who needs to budget.
Three case studies of people with different financial backgrounds	Case studies help pupils to see that people's needs are different and everyone therefore must budget differently. Pupils work in pairs to draw up budgets and evaluate them using a questionnaire.

Spending affects local community

Plan of local Main Street	Class lists shops in a particular street. Survey on how many types of shops there are and

why some are more popular than others.

Questionnaire — Price survey to establish which brands are bought, why and from where. How they make the right choice of which brand to buy and where to buy it. Conclusions presented graphically.

Advertising

Newspapers and magazines — Different ways of marketing investigated. Pupils classify advertisements into informative or persuasive. Pupils suggest the advantages and disadvantages of advertising – these are recorded on an OHP.

Term Two

Advertising and market research

'Tiny Atom Radio' — Class works on stimulus material to recognize the problem with an obsolete radio. Individual pupils advise the firm on what ought to be done and carry out a market research exercise as homework. Groups plan a replacement product based on the market research findings. An advertising campaign is planned.

Consumer awareness

'Alternatives' — Teacher explains what a medium of exchange is. Class is shown slides and discusses the methods of payment shown in the slides. A checklist is made of the characteristics of particular methods of payment and comparisons made between cash and credit transactions. Groups use a worksheet to devise wallcharts which show the results of their discussion and conclusions reached.

Consumer protection

Schools' project — Pupils role-play a consumer complaint. Pairs of pupils evaluate the scheme and write down what they see was wrong and their suggestions for complaints procedures. Teacher explains organizations which help and advise consumers. Aspects of consumer legislation are introduced.

Term Three

Setting up a business

'Price of a Perm' — Teacher and pupils work through stimulus resources and worksheet concerned with a small business. Groups consider how a business might tackle its problems. Accounts are constructed to give the owner a clearer idea of her financial position.

Jobs people do

'The Ice Cream Factory' — Stimulus material used to introduce pupils to ideas, capital labour costs, piecework, bonus and the notions of job satisfaction. Visit to local factory to catalogue the resources in use and to establish its capital structure.

Appendix 4: Fourth year Economic Awareness scheme

To use situations that pupils are familiar with to prepare them for the world outside; to make them aware that their actions affect not only themselves but others as well. Two 35-minute periods a week over six weeks.

Section One

Study of the three units 'Vandalism', 'The Accident' and 'Who Pays'

The Accident

Based on a car accident and intended to stimulate the pupils' oral and written responses.

Pupils will be able to identify a range of costs associated with a road accident and categorize them into monetary and non-monetary, private and social costs.

Who bears the burden of the accident costs and what choices face individual motorists and society over who should pay these costs?

Go on to look at the measures that could be designed to prevent accidents, and also to consider insurance.

Vandalism

Looks at reported attacks on people and property to stimulate written and oral responses.

Again looking at costs both monetary and non-monetary, private and social.

What responses can society make to reduce or redistribute these costs?

Could lead on to a field study of some aspects of vandalism and pollution which impose costs on the local community.

Who Pays?

This looks at public spending through the topics of housing, defence and the Welfare State.

Section Two

Study of the three units 'Two Workers', 'The Rate for the Job' and 'What is Work?'

What is Work?

Encourages pupils to examine the meaning of the word 'work' both in terms of its being a contribution to the welfare of the community and in terms of conventional categorizations, for example employment/unemployment, paid/unpaid.

Looking at teenagers' working situations.

The Rate for the Job

Looks at job advertisements and a sheet of wage rates which will introduce the idea that the wage rate paid for a particular job is influenced by factors on both the demand and the supply sides of the labour market.

Discuss the individual items which make up the wage packet and why people are paid more or less than others.

Two Workers

This looks at the nature of production and the variety of jobs involved in it. Photographs will provide an opportunity to raise issues of the pupils' own attitudes towards different types of work and of stereotyping in employment.

Looks at job choice and the chain of production both here and abroad.

Resources

Units from *Understanding Economics*, Longman, 1985.

Appendix 5: A closer look at the fourth year scheme

Lesson/week 1

'Accident' unit; OHP of accident picture

Brainstorming based on stimulus. Class discussion on observations. Teacher explains and illustrates examples of costs and benefits. Pupils not always aware that costs can be more than just financial. Class discussion groups. Topic: How would they feel if they were stuck in traffic behind the lorry.

Lesson/week 2

Clippings from local newspapers

Class investigates local newspapers to identify examples of stories where there are private and social costs (1 week). Class discussion to draw conclusions on who bears the cost of an accident. Constraints of time and the ability range of the group may cause slight amendments in the programme and activities.

Lesson/week 3

'Vandalism' pilot material; costs and benefits; published materials

Group work using amended stimulus from early pilot material — pictures of vandalized telephone kiosk and car provided. Pupils asked to list the cost of vandalism and to suggest who may have to pay for it. Pupils have been asked to identify examples of vandalism in home town of Bangor. Still in groups, findings collected into a table. Class compares findings from groups.

Lesson/week 4

To date, without teacher input, one group has provided local examples of pollution as a form of vandalism in the local community. This tends to be a fairly open lesson as much depends on what exactly the class provides as examples of vandalism.

Lesson/week 5

'Who Pays?'

Teacher poses general questions on health issues for class responses: e.g. frequency of obtaining prescriptions; attending hospital; having hospital care; who pays for such treatment? Pupils need stimulus sheet relating to the declaration on the back of a prescription. Pupils work through questions on the student worksheet, S1 individually, except for question 6 where they work in pairs.

Between classes, teacher collates class results and prepares a presentation of them for the next lesson.

Lesson/week 6

Class discussion on personal and family use of state services. Class asked on their use of services provided by the State. (Teacher takes care not to expose any individual family financial backgrounds which might cause embarrassment but to date, this has not caused difficulties.) Revision of module—general discussion to recap on issues which have been raised throughout the course.

8 Developing economic awareness in the 'core'

Margaret Walters

Waldegrave School for Girls, Twickenham

Formed by the merger of Kneller and Twickenham Girls' schools in 1980 and the only single-sex school in a borough which now has eight 11–16 schools and a tertiary college, Waldegrave has no particular catchment area. Girls come from all over the borough. The building is spacious and well-equipped, with extensive playing fields.

The school believes that girls blossom socially and intellectually when boys do not dominate the classroom. Students are encouraged to take physics, chemistry, technology and computer studies, and to consider careers that have traditionally been the preserve of men. The contributions of girls of differing abilities, interests, backgrounds and cultures are welcomed. The importance of academic standards and examination results is basic to the ethos of the school.

Much of the teaching is in mixed-ability groups, but pupils are set for mathematics after one term in the first year and for French at the beginning of the second year. All students are expected to offer some subjects to public examination level. English, mathematics, religious studies, careers, physical education and the general studies module (e.g. study skills, political education, electronics, computing, tourism, health education, theatre studies) form the compulsory core. Approximately 85% of pupils take French or French studies. Four options are chosen to include a science/technology and a humanities subject.

Economic awareness: the beginning

In January 1985 the Headteacher produced a paper on economic awareness (see Appendix 1). The paper was inspired by the response of the LEA's Business Studies Adviser to Government papers and by the ideas of the Economics Association and the Economics Education 14–16 Project.

The paper was circulated to Heads of Departments and, after a lengthy review at an interdisciplinary meeting, some concepts and areas of knowledge already covered in different parts of the curriculum emerged as well as ideas for other coverage.

In the first year, primary industry and supply and demand were taught in geography. Work on percentages in mathematics could be extended to include a wide range of commercial institutions, and economics topics could become part of computer studies and information technology.

The mathematics department was to be asked to ensure that examples relevant to the business world appeared in second and third year courses. During the second year of world studies (taken by all pupils not studying a second foreign language) comparisons were drawn between aspects of the British economy and that of a developing country. China was studied extensively in the third year with some mention of her differing modes of production and distribution, and different work ethic. UK government and local authority spending were covered as well as taxation and rates. In geography all third year pupils studied urban areas, new towns, transport, the import and export of goods and raw materials, and primary, secondary and tertiary industry together with industrial change.

In fourth and fifth year 'core' courses, income tax, wages and salaries were tackled in different ways in both mathematics and careers. 'Careers' was interpreted in its broadest sense. The lessons included games to illustrate wealth creation, the structure of a firm, the changing pattern of employment, government spending and personal budgeting. The computer studies core module gave some understanding of the potential of computers for commerce and industry, while a module about travel and tourism provided an opportunity to study an expanding service industry.

At the same time a number of noticeable 'gaps' emerged, particularly for those taking a second foreign language who missed the foundation work in economic awareness in world studies. Other topics thought important by the Headteacher but which were missing were trades unions and industrial relations, marketing, savings, practical office skills, the stock exchange and the finance of industry. It was agreed to continue discussions and to decide where best to include these.

It was at this stage that the secondment of the writer to support work in all the LEA's schools was agreed. However, the movement for economic awareness at the school continued with two events in the 1985 summer term. An in-service training day for teachers from all of the schools and the college was organized by a Field Officer from the Economics Education 14–16 Project. Participants included the writer and the Head of Sociology and Commerce. Most of the teachers who attended were about to begin the Hampshire Business and Information Studies course, a scheme rejected by Waldegrave, where commerce, typewriting, office practice and computer studies were preferred as options and sociology was chosen as a key TVEI subject for community care. The second event which served to keep up the momentum was an Open Day at the University of London Institute of Education in July, attended by the Head, the Adviser and the writer at which work in London network schools was displayed and a number of activities arranged.

Planning for economic awareness

Given the enthusiasm for economic literacy and the availability of *Understanding Economics*[1] planning was concerned mainly with how to make the best use of the materials. Core studies (careers, general studies, health education), the pastoral

curriculum, world studies, commerce and geography were thought to be appropriate. The Headteacher, Deputy Headteacher (curriculum) and appropriate Heads of Departments had discussions with the writer about which units might be used in particular courses. At the same times units were tried out with different classes.

Core studies

Political and economic awareness are part of the modular programme for general studies and careers. Each subject has one double lesson a week for a term in the fourth year and about two-thirds of a term in the fifth year. All pupils (with the exception of a small minority who take art or music as an extra option) attend these lessons in mixed-ability form groups. They are taught by the Head of Core Studies and the Head of Sociology/World Studies/Commerce, with the help of two teachers of English.

It was easy to substitute units from *Understanding Economics* for other materials in careers lessons where topics such as government spending, taxation and personal budgeting were already on the syllabus. Trades unions had previously been discussed after viewing a video, but it was decided that attitudes could better be examined via a role-playing exercise (in this case 'Wages' from the *Understanding Economics* pack).

In a similar way other units were incorporated into the eight-week health education module which is taught by a home economist.

Following the writer's discussions with the TVEI Coordinator and the Headteacher, who was concerned with improving school/industry links, it was decided to have a new 'industry' module (eight weeks with one double lesson a week) based on the 'Young Person as Producer' units and a game such as *Dart Aviation*,[2] or one using Lego. General studies was to remain unchanged since it involved outside speakers (the police, for example, for a mock court) and visits.

Pastoral curriculum

The Deputy Headteacher (curriculum) was concerned with the development of personal and social education in the school and in the LEA as a whole. She felt that economic awareness should be an important element in the LEA's scheme.

For Waldegrave in particular it was decided that some *Understanding Economics* units could be broken down to fit 20-minute slots in tutorial time. It was decided to try 'Consumers' in the fourth year and 'Ice Cream Factory' as part of the preparation for option choices in the third year. The problems in adopting this approach were recognized. There would be a very short time span, many staff with diverse backgrounds would be involved, and their in-service training needs would have to be recognized.

World studies

The teacher was already using 'The Accident' and a series of 10 video programmes called *Foundations of Wealth*[3]. However, it was felt that work on the community could be enhanced by including 'Costs and Benefits', 'Community Expenditure', 'Local Authority Rates' and 'Who Pays?'. The teacher was also well used to group work and active-learning methods, so the units would add to her bank of materials rather than demand changes in teaching style.

Commerce

Bank Loan[4] has featured in the 'O' level/CSE course since it was produced by the Banking Information Service in 1984. Other units such as 'The Price of a Perm' and *Teddytronic*[5] were seen to be useful, but negotiations will be necessary to decide which units will be fitted into Commerce and which into the 'Industry' module.

Geography

The Head of Geography was already using the CAL unit *Location of Steel*[5] and welcomed the *Understanding Economics* materials. 'Andy's Car', 'Land Use Planning', 'Local Shopping', 'Moving About' and 'Journey to Work' could be introduced into the third and fourth year syllabuses. 'Lamb' might be used for first years who study farming. The CGSE criteria for geography indicate that such materials will be even more useful than was thought originally, since they give a greater emphasis on experiential learning.

TVEI

A group of teachers including a mathematician, a biologist and a technologist, all of whom had some responsibility for TVEI pupils, had decided to run a mini-company. They favoured the mini-enterprise idea of a structured company with formal roles of managing director, accountant, personnel manager and workers. However, following discussions with the Deputy Headteacher (who had been seconded for a school/industry links course) and the writer, they agreed to try starting on the basis of small group work. Each group would brainstorm for ideas and then organize itself. Information would be supplied by the teachers as and when the need arose. Units from *Understanding Economics* like 'Price of a Perm' could be introduced when, for example, pupils needed to know about fixed and variable costs.

Initially, the Headteacher would allow the 33 fourth year TVEI pupils to be withdrawn for a double lesson to start the mini-companies. They would then be allowed one single lesson a week on a rota basis. The rest of the work was to be done in their own time.

The planning and negotiating process which led to the decisions described above extended over six months, during which time some informal staff development activities were begun.

Staff development

Teachers' industrial action affected the possibilities for staff development during the whole year. For example, no one was able to attend the formal in-service training days at the University of London Institute of Education, and school-based sessions proved to be impossible. The most help that could be given by the writer to support the work of colleagues was through team-teaching in the classroom.

Careers lessons offered the greatest opportunities for this, and *Dart Aviation*, a business game, was used by the Head of Core Studies and the writer. A demonstration lesson was given for health education, and teaching strategies were discussed for commerce and world studies.

Team-teaching was rewarding for both teachers since the lessons were so enjoyable. At first the writer took the lead, but as a pattern emerged and the materials became familiar, both took an equal part. The Head of Core Studies is now very confident in the use of *Understanding Economics* units and has tried many others on her own.

The start of the TVEI mini-companies involved a team of five teachers, four of whom were sceptical about the pupil-centred approach and, indeed, the TVEI coordinator gave a formal introduction. Pupils divided themselves into five groups. A short brainstorming session followed in which all their skills were noted, and ideas for their own business formulated. Pupils quickly became involved, coming up with dozens of ideas in an atmosphere of increasing, but controlled, excitement which was directed towards the goal of deciding on a product they could make or a service they could provide. The teachers, rather anxious at first, wanted to interfere and direct, but gradually saw that this was unnecessary since the pupils were motivating themselves. Individual pupils appeared in a new light. One, for example, thought to be rather weak academically, had taken charge of her group and shown she had initiative and was articulate and well organized. The teachers commented on the change of relationship that had occurred – 'They have never really talked to me before.' Although the occasion was unusual, with five teachers for 33 pupils, it had made the teachers aware of a different strategy for organizing learning. The pupils' undoubted enthusiasm encouraged the staff to continue the business ventures with the individual groups.

No progress was made during the year with staff development for pastoral curriculum work in economic awareness, but school-focused work for form tutors is the main proposal made by the Waldegrave TRIST planning group for 1986–7.

The impact of experiential learning on pupils and the development of economic awareness

Observations were made in about 12 fourth year careers lessons. These were followed up by discussions between the two teachers and by pupils' written work.

Using Dart Aviation

The introduction to active learning was through *Dart Aviation*, which had been adapted for use with mixed-ability fourth year classes in two double lessons. Groups compete with each other to make and sell paper aeroplanes with the aim of making the most profit. Decisions have to be made about the design, use of materials, use of labour, cost and price. The criteria used by the buyer (usually the teacher) are the ability to fly, and a low price.

The first session usually proceeds on a basis of trial and error, but later the groups organize themselves (sometimes with division of labour, sometimes not) and plan the work. Nearly all the pupils responded positively:

'I enjoyed this game as we were left on our own to see how well we could do without any advice from teachers. We had to use our own skill.'

'I enjoyed it because we could use our own ideas and organize what we wanted to do without people interfering.'

'I learnt to think things over clearly and not to jump in at the deep end. ... I enjoyed *Dart Aviation* because we were not continuously writing and we were left to think for ourselves without the teacher interrupting.'

One or two, however, complained that it dragged on too long.

The game is followed by a debriefing to discuss what they have learnt:

'Streamline did better than the other groups because their planes were cheaper than the rest, they flew well, their design was reliable and was quick to make.'

'The other groups had the same problem, e.g. it cost too much to make and a lot of the planes that were made did not fly.'

'We found that if each one had a certain job to do then the planes were made quicker and less money was spent and so it contributed to the overall profit.'

'It shows how people have to work as a group.'

'You are constantly in competition with other companies. You have to learn to get on with other people, maybe as a team or a partner, and you have to be a good judge on how to spend your money wisely.'

Was winning important? The girls were divided in their opinions:

'Winning the game is important because the aim of the game was to see how you could compete in a real business situation.'

Most were able to apply what they had learnt to the outside world, though from one or two the response was 'I didn't see the point of it.' More usual comments were:

'I learnt how real business would be run and found out what it is like to gain and lose profits and the competition between others, and co-operation. I thought it was great fun to have a go at having a company.'

'It made me think more about how a company is organized and what a lot of hard work and thinking is going into produce a few aeroplanes.'

'The game made *me* think about real aeroplane manufacturers such as British Aerospace and the time it takes to produce a good designed aeroplane and the money wasted when an aeroplane crashes.'

and even:

'I think it is a skilful technique of teaching, and you learn quite a bit about large companies. It also helps you if you are going to be involved in large companies in your career.'

'Talking to my parents about it they thought that it was a very good idea.

As for economic awareness – *Dart Aviation* contributed to the understanding of the world of business. It gave pupils some insight into the economic base of our society and the importance of the wealth-creating process, but there is little consideration of values. Maximizing profit is the aim of the game. Scarce resources are time and raw materials: their allocation is confined by the rules of the game.

From the pupils' written comments (taken from three classes), talk in their groups, and discussion in the class debriefing, it is clear that they learnt a great deal – and enjoyed the learning. From the classroom management point of view, the teacher has to be well-prepared so that instructions are clear, and salient points can be drawn out in the debriefing. A classroom with space to fly the aeroplanes and where desks or tables can be arranged for group work is essential. The lessons are bound to be noisy but it is busy talk. Pupils are almost all enthusiastic, well-motivated and involved.

Using 'Public Spending'

'Public Spending' (*Understanding Economics*) is a unit that considers the opportunity costs of different patterns of government spending. It is based on a role-playing exercise in which students decide upon levels of taxation and government spending as well as upon the mix of government expenditure. Information is given about past, current and future choices of spending by British governments and about tax revenue. For the role-play, groups of four or five pupils form a political party. Their task is to produce a government spending and taxation programme for inclusion in an election manifesto. Using the figures for 1981–2, the political parties have to decide which items of public spending they might want to increase and which items to decrease. The election manifestos are read out to the class and an election takes place.

This exercise suited the more able pupils very well. They quickly grasped the concepts and began the discussions and negotiations necessary to agree to an electoral programme. Where there were political disagreements the argument became quite heated. The teacher's help to explain a statistical table showing government spending was needed by some groups. Other pupils struggled with the exercise, but were, however, able to suggest what they thought was important:

'We have put up education so that schools can get more money and teachers get more pay.'

'Increase industry ... this would help the unemployed.'

In the election that followed, the presentation of the ideas in the manifesto proved to be as important in the role play as it is in reality.

Value judgements and political factors in relation to economics were well-explored:

'We will increase overseas aid ... to give relief to the starving and homeless. ... We feel that industry and employment are a very important part of the government's responsibility, therefore we increase this ... to create jobs.'

'On the decrease side, we have decided to scrap Defence completely, because we believe in spreading peace throughout the world. ... We have increased certain things, like social security, to accommodate for the jobless we have made in decreasing the defence. ... We are generously increasing the government's lending to national industries, and industries of the future are the answer to all our problems. ... Income tax you will be pleased to know we have decided to decrease by 2p which is an extra two pounds a week to the general public.'

The relationship between taxation and spending was well understood and much thought and debate went into the choices made about the use of resources. The costs and benefits were assessed and the opportunity cost was taken into account.

A lot of economic ideas therefore emerged from the lesson. The group work involved all the pupils in thinking, discussing, making value judgements and contributing to their manifesto. The election was so engrossing that one group class sacrificed its break to count votes. Social skills such as listening to and negotiating with people who hold differing views are developed by group work. The pupils also learnt how to prepare arguments to support a point of view and gain confidence in presenting that view to a wider audience.

Using 'Wages'

The 'Wages' unit (*Understanding Economics*) uses newscuttings and wage-negotiation role-play to introduce the institutional framework of industrial relations and the processes involved in pay bargaining. Once again value positions are highlighted in a particular field of economics. Attitudes to the role of trades unions and employers in wage determination can be explored through the roles, along with the ideas of subsidizing production. The notion of fairness in wage distribution can be discussed. The validity of other people's views must be taken into account and an opportunity is provided for negotiating skills to be developed.

Initially, pupils have to comprehend the information given in written passages and numerical tables which set the scene for the wage bargaining. The bias of the newspaper reports is a topic for discussion.

For the role-play the class is divided into an even number of teams of two or three, each team representing either the management of a local bus company or the trade union. Union representatives ask for a wage rise, but management want to increase productivity by moving to one-man operated buses and creating redundancies. One alternative is to ask the local council to increase the level of subsidy.

When the activity was run, everyone except two children (with learning difficulties) became very involved in the negotiations. Arguments were heated:

'The negotiations were totally unsuccessful due to the bombastic attitude of the management.'

'They said in rage that *everyone* would be sacked. This is a totally irrational attitude as they would lose on passengers and money.'

Pupils who, in formal situations, would not utter a word became very involved. The roles were real enough even if the validity of other people's views was forgotten. Calculations of wage rises proved difficult for some groups, but the teacher was able to act as helper and adviser when required. Practically all pupils understood that increases in wages affect costs and might have implications for prices and employment levels. They also grasped the concept of 'productivity', a term they had heard on radio and television, but at the beginning of the lesson could not explain.

The quality of the written management and trades union reports varied from group to group, but economic ideas came through:

'The management (us) are against the strike because they (the workers) would lose more money.'

'Shop stewards feel we could pay for their increase by raising fares, but this means that fewer people will want to go on buses as it is more expensive.'

'To increase productivity we intend to make a few people redundant and move to one-man-operated buses.'

'The management think one-person buses could be the answer because they would have to pay fewer people for jobs and therefore would make a profit. Our members objected to this because they would be making some people redundant. We, and the management, are keen to avoid the strike; the management want to avoid it because they will have to pay off things, with no incoming money, and we don't want it because we will have no pay.'

'The introduction of driver-only buses is not desirable for our union for several reasons:
a) loss of jobs
b) no conductor leads to vandalism and even violence which the driver is powerless to stop
c) this could and has led to loss of custom as the public doesn't feel safe on driver-only buses
d) this leads to more cars on the roads and more loss of custom as the service becomes unreliable
e) and so the proposed cut in expenses would be made non-existent by the loss of custom, repair-bills and general maintenance that will be needed.'

'Increasing productivity on low wages leads to dissatisfied drivers giving a less pleasant service, once again leading to loss of custom.'

Most management groups were intimidated by the threat of strike action and agreed to natural wastage rather than redundancies: 'We will not be sacking anybody, it will be voluntary redundancies by the old and infirm', or 'finding alternative employment for the few made redundant'.

Talks broke down into two groups, resulting in a work to rule or a ballot of union members on whether to strike. Unfortunately, in only one double lesson there was not time to go to arbitration or extend the work further.

With the time available in the new module as well as in careers, extension work will be possible. The trials of the two units convinced the teachers of the value of the learning for the whole ability range as well as that lessons like these are fun.

Conclusions

The 'Industry' module has been incorporated into core studies for a term now (December 1986). Fourth year classes have a double lesson each week for seven weeks – but pupils have responded to the work so well that the teacher wishes the course could have been longer. As a non-specialist she has found it reassuring to use the television series *Economics: A Question of Choice*,[6] with activities from the teacher's booklet as a stimulus for discussion. 'Consumers' and 'The Price of Pop' (*Understanding Economics*) have been incorporated into the follow-up work, together with a Lego production simulation and the school's own version of *Dart Aviation*.

References

1 Economics Association, *Understanding Economics*, Longman, 1985.
2 *Dart Aviation*, Careers Research Advisory Centre, 1978.
3 *Foundations of Wealth*, a series of ten video programmes, 1980–82, available from CFL Vision, Chalfont Grove, Gerrards Cross, Bucks SL9 8TN.
4 *Bank Loan*, Banking Information Service, 1984.
5 *Computers in the Curriculum*/Economics Education 14–16 Project, 'Teddytronic' and 'Location of Steel', *Understanding Economics*, Longman, 1985.
6 *Economics*: A Question of Choice, British Broadcasting Corporation, 1986.

Appendix 1: Outline of Economic Literacy paper presented by Headteacher in January 1985

Aims

1) to increase pupils' knowledge and understanding of the business world and the working of a modern commercial and industrial society
2) to promote an awareness of the ways in which society is changing and the need for adaptability to the effects of rapid technological change
3) to contribute to the improvement of communication skills such as problem-solving and decision making in order to help pupils in their future lives as consumers, producers and citizens
4) to help to develop in pupils an orderly and systematic approach to work, an ability to work with others, a willingness to consider different viewpoints and ways of life, a critical awareness, the ability to order priorities and a respect for evidence as a basis for forming judgements.

Knowledge to include elements of the British economy, the EEC, production and distribution, money and financial institutions, prices, wages, government and taxation and trades unions.

Skills to include finding and organizing information and being able to: discuss economic and business problems meaningfully; distinguish between fact and opinion; read/listen to/watch articles or programmes with a business content; make informed personal financial decisions; understand the power of marketing and advertising; and use a keyboard.

Attitudes to include demonstrating, respect for evidence in decision-making, which are not ill-informed or prejudiced as a result of incomplete or biased knowledge, and which demonstrate a concern for the responsible use of resources for promoting the economic welfare of our own and other societies.

Concepts to include wants and needs; resources, their uneven distribution and their alternative uses; the role of individuals in society as producers and consumers; production and its dependence on the combination of factors of production; investment and its relation to saving; exchange; the relationship between price, supply and demand; economic growth; inflation; the balance of payments; unemployment; the standard of living; specialization; interdependence and the interrelationship in the economy and between countries.

Section 2 *Economic Awareness through Subjects*

9 Economic awareness through geography

Peter Davies

Leek High School, Staffordshire

The school

The school is a 13 – 18 comprehensive in a small town with a large rural catchment area. The organization of the curriculum is based on departments accustomed to working independently, and examination results are very much the dominant criterion for evaluating departmental performance. In the life skills area of the curriculum all fourth and fifth years had to follow a general studies course unless they opted for religious studies (top third of ability range only) or a mode-3 humanities course (bottom third of ability range only). The general studies and humanities courses were broadly similar and both had detailed content and method specification (for example, specifying which page of which book and with which worksheet).

Economic awareness in the curriculum

The only economics specialist on the staff was Head of Geography, Economics, CPVE and Work Experience. Of the three other full-time geographers, one was a Deputy Head. Two PE teachers also taught a few lower-school classes.

Previous attempts to gain a place for economics in the fourth and fifth year curriculum had been carefully deferred by the Headteacher (on the pragmatic grounds of who was going to teach it, the effects on staffing of falling rolls, etc.).

The areas targeted for economic awareness were general studies/humanities, geography and CPVE. This restricted development to two departments: the one over which the writer had the most influence and the one which was the most obvious candidate. The judgement that a broad-based use of units from *Understanding Economics*[1] in many departments would be unlikely to achieve significant long-term change was a considered one and a number of factors contributed to it:

1) the emphasis on independent departments within the school
2) the perceived difficulty of coordinating and implementing cross-curricular work
3) the suspicion that using units would be regarded as synonymous with achieving successful 'delivery' of economic awareness and therefore blunt any further attempts to achieve change
4) the judgement that the school coordinator (the writer) would not have enough time to support the use of materials by a larger number of staff
5) the existence of a 'computer awareness' programme which departments were being expected to implement – thus leading departments to be wary of demands being made on them
6) the failure to identify a second member of staff who could be encouraged to act as an agent of support and change *in relation to other staff.*

Clearly, this list involved a series of 'hunches' which seemed reasonable at the time (and still do).

However, point 6 was a critical failure and had implications well beyond the wisdom of deciding to concentrate the development on two departments.

The strategy in geography

The third year course was badly in need of improvement. In years four and five, geography was an option attracting between six and seven groups per year. All students followed the Avery Hill scheme.[2] The most able were entered for the Avery Hill WJEC/SUJB 'O' level; everyone else was entered for the Staffordshire mode-3 16+ exam.

The third year course

Through departmental meetings, members of staff collectively identified the major headings under which they wanted the new course to be planned. These were:

1)   local studies: the potteries
2)   industry
3)   the effect of the physical environment
4)   glaciation and coastlines
5)   world differences and development

Two of the modules were seen to have more potential than the others as vehicles for economic awareness: these were 'industry' and 'living standards and development'. Each member of the department took responsibility for drawing up suggestions regarding one module. Figure 1 shows the scheme drawn up to guide the thinking on the industry module.

It was originally expected that three of the units from *Understanding Economics* would be used. However, the intention was always to design modules that were coherent within their geographical parameters rather than to attempt to build part of the course around particular resources.

When the course reached the detailed planning stage it was apparent that only one of the *Understanding Economics* units remained appropriate. This left the problem of how to *design* work which

Figure 1   Proposed third year scheme for the industry module

Processes	Resulting patterns of employment	Resulting patterns of land-use
Characteristics of an area may give it an advantage in the development of a particular industry	Dependency on one main type of employment	Effect on population growth (in-migration due to employment); size of built-up area; type of housing built
The nature of employment in an area will be affected by technological change	Effect on the type of skills required; effect on employment/unemployment	Factory and office location and type; use of the home as the working environment.
The nature of employment in an area will be affected by market conditions in a market economy	Effect of changes on employment structure	Links between local industry and number of people working in the town; standard of living and demands for housing type

would encourage the development of economic awareness in geography lessons. This was always going to be a longer job than using an existing unit. In particular, notions of 'what is economic awareness?' and 'what is the relationship between economics and geography?' were at best half-formed. Such notions as existed were derived more from classroom experience than vice versa. The extent of any underlying rationale can be summed up in the statement that

economic processes are important in determining the way in which resources are used in a particular location and economics provides one way of evaluating the implications of that use of resources.

Some reflections

What effects did the changes have on pupils, staff and school resources?

The pupils

It is possible to identify differences between the new third year course and the old. Given that all members of staff used the new course materials, it is reasonable to assume that these differences carried through to lessons. Whether, as a result, there were any material differences in pupils' experience and learning is, of course, much harder to judge. The following list might be useful in pinpointing these differences and difficulties.

1) pupils were asked to learn and interpet more information relating to production and living standards

2) pupils were expected to use some concepts (e.g. the link between financial costs and production decisions, the link between industrial land-use and the use of resources in urban areas, and the meaning of an improvement in standard of living) which had not been explored in the previous third year course

3) the introduction of two case studies and simulations entailed more problem-solving

4) evaluation of the 'best use' of resources received minimal attention – pupils were asked to use the perspective of the resource owner (e.g. the steelworks) without attention being drawn to alternative viewpoints

5) despite the intention of changing to work which emphasized explanation and problem-solving rather than description, the nature of many of the teaching materials encouraged the latter (see comments on school resources below)

6) despite initial plans, pupils were not asked to consider links between production, demand and government, and little attention was given to the link between production and employment

7) given points 4, 5 and 6 above, and the prescriptive nature of many of the teaching resources, whether the course helped pupils to make informed judgements about issues such as 'How should land be used?' must be in doubt.

A brief look at one of the teaching resources (shown in Appendix 1) may help to clarify some of these points. Apart from the development of basic mapwork skills, the ground covered by questions 2 and 3 is shown by the italicized items in the accompanying analysis. The questions thus stop well short of allowing an investigation into the issues raised by all the evidence. That is, they do not allow consideration of the social costs and benefits that accrue to the community; they do not allow discussion of whether profit should determine the use of land; and pupils are not encouraged to ask the questions which would help them to make sense of the processes underpinning the evidence in front of them. At first sight question 7 appears to leave the way open for greater investigation. In practice, however, pupils were not expected to move beyond the first stage of limited explanation apparent in question 3. In this case it is the teacher rather than the printed question who creates the limitation.

The teachers

All the teachers were involved in planning the curriculum change. The department drew up the overall structure for the course in the light of suggestions from each of the four main teachers of geography. Each of these four also had responsibility for producing a coherent module and the resources to support it. Resulting from this was the need to communicate to other members of the department how they expected the module to operate.

The intention behind this arrangement was to force them to develop resources and teaching strategies for each other. Learning from one another had previously been rather limited despite a very extensive shared bank of paper-based resources. The pace of change was also forced by spreading the load of work through specialization. Moreover, this pace put the development of the teaching ideas and materials under the pressure of urgent need. Thus, as the year progressed there was a great emphasis on the production of virtually 'ready-made' lessons and little time for careful thinking and reflection on what had, and indeed was, happening.

So, how does this relate to 'economic awareness'? A climate of learning from each other and using each other's resources provided the context for people to work with ideas which were not necessarily drawn from their own teaching experience. This opportunity was not, however, fully exploited. Changing a whole year's course also prompts discussion of the question 'what do we really think is important enough to be included?' It is much easier to examine the case for 'economic awareness through geography' if the nature of a course is *already* being questioned. Also, changes which come as part of a complete course revision are more likely to last than discrete teaching units introduced into an existing framework.

Given these favourable circumstances, it is reasonable to ask why more was not achieved. Two members of the department had designed modules and teaching materials expected to lead to some increase in economic awareness. One of these (the writer) had an academic background in economics, while the other was very much a geographer, in his second year of teaching. All members of the department had taught lessons based on these materials.

Suppose that the following objectives had been established for staff development:

● to be able to identify economic awareness issues involved in teaching particular topics

● to be able to use teaching materials to develop economic awareness in a way consistent with the objectives of a course in geography

● to be able to develop their own teaching materials which develop economic awareness through geography

These objectives were not achieved during the year, but the changes effected did at least create a more likely context for their realization in the future. Why was progress slow?

The fact that the writer was trying to come to terms with what economic awareness in a third year geography lesson really entails meant that he was not in a strong position to help other members of the department to develop their own lessons. Moreover, the opportunity to team-teach some third year lessons with others in the department was also lost. Perhaps the explanation for this lies in the fact that the writer had not been exposed to team-teaching as a way of teachers helping teachers. (Instances of teachers working together in the classroom arose only from 'doubling up classes' for films, fieldwork, etc.) On the other hand, perhaps it had not appeared as a problem. A reason for accepting the latter explanation lies in the preoccupation with the production of lesson materials, which in itself arose from the pressure of the speed at which the changes were being introduced.

School resources

By the end of the year the department was equipped with teaching resources for the entire course. Moreover, as discussed earlier, these resources were generally very prescriptive and in fact gave little room for the development of economic awareness. Therefore their use in the future may tend to limit rather than enable change. The potential for the future may lie in the ability of staff to develop new teaching strategies rather than in the bank of resources which was the focus of so much effort during the year.

Appendix 2 shows an example of the type of resource which may be more likely to point the way forward. Taken from a Staffordshire Education Committee source, it is the result of the application of what was learnt over the first year of the course. Included in this learning was the experience of using some units from *Understanding Economics* and adaptations of the same in the fourth and fifth year geography course (see below). The range of questions and concepts which the use of the material is intended to pursue are described. The unit of work is intended to structure answers towards the key points of economic awareness (question 1) and geographical enquiry (question 2) raised at the bottom. The diagram is intended to aid classification, identification and causal links and the placing of values on outcomes which provide that structure.

The suggested classroom use of the material is also shown in Appendix 2. The product of two third year classes in response to question 4 is illustrated. The next stage was to expose these lists to questionning:

● why do you think this *will* be an outcome?

● why do you consider this outcome to be better or worse?

● for whom will this outcome be better or worse?

● what value do you place on this outcome?

The fourth and fifth year courses

Geography was a popular option for the fourth and fifth years, attracting between two-thirds and three-quarters of the pupils. The subject was available as a choice to pupils of all ability, but the take-up was skewed towards the more able. All classes followed the GYSL syllabus[2] towards an examination either at 'O' level or at 16+.

The GYSL syllabus

There is no doubt that geography courses for the 14 – 16 age group deal with topics which may be used as a context for developing economic awareness (e.g. the exploitation of mineral reserves and forests). There have been calls from teachers of geography for teaching contexts to be chosen through which economic awareness can be developed.[3] Indeed, the GYSL 'O' level and CSE syllabuses could certainly claim to be the ones which travelled furthest in this direction. However, the 'point-form' of the 'O' level and CSE examinations encouraged a style of work which was unlikely to bear much fruit in terms of economic awareness. This style of work is most clearly exemplified in one recent and popular geography textbook for the 14–16 age group.[4] Indeed, the success of the department in terms of examination results was based in no small measure upon the teachers' ability to induct pupils into the technique of 'point-form'. An illustration of the type of work involved is shown in Appendix 3.

Under these circumstances lessons intended to develop economic awareness were likely to be peripheral in terms of examination goals. Therefore the fourth and fifth year course was the scene of experimentation with home-produced units alongside *Understanding Economics*, to try to discover the extent to which these different objectives could share the same time and contexts. Planning proved to be the most fruitful syllabus area to attempt this marriage, and Appendix 4 provides an example of a school-produced unit in this context. However, it proved very difficult even to attempt such a process within the economic geography section of the syllabus. None of the *Understanding Economics* units, for example, shared the same contexts, and it

proved more difficult to overcome the constraints of the 'point-form' approach than it was in the case of planning and transport. The reason for this was that problems in the realms of planning and transport were frequently posed in terms of searches for best solutions. Thus, the points sought were arguments attributable to a viewpoint in relation to a desired solution. When a problem is already set in terms of 'what is best, and for whom?', then understanding what that means in terms of economic awareness only involves extending the given structure. In economic geography, apart from the area concerned with the effect of industry on the environment, the emphasis was on explaining observed changes and patterns (e.g. the distribution of types of industry within a town, the closure of a steelworks). To approach these issues in terms of economic awareness would require a complete change in, rather than an extension of, the structure through which they were investigated. Explanations would, for example, need to be cast more in terms of the interaction of many variables and less as discrete effects. So, explanations for the closure or establishment of a business would need to take account of the interaction of profits or losses (determined by the relationship between costs and revenue) with other factors such as social costs and business motivation.

These considerations were a factor in determining the choice of GCSE syllabus. The GYSL project syllabus[5] clearly represented a shift in thinking towards the evaluation of industrial and employment change, whilst the 'Avery Hill' syllabus[6] produced by Regional Boards enshrined previous practice. Thus choosing the new GYSL GCSE syllabus should provide a more favourable vehicle for the development of economic awareness in the fourth and fifth year geography course at the school.

Appendix 5 is included to provide some impression of the syllabus. For example, an adaptation of 'Price of a Perm' (*Understanding Economics*), reset using a case study of a local dyeing firm which closed in the 1981–2 recession and re-opened after a management buyout, has been developed for use in the new course.

Notes and references

1 Economics Association, *Understanding Economics*, Longman, 1985.
2 The 'O' level syllabus based on the Geography for the Young School Leaver (GYSL) scheme was known as the 'Avery Hill' and was offered by the Welsh Joint Education Committee (WJEC) in conjunction with the Southern Universities Joint Board (SUJB).
3 See, for example, Richard Kemp, Is What You Teach About Industry Really Relevant?, in *Teaching Geography*, Geographical Association, January 1985.
4 Waugh, D., *The British Isles*, Nelson, 1983.
5 The GYSL project team produced a complete and radical revision for the GCSE. This is offered through the WJEC and MEG.
6 See, for example, MEG, Geography Syllabus C.

3) Which of the following would have been good reasons for factories and warehouses being built in grid square 1975?

   a) the land is flat so it costs less to build large factories
   b) a factory in grid square 1975 would be in a good position to send out what it makes by rail or ship
   c) it is close to the beach
   d) the land is lying close to the sea, so it was probably marshy before the area was built up

7) Look at the house in Grangetown (grid square 1774). Think of the people who live there.

   a) what sort of jobs do you think they have?
   b) where in Cardiff do you think they might work?
   c) what is it like to live in Grangetown?

Appendix 1: Example of a third year course worksheet refering to pages 24 and 25 of *Metric Map and Photo Reading* by T. W. Birch

Analysis of industrial location issues arising from the worksheet

Identify what is there: *almost entirely industrial; factories, warehouses, docks, railways; flat land near mouth of estuary*

Why these industries established themselves here: *land, transport; type; cost variations; demand, profit*

2) Look at grid square 1975. Do you agree or disagree with each of these sentences about the square?

   a) all the land seems to be used for industrial purposes
   b) several main roads pass through the area
   c) goods can be loaded off ships in the dock and put straight on to railway wagons
   d) the factories probably included warehouses for storing goods before they were shipped
   e) it would be a pleasant place to live
   f) the land is very flat and low-lying

Appendix 2: Example of a better third year resource

CHANGES IN WORK AND HOME

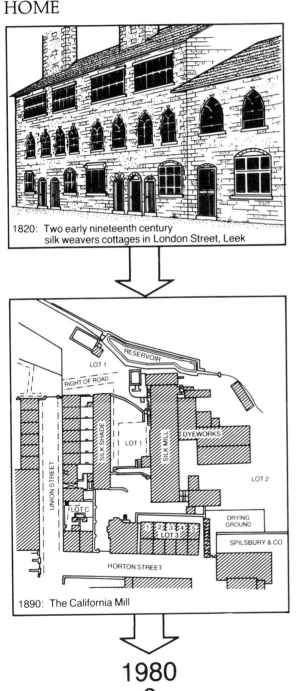

1820: Two early nineteenth century silk weavers cottages in London Street, Leek

1890: The California Mill

1980
?

QUESTIONS AND CONCEPTS TO BE PURSUED

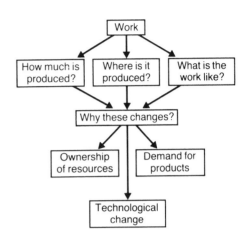

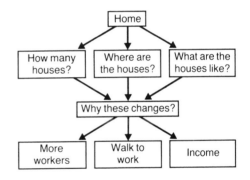

1) Are these changes an improvement?
2) How are changes in work and home linked?

Classroom use of silk industry stimulus (first lesson)

1) pupils produce five words on each picture, individually and then in groups
2) suggestions from each group are recorded using the following classification: 1820/work, 1820/home, 1890/work, 1890/home
3) identification of changes between 1820 and 1890 under the headings 'work' and 'home'
4) are these changes an improvement?

The responses of two third year classes

Stream 1

'Better'

efficient, organized, more products, more room at home, many buildings put into a small area

'Worse'

loss of independence, no choice in housing, no control over pay, travel to work

Stream 4

'Better'

produces more, houses close to factory, better houses, more jobs

'Worse'

less quality, more machinery breakdowns, takes up good land, people didn't have to work so hard, more pollution, worse view from houses, not working for yourself

Appendix 3: Extract from model answer to question on industrial decline (Avery Hill 'O' level question 7, 1979)

a)(i) The Steel industry has declined in this area because:

1) closure of local shipbuilders INCREASED/ REDUCED the demand for steel
2) lower demand for the steel meant that the plant WAS/WAS NOT able to sell enough steel to remain profitable
3) exhaustion of local iron ore leads to the need to (------) iron ore RAISING/LOWERING costs
4) old plant ABOVE/BELOW the most efficient size raises costs of production
5) increased costs of production mean that the plant IS/IS NO LONGER profitable to run
6) therefore the plant is closed as part of a RATIONALIZATION/NATIONALIZ-ATION plan by British Steel

Appendix 4: A questionnaire on travel to Hanley

1) If you travel to Hanley would you be more likely to go there for
   a) work
   b) shopping
   c) leisure? ...
2) If you travel to Hanley would you usually go there by bus or by car?

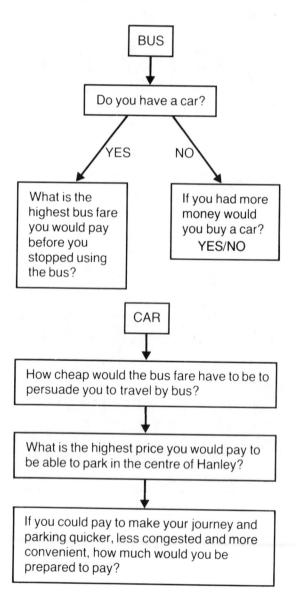

Appendix 5: An extract from the syllabus, and sample questions for the GYSL GCSE Geography (WJEC)

The nature of work and employment (teaching time: 1 week)

Work and paid employment are not necessarily the same thing.
How is work defined, and by whom?
How does work differ from paid employment?
What factors affect an individual's employment opportunities?

Variations in employment opportunities: pattern and process (teaching time: 7 weeks)

1) Employment structures and opportunties vary at local, regional and national scales.
   How do employment opportunities and structures vary?
   Why do variations occur?
   Are these variations inevitable?
2) Distributions of employment structures and opportunities vary over time.
   How have employment opportunities varied over time?
   Can we predict future developments?
   What are the alternatives to the present structure of employment opportunities?
3) Employment opportunities in any area may vary through time and space for a variety of reasons.
   How do national and world economic processes affect employment opportunities of an area?
   How do the physical, historical, social, economic and political characteristics of an area, and changes in these, affect employment opportunities? What factors attract or inhibit economic investments?

How might decisions on the use of technology, and changes in organizational structures, affect employment opportunities?
What role do governments play in influencing the nature and location of economic activity?

Whose economy is it? (teaching time: 2 weeks)

There may be alternative ways of organizing economies.
What are the alternatives to the present system of power and decision making?
How can people, organizations and governments affect the nature and location of work and paid employment?

Sample questions

Question 4(d)

Work opportunities in a country or region may be improved by:

1) developing new sources of energy
2) developing new mineral resources
3) improving accessibility
4) creating cooperatives or communes.

Choose *two* of the ways listed above, and by naming a country or region you have studied, show how work opportunities have been improved.

Question 5(c)

Penrikyber mine in the Cynon Valley (Block Diagrams B) is threatened with closure. It employs 660 men, most of whom live in the nearby town. It is one of three mines left in the valley. There is enough coal underground to last another 20 years. The Coal Board says it cannot produce coal cheaply enough and is losing money. An enquiry is to be held into the possible closure.
Write a letter to the Enquiry stating as many good reasons as you can think of as to why the mine should not be closed. Start you letter 'Dear Chairperson, I wish to make the following points regarding the possible closing down of the Penrikyber coal mine . . .'

10 Economic awareness through GCSE Business Studies

Angus Taylor

Cramlington High School, Northumberland

This case study considers GCSE Business Studies courses as a potential vehicle for economic awareness education in the 14+ and 15+ years of compulsory education. It refers briefly to GCSE national criteria and the opportunities offered for syllabuses and schemes of work in business studies. Aspects of a business studies course in one school are examined and related to economic awareness.

The SCDC Planning Conference on Economic Awareness held in July 1986 agreed on an impressive agenda for future action, 'the principles upon which subsequent planning will be founded'.[1] The HMI contribution to the conference described economic awareness as 'a continuum that begins with economic awareness, progressing through economic understanding to economic competence and capability'.

What is anticipated clearly lies between the extremes of an in-depth academic course in economics (such as 'A' level) leading to 'a sort of club of economists' on the one hand, and a superficial acquaintance with 'the economic base of society' and 'the importance of the wealth creating process'[2] on the other. It is an ambitious intent. To quote again from the SCDC report:

'Economic awareness should permeate the curriculum for the full age range 5–16/18 and the full ability range ... its purpose is to enable young people to make informed decisions throughout their lives ... in which they will be producers, consumers and citizens.'

Clearly this ambition cannot be effectively met through short modules in personal and social development courses, in spite of the care that has been put into the development of many such courses. Nor can we hope to get substantial core curriculum time set aside for a two-year, four-periods-a-week course leading to GCSE Economics. The opportunity cost would not be possible to justify for a curriculum which aims to be broad, balanced, relevant and differentiated.

This case study accepts that curricular accommodation of learning leading to an ambitious definition of economic awareness will have to start in the primary phase of education (ages 5–11) and continue through to 16 (or 18). It will also have to be across the curriculum in an effectively coordinated way. But GCSE Business Studies also has a potentially powerful role to play, and we should be aware of this.

Until very recently, business studies in the main school pre-16 curriculum referred to various courses in business skills, and especially typewriting. 'O' level syllabuses in business studies grew out of successful 'A' level developments, and involved the study of the business environment, business organization and various aspects of business behaviour. However, it did not involve many candidates; it seemed an inconsequential vehicle for education for economic awareness.

Two developments are changing the situation, probably reflecting the increasingly utilitarian approach to curriculum design and the emphasis on 'relevance', an emphasis that is reflected in the HMI view that 'the curriculum should be relevant in the sense that it is seen by pupils to meet their present and prospective needs'.[3,4] The two developments are the selection of 'business studies' as one of the 19 titles for which subject-specific national criteria were to be developed ('economics' was added as a twentieth subject later) and the MSC-funded Technical and Vocational Education Initiative (TVEI).

The selection of business studies as one of the 20 subject titles not only led to the creation of GCSE national criteria in business studies, but also ensured that each of the five examining groups in England and Wales submitted at least one mode-1 syllabus in business studies for approval by the Secondary Examination Council (two groups submitted two syllabuses). The marketing that followed saw these syllabuses circulated to schools around the country.

TVEI aims to 'enhance' the curriculum, usually of a limited number (cohort) in the 14 + year and beyond, in a limited number of secondary schools in those LEAs (the vast majority) who apply to be involved.* Business studies (and various related enterprise activities) is a common, and sometimes dominant, feature.

As a result, business studies is a rapidly growing feature of the 14 + and 15 + curriculum. GCSE is the main target and TVEI has ensured a practical and experiential approach. In some schools a substantial proportion of a year group follow such courses. The number of schools offering courses is growing rapidly. It is a subject which attracts equal numbers of boys and girls.

How then is education for economic awareness served for those following GCSE Business Studies courses?

The GCSE national criteria for business studies offer no immediate commitment to education for economic awareness.[5] In fact, the only reference to anything 'economic' occurs but once, in an example of business behaviour, and the inclusion in the course of 'an awareness of central business and economic problems'. Most significantly, 'the educational aims of all courses in Business Studies' (quoted verbatim in all the syllabuses approved in 1986) make no reference to economic understanding or the sorts of concept that might be anticipated in courses leading to that understanding. And yet the aims, assessment objectives and core content encourage educational experiences ideally suited to the acquisition of economic awareness in

the full sense anticipated earlier.

This is not the place to list all the aims contained in the national criteria. However, they include developing a knowledge and understanding of the environment within which business activity takes place, of the major groups within and outside business, of the roles and purposes of business activity, of the main types of institutions and of the language, concepts, techniques and decision-making procedures in business behaviour. The implication, in the introduction to the core content, is that those following the course should have far more than a descriptive knowledge of institutions. Business behaviour and experience of the roles of producer (especially), consumer and citizen should give students an active understanding of the subject.

The result is a panorama of experiences which keep the student in active contact not only with business studies but also with many aspects of economic awareness – what we would consider necessary as a part of economic competence and capability. Thus, students will acquire a working understanding of the structure of the mixed economy; the role of price and profit in influencing patterns of production; costs, revenue, break-even and profit and loss; consumer protection; competition and imperfections in the market; the role of government in supporting and controlling economic behaviour; and many other key features of the economic system and economic behaviour.

Of course the question can be asked, 'why choose business studies as a way of contributing to economic understanding?' Most of us who are teaching in this area are economists by training and have found our way into 14–16 education from 'A' level work. Why not, therefore, follow a GCSE course in economics?

Clearly the GCSE Economics course is less descriptive, which can be seen as an advantage, and takes a broader view of the economic system. There are more opportunities in economics compared with business studies for discussing value implications, for example on the standing of advertising.

My view is that we are seeking to serve broader education aims than a course specifically in economics will achieve. Some 20 years ago the route that was explored was that of social science. However, the emphasis of sociology as a discipline

* The TVEI extension phase is available to all students 14–18 in all schools.

made it very difficult to pursue experiences of economic thinking and behaviour. Business studies could be valued as a course in itself without any considerations of the achievement of economic understanding. This is the main reason why it was introduced into the curriculum and reinforced by such initiatives as TVEI. Those following the course are, or could be, quite unaware of any economic understanding being achieved. The economic understanding is a bonus rather than intention of the course. In addition there are clearly advantages in choosing business studies rather than GCSE Economics, particularly in the facility for making abstract ideas more concrete and relevant through the study and even the operation of a business. Our feeling is that business studies will prove a very popular GCSE title because of the pre-vocational influence on the 14–16 curriculum at a time of uncertain job prospects. That is the *de facto* situation. We suspect that economics will not prosper on quite that scale, particularly as social science, in our experience, is proving another popular title. If economics education is going to be available within an options system the positive rather than the normative situation is that it is more likely to be through the facility of a business studies course than an economics course.

GCSE Business Studies at Cramlington High School: a vehicle for economic awareness

The origin of the scheme of work is not in GCSE. The school had introduced GCE 'O' level Business Studies (following the Cambridge syllabus) and written a CSE syllabus to allow joint teaching. The course followed a fairly traditional route, with some experiential learning. Coursework for CSE was based on three projects, two based on a common practical activity. Those responsible for organizing the course were simultaneously responsible for developing a very successful and popular BTEC General course in the sixth form, with its emphasis on practical assignments and cross-curricular exercises. When the school became involved with TVEI in 1984, business studies was available

as a TVEI option while continuing as an option for students not in the TVEI cohort of 20% of the year group. Business staff were involved in writing a series of assignments in the BTEC style – primarily to respond to the more practical, enterprise approach to business studies encouraged by TVEI. This scheme of work has been developed to extend to all students following a business studies course and to respond to the aims, objectives, core content and coursework expectations of GCSE – in this case the Northern Examining Association's Syllabus A.

The first term's work follows four assignments in the following order:

1) the local business environment
2) a small business and its finances
3) a marketing exercise
4) advertising

The emphasis is very much introductory – introducing students to the practice of working in small groups and extended assignments and providing them with an introductory feel for the business world and the roles of individuals within it. Incidentally a good deal of economic understanding will be available even though, at this stage, a conscious recognition of this potential is not written in.

In Assignment 1, the objectives are stated as to make pupils aware:

● of what industry exists locally, where it is and why it should stay in Cramlington or come here originally
● that our economy is divided between public and private sectors and understand the basic differences between the two

Students are placed in a 'situation' and given exercises to work on together (see Appendix 1).

Resources are limited to the town map, which contains details of industrial and retail premises; the planning department's list of businesses – when they were established in the new town and what their main product is; and the teacher. Teachers are free to create their own materials and exercises on the differences between the public and private sector and basic factors influencing industrial location. Both texts and newspapers contain examples of the sort of advertisement they are asked to design.

Assignment 2 places the student, or groups of students, in a situation which grows out of and maintains the narrative of Assignment 1 (see Appendix 1).

The first task is to work through 'Price of a Perm' (*Understanding Economics*).[6] With the concepts and information gained there, and with teacher support depending on the nature of the teaching group, further tasks are tackled.

The economics learning is that identified in the unit's key ideas. The rest of the assignment puts that unit into an experiential context and reinforces understanding. The course is still at an early and elementary stage, but already a variety of economic ideas and concepts have been met in the context of the mixed economy, its environment and institutions.

Assignment 3 leads on from the extension exercise to Assignment 2. Using 'Tiny Atom Radio' (*Understanding Economics*), it involves students in experiences and exercises which help them explore the role of the market in influencing what is produced, factors influencing demand, the various features of the marketing mix, and it reinforces understanding of concepts such as costs, revenue and profit. By the end of this assignment, with the first term still unfinished, students have become confident learners in business studies. They also have the beginnings of economic understanding.

Depending on the group, its ability and motivation, there will have been several opportunities for extension, reinforcement and variety. The department has a range of good films on video giving practical examples of small firms and of marketing at various levels. Although there are two computer laboratories a few yards from the Business Studies Department, we have our own mobile unit and most teachers in the department have good experience of integrating its use into the overall organization of learning. For example, the program 'Teddytronic',[7] played as a competition between the learning groups in a class, fits well into work towards the end of Assignment 3 with students becoming more familiar with costs, revenue and profit and loss, and a marketing mix of price and advertising.

The advertising Assignment 4, which draws the term to a close, is popular but would appear low in economics. However, having to plan a product launch from a limited advertising budget, with a schedule of media prices, is a useful exercise in resource constraints and opportunity cost. But there are other features of this assignment which would properly be part of an economics education, including recognizing the difference between the positive and normative and developing the ability to argue a point of view.

Thus after a term of business studies the student, in his or her 14 + year, with no previous economics education, has already economic awareness, has economic understanding in some areas of the subject and, by being able to make informed judgements (for example in playing the 'Teddytronic' business game) has a degree of economic competence – and all of that without having set out to learn economics.

A genuine education for economic capability and competence cannot be left to a business studies option. That education to be adequate needs to be spread through time from 5 to 16 and, in the later years especially, have a natural home across the curriculum. But during this phase of whole curriculum development, business studies courses can ensure substantial economics education for students who might otherwise miss out.

References

1   SCDC, *Report on Planning Conference on Economic Awareness*, July 1986.
2   DES, *The School Curriculum*, HMSO, 1981.
3   DES, *Better Schools*, HMSO, 1985.
4   Her Majesty's Inspectorate, The curriculum from 5 to 16, *Curriculum Matters 2*, HMSO, 1985.
5   DES, GCSE *The National Criteria for Business Studies*, HMSO, 1986.
6   Economics Association, *Understanding Economics*, Longman, 1985.
7   *Computers in the Curriculum*, Longman, 1985.

Appendix 1: Details of assignments 1 and 2

The local business environment

You and a number of friends have decided to set up a small business enterprise, confident that your wide-ranging skills and enthusiasm will bring success. Before starting production/service you have decided to examine the potential of the area, what is existing and where the best opportunities are likely to be.

TASK 1
Present an account of what industry exists in Cramlington at the moment, showing what is manufactured, by whom and whether the organizations are involved in the *public* or *private* sectors.

TASK 2
Many of the firms in Cramlington are household names. Why should they have chosen this area to set up? For example, American Air Filters supply goods nationally and export all over the world, yet they choose to have their main factory in the far north of the country. Why?

EXTENSION EXERCISE
Design an advertisement to persuade companies thinking of setting up in the north-east of England that Cramlington would be a suitable place to choose.

A small business and its finances

As a final step before organizing your own enterprise you decide to study closely the costs and problems associated with one particular business, that of Jackie who owns a hairdressing business.

TASK 1
Describe the exercise on Jackie's costs, which will provide the background to making decisions regarding your own business costs.

TASK 2
From the following list of business ideas, choose *one* to develop and give it a name:

> window cleaner
> office services
> garden services
> sandwich service

TASK 3
List any equipment you will require, with prices where possible.

TASK 4
Calculate your monthly fixed costs and *list* any items you consider as *variable costs* connected with your business. The leaflet 'Working for Yourself' will help with ideas of costs, but take into account:

rent of factory/office	£25 per week
electricity	£15 per week
insurance	£5 per week per person
wages	
equipment	for you to discuss and decide
materials	
vehicles	

EXTENSION EXERCISE
Design an advertisement for your business and say how you would obtain customers for your product/service.

11 Economic awareness through economics

Paulette McLoughlin

Droylsden High School for Girls, Tameside

The school

The school is a secondary comprehensive for girls aged 11–16 years. There are presently 842 girls on roll and a normal annual first year intake of 150 pupils. The school is committed to welcoming pupils from different cultures and backgrounds.

The curriculum is timetabled for a week of 40 lessons each lasting for 35 minutes. In the first three years, pupils are arranged in three ability bands, with movement between bands encouraged. In years four and five, pupils are set for certain subjects but are generally taught in mixed-ability groups.

In year one, pupils study languages, mathematics, science, humanities, technology, religion and creative subjects. In years two and three, although the basic core of the curriculum remains unchanged, there are some additions, including 'economic understanding' which is introduced to all pupils. In years four and five all pupils undertake work in key areas of study, plus chosen options. GCSE Economics features as an option course.

Economic understanding in the curriculum

During 1985 the local authority Adviser with responsibility for this area of the curriculum wrote to all schools in Tameside in the following terms:[1]

'It has widely become acceptable in educational circles that there is a need to promote a better understanding in the world of commerce and business.'

Further:

'What I think may now be needed, but only for those schools who feel they are able to take part, is a more concerted attempt to promote a course for all pupils concerned with helping them to a better understanding of the world of business and commerce. ... There is the possibility of including within the fourth and fifth year options, a course based around GCSE Business Studies for which national criteria have already been published. The two issues not dealt with in the above are:

1) general economic issues of how the country earns its living
2) the structures and purposes of large and small businesses and commercial ventures.

These, I believe, could form the basis of a course for all pupils.'

As a result of this initiative and others, by September 1986 decisions had been taken to create the following opportunities for economic understanding to be developed:

1) all second and third year students would experience one 35-minute lesson each week throughout the year
2) GCSE Economics would be offered as an option course to all fourth year students
3) two teachers would be seconded to the University of Manchester for 30 days to work with teachers from other Tameside schools on the development of economic awareness in general and, in particular, to develop new modules for the school's fourth and fifth year personal and social development programme.

At the time of writing the second and third year economic understanding courses are in full operation and more than 40 students are following a GCSE course. Two new modules have been developed for the personal and social development programme, one by the Head of History and the other by the writer. These link economic with political awareness and introduce students to aspects of earning/spending and the world of work.

The details which follow relate to two of these areas of development only – the introduction of economic understanding in years two and three.

Aims for years two and three

The aims which have been established for lower-school courses are two-fold: first, to impart conceptual matter that is economic in character and which enables pupils to recognize economic processes and understand economic situations; and second, to provide a skills-based teaching platform. It is hoped that the courses will enable all pupils to be aware of their role as part of society (active or passive) and to recognize the influence of any economic system on individuals.

It is hoped that economic understanding will provide a means for pupils to assess and evaluate situations by encouraging a 'way of thinking' and by relating classroom studies to what goes on outside school as part of their preparation for working life. The courses will also aim to provide some cultural evaluation by indicating the process of economic development, and by illustrating the degree of global interdependence which exists between nations.

Course materials and teaching approaches

Drawing up new course materials has proved to be demanding of both time and energy, but certain characteristics to the course are considered to be vital if the education of individual pupils is to be best served. The subject matter of any economics-based course can all too easily involve abstract

concepts which, to younger pupils (and especially younger, lower-ability pupils), present learning barriers. Learning needs to be active and where possible along the lines that 'to do is to understand'. Activity means involvement and less opportunity for passive boredom to creep in. A variety of approaches to individual lessons is therefore seen to be of paramount importance if student interest is to be a key to learning. For example, a variety of lesson approaches has been achieved by 'low-tech' learning strategies and in the face of financial shortage.

Approaches which involve pupils working in pairs or groups are used. Guidance and prompting are then required, especially where pupils lack confidence, but those who have no need can work without referring directly to the teacher. In many lessons the teacher's role is to guide and oversee, and to provide help on a one-to-one basis. Activities used include role-play, group discussion, brain-storming, investigative group project work, picture response work, video and written stimulus, and mini-company creation, all aiming to give individual pupils as many opportunities as possible. It is hoped that the pupils will begin to think of the links which exist in interdependent relationships, and can therefore be used by the teacher as a resource for the lesson.

The second year (foundation) syllabus

Aims

The course aims to provide a first introduction to the processes of economics and to enable pupils to identify economic situations. It acts as a 'taster' to the whole subject. A familiarity with some basic economics terminology is felt to be important at this early stage, jargon being used where necessary but not for effect. The course offers glimpses into micro- and macro-economics, skimming over the theoretical and abstract, and paying attention to themes with which 12-year-olds might have had more personal experience. Some aspects of the course content challenge pupils to understand concepts like the demand schedule, and other areas aim to give reason and meaning to everyday concerns, such as the origins and purpose of money.

Content

The nature of the course should encourage pupils to practise and develop skills in the following areas: literacy, numeracy, sociability, communication, participation in group discussions, analysis of data, classification of data, comprehension of written and pictorial stimulus, and distinguishing between facts and opinion.

The course content aims to provide an awareness of the mechanisms, techniques, constraints, values and motivations of the economic framework of society, and is outlined as follows:

1) the central economic problem of scarcity of resources and the need for choice; terms 'unlimited wants', 'types of resources' and 'opportunity cost'

2) who are consumers? why do they behave in certain ways? who are suppliers and why do they react as they do? why bother with prices? do prices mean money?

3) practical work in the local areas is encouraged at this stage to look at local shops and allow application beyond the classroom to be made

4) pupils are introduced to the origin of money; coins, notes and 'plastic money'; the purpose of banks (relating to the school bank and their own methods of investment); and finally to examine the earning, spending patterns and money-management of 12-year-olds.

A sample activity involves the use of a short story about four girls choosing presents to buy for Mothering Sunday. The story aims to illustrate factors which affect consumer decisions about whether or not to purchase an item, including the price of the goods, the price of other goods, an individual's tastes or fashions, and the level of disposable income.

Pupils act out the story as a short play with each pupil taking the part of one of the four characters. The lesson proceeds with a 'matching' exercise, in which for each one of the imaginary girls, the present bought and the reason for its purchase are identified. This is done as a group activity using 'flip-charts', in pairs or individually. Words or diagrams are used by pupils to represent their information. At this stage the teacher has the opportunity to deal with individual problems and help lower-ability pupils who may need some guidance. Finally, pupils report back on their findings.

When this is done via group work, pupils invariably supplement the information given to them with personal anecdotes of similar situations. Alternatively the teacher may prefer, after 'debriefing', to outline factors which affect effective demand in a more orthodox way using an additional information sheet or by using the blackboard.

With some groups this lesson can be used to look at the theory of demand – the demand schedule, factors affecting demand, the nature of substitutes, compliments, inferior, normal and Giffen goods. However, by itself it is sufficient to enable awareness of economic behaviour to be developed.

The third year syllabus: industry, its place in society

The course aims to build on second year work and help pupils to appreciate 'how a nation earns and maintains its standard of living'. Pupils are made aware of 'the essential role of industry and commerce in this process' and shown how to recognize the growth of world population and its implications for the use of scarce resources. How a country makes best use of its resources is related to its economic functioning and level of industrial development. A comparison between industrialized and developing nations is made, showing different standards of living experienced by different communities. Pupils become aware of the divisions of industry and consider the role of industrial specializations.

At this stage in the course, primary, secondary and tertiary sectors of industry are explored with examples of each being considered and the meaning of the terms 'production' and 'productivity' explored. To help in this process pupils engage in a classroom activity which also provides a basis for examining the roles of workers and machines in industrial development.

First, a formal definition of the two terms is presented in the form of a written handout which is used for future reference. The terms 'inputs' and 'outputs' are represented by raw materials, workers and machinery on one side of the equation and outputs as products on the other. (Diagrams of this type appear to improve levels of comprehension, with pupils remembering the pictures if not the words.) The class is then divided into two teams. One team acts as an assembly line with each pupil performing just one operation, whilst the other team acts as individual workers, each pupils performing all the stages of the production process. The task involves assembling items of stationery – paper clips, treasury tags, punched paper – to produce items with no functional value, but the construction of which involves manual dexterity and nimbleness of fingers. Once each finished item is complete, it is passed to a team checker who can act as quality controller. A time limit for 'production' adds to motivation. The teacher records the scores passed on by the checker, and responds to calls for 'more treasury tags' and 'more paper clips, please' from various points of the room.

When time is up, totals for each of the teams are tallied and productivity rate per team is calculated. Usually the production line team has the more efficient level of output, but this result is by no means essential. Each team reviews the method of production using either flip-charts or a rapid yes/ no response questionnaire.

As the course develops pupils will visit a local factory. A home-made video about a local factory will seek to further illustrate the importance of the place of workers and their changing role in industry. Pupils will examine employment structures from managing director to shop floor worker, professional to unskilled, and consider the rewards to factors – wages, interest and profit.

Pupils will be encouraged to work on a mini-enterprise project, with the option to develop their scheme with help from a local firm. They will deal with issues relating to the cost of running a business, find initial capital to finance the venture, adopt specific roles by applying for vacancies within the company, and consider ways to promote and develop on-going marketing strategies. Finally, guests will be invited into the classroom to give first-hand knowledge of their experience in the world of work.

Review

The past 15 months have seen not only the launching of economic understanding as part of the curriculum, but also its development along the lines referred to earlier.

At present limitations are imposed by the brevity of the contact time per week with each pupil – 35 minutes seems to hurry past all too quickly. However, the time allotted represents considerable and rapid progress and developments in the personal and social education curriculum should enhance pupil opportunities for development in the first year as well as in years four and five.

Obviously the broadening of any areas of experience to all age levels is frequently constrained by such things as the number of lessons in a week, staff availability, and so on. However, the presence of mini-enterprise schemes in primary schools suggests that some input into the first year may well be necessary to provide for continuity of experience.

Reference

1   Tameside Education Department, *Economic Understanding for All*, a letter from the General Adviser to all schools, May, 1985.

12 Introducing economic awareness at 14 and 17 years

Joy Muir

The Wallace High School, Lisburn, N. Ireland

This case study considers the development of two separate economic awareness programmes in an examination-orientated grammar school in Northern Ireland. The Wallace High School caters for over 1,100 pupils of well above average ability, the majority having successfully come through the selection procedure at the age of 11. A small number of fee-paying pupils is accepted each year.

The changing curriculum and a new opportunity

Over the last 10 years the traditional Ulster grammar school curriculum has seen many changes and the curriculum of Wallace High School is no exception. New examination subjects such as computer science, business studies, technology, accounting and economics have found their way on to the timetable and there have been major innovations in non-examination courses throughout the school. The latter area, especially, has received a great deal of attention from the school's Curriculum Committee in the last three years. In 1984, a change was made in the subject choice for third year pupils to allow a small number to take up an extra language (German), thus leaving an empty space in the timetables of the remaining pupils. Here was the perfect opportunity for introducing the non-examination subjects which were felt to be a vital part of preparing a pupil for life in the outside world.

After much discussion the decision was made to introduce a liberal studies programme and a tu-torial system. The former already existed in the first year of sixth form but with a heavier timetable commitment than that envisaged for this new third form course. The sixth year programme involved two sets of modules operating on two afternoons each week, with each module lasting for six weeks. Finding room for such a sixth year course was relatively easy as most pupils are occupied in classroom examination work for a maximum of only 24 periods out of a 40-period week. (The only exceptions are those pupils taking four 'A'-levels.) At third year level it was impossible to allocate four periods per week to this programme, given the desire to also introduce a tutorial system, and the fact that the German class, against which liberal studies and tutorials were to be timetabled, had been given just two periods per week.

The third year liberal studies programme was thus set up on the basis of just one single period per week. There were to be six modules, each of which was to run for six weeks. The pupils were to be removed from their traditional class groupings and formed into small sets of around 20 pupils for this work.

The beginnings

It was felt that the new course should provide the opportunity to help pupils deal with situations they might encounter outside the classroom, and which would not be considered during the normal examination syllabuses they followed. In addition, it was felt that they should have the chance to see some of the uses of a computer (apart from playing games!) and receive some gentle careers guidance with a view to choosing the subjects to be studied in their fourth and fifth years. The decision on what to include as modules in the course was also constrained by the expertise of the staff who had time available to teach in the programme. Eventually the subject matter of each module was determined, and the one which concerns us most is that which was entitled 'Money Management' – the words 'Economic Awareness' had not yet reached the ears of the committee!

The third form liberal studies programme finally got under way in September 1985 with a geography teacher taking the module on Money Management. The module looked at budgeting, banking services and building societies, with the manager of the local society visiting the school to talk to the pupils. The pupils' role was largely passive, and as the year progressed it quickly became apparent that they were not showing a great deal of interest in the course. Was it asking too much of a non-specialist teacher to work in a new field with someone else's materials which included a view of classroom which left little room for pupils' involvement and enthusiasms?

The writer joined the staff of Wallace in September 1983 with the task of introducing economics and related subjects into the curriculum, initially at sixth form level. These subjects took time to develop, and as a result an Economics Department was not officially born until 1986; thus the writer was not involved in the early talks about liberal studies and what should be included in the modules. However, during 1985 Wallace was approached about becoming involved in the Northern Ireland Council for Education (NICED) Economics Education Project. After discussion with the Principal and Senior Vice-Principal, the decision was taken to join the growing network of schools.

The basis for the work of the NICED project was the exemplar units of the Economics Association's Economics Education 14–16 Project (*Understanding Economics*).[1] The major appeal of these materials lies in the fact that they are pupil-based learning resources and involve many and varied learning situations. Opportunities are provided for role-playing, group work and individual research and a local flavour can easily be introduced into the

work. Teacher involvement can, in many instances, be kept to a minimum with pupils having the chance to develop some of the personal skills they need but which have often not been encouraged by traditional teaching.

Wallace was one of a number of local schools to become involved in the NICED Project and who were to meet as a group once per term to discuss their use of the 14–16 Project materials. Two teachers from the school were involved in these meetings – the writer and the Senior Vice-Principal, who is very concerned about the social and personal skills which pupils should be encouraged to develop. The involvement of the Senior Vice-Principal in the work quickly convinced him that it is the right of every pupil to become economically aware. The Headmaster was also very supportive and this smoothed the path for the development of economic awareness courses in the school.

The changing scene

As the pupils' lack of interest in the Money Management module became clear, the need for change was recognized. The Curriculum Committee was agreed that some form of business-world/money-type course is an essential requirement for the third form liberal studies programme, and the Senior Vice-Principal suggested the development of an economic awareness course to replace the Money Management module. At the same time he proposed the development of a similar course for the lower sixth liberal studies programme which, until then, had tended to contain leisure modules such as photography, musical appreciation and woodwork.

The aims of the third form course were considered – what did making a pupil economically aware actually mean? There appeared to be no hard and fast definition of this, but we felt that if the following aims were achieved then we would have gone some way towards helping our pupils to become economically aware:

1)   to make pupils aware that every action of an individual involves choices, and that these choices may imply costs and benefits not just for the individual but for society as a whole

2) to help pupils consider the productive resources at our disposal, how these can be organized and substituted for one another, and how new technology has had an impact on methods of production

3) to show pupils how spending is constrained by income and influenced by many other factors such as advertising, and to encourage them to recognize the benefits of planning ahead in their spending and saving.

The aims for the lower sixth course were, in a sense, slightly narrower. It was felt to be important to emphasize the first of the aims listed above, and especially to let pupils consider the criteria which are used in decision-making by politicians, business people, trades unions and local councillors. Above all, the aim was to make them question the ways things are done in our society and, by putting them in the position of the decision-makers, to see how difficult it is to make decisions, given all the constraints that exist in our real world.

The Senior Vice-Principal and the writer took the project materials home and selected units which it was felt would best meet the needs of these two courses. A meeting was then held to consider the units which had been chosen and to agree on a core of eight units for each of the liberal studies programmes. It was agreed that the selected units would be tried out with various classes throughout the school and, if necessary, altered to give them a local context. After a further try-out, six units for each of the programmes were to be chosen for the courses beginning in September 1986. The eight core units are listed in Appendix 1.

Some of the units chosen, especially for the lower sixth course, had to be altered owing to the different system of local government existing in the province. However, this proved to be no problem and the units were soon being tried out in the classroom situation. The writer was helped in this process by colleagues from other departments who used units and then reported back with their opinions and findings. The Head of English was particularly enthusiastic and commented on the units as follows:

'They help pupils to develop many important skills, such as understanding and interpreting both pictorial and written data, and using evidence to support an argument and come to a decision. ... They help pupils to become more sensitive to the needs, views and feelings of others, especially through cooperation in group work. ... They provide a forum for pupils to state their attitudes, discuss and debate them, and gain confidence in their abilities to do so.'

The response of the pupils was marvellous. It was such that many of the units needed little or no alteration at all, as they were received with enthusiasm and appeared to achieve the aims of the courses. Others were changed purely to bring in local flavour. In the case of 'Vandalism', for example, newspaper reports and photographs of vandalism in and around the local area were used in place of the resources in the project unit. This was done because it was felt that the children can better relate to something on their doorstep which directly affects them or their families. This proved to be a correct decision. The reports which the third form groups produced showed just how angry they were at the destruction of their local environment and how ruthless *they* would be in the punishment of culprits, should those individuals ever have the misfortune to be caught! They also put forward some interesting ideas as to how vandalism might be prevented in the future.

The choice of the final six units proved difficult because there were no obvious failures among the core units that had been tried out. In the end the units were selected on the basis of those that had provoked the most response from pupils (marked with asterisks in Appendix 1). The other point which emerged from trying out the units was that teachers from subject areas other than economics/business studies did not feel confident in their use of the units. The fact that in a selective school pupils are able to challenge and push teachers to explain things about which they feel they have little knowledge might account for this. Whatever the reason, it led to the Economics Department taking on the teaching of both economic awareness courses in 1986–7.

The modules have now been under way in their present form for a number of months and are being received by this year's third form and lower sixth with the same enthusiasm as when they were first tried out. As the year proceeds, however, the modules will be reviewed and changes, if any, decided upon. If the development proceeds as intended, then more time will be spent sifting through possible materials and trying out new units. This would be as a result of three things — more time being given to the third form economic awareness module so that *all* pupils can become involved, other years being drawn into the economic awareness programme, and economic awareness being introduced in a cross-curricular manner throughout the school.

The future

The management and the Board of Governors of Wallace accept that economic awareness is a very important part of the non-examination curriculum of the school, but the obstacles to extending this initiative elsewhere in the school are many. Where is the time required to be found? Would, for example, another subject be willing to have its time with a class reduced? Who would teach these extra classes? The Economics Department is already fully stretched and there is an unease about the use of non-specialist teachers. Whatever the outcomes of the discussions that will take place, one thing is certain — economic awareness is a firm part of the curriculum at Wallace.

Reference

1   Economics Association, *Understanding Economics*, Longman, 1985.

Appendix 1: 14–16 Project units selected for use in third and sixth years, 1986–7

Third form Economic Awareness module

1) The Accident (Young Person as a citizen)
2) Vandalism (not published but incorporated into a unit entitled 'Costs and Benefits')
3) Budgeting (Young Person as a Consumer)
4) Paying (Young Person as a Consumer)
5) Production Record Sheets (Young Person as a Producer)
6) The Ice Cream Factory (Young Person as a Producer)
7) Wanting (Young Person as a Consumer)
8) Two Workers (Young Person as a Producer)

Lower sixth Economic Awareness module

1) Public Spending (Young Person as a Citizen)
2) Local Authority Rates (Young Person as a Citizen)
2) Wages (Young Person as a Producer)
4) Journey to work (Young Person as a Consumer)
5) Whose Health is it Anyway? (Young Person as a Citizen)
6) Land Use Planning in the Local Community (Young Person as a Citizen)
7) Community Expenditure (Young Person as a Citizen)
8) At the Bus Stop (Young Person as a Consumer)

13 Introducing economic awareness

Aidan McMahon

St Patrick's (Boys) Academy, Dungannon, N. Ireland

The school

St Patrick's (Boys) Academy is a single-sex voluntary grammar school with some 620 full-time students. The school's catchment area is extensive, and includes the large towns of Portadown, Dungannon and Cookstown. The student population is fairly evenly divided between town and country. The school moved premises in 1975 and now occupies a site with two other large secondary schools, one grammar and one secondary intermediate.

One tradition in the school over the past 10 years has been to offer optional business-related subjects. In the late 1970s and early 1980s, for example, 'O' level Commerce and 'O'/'A' level Economics came to prominence amongst optional subjects. Commerce, however, has now disappeared, giving way to 'O' and 'A' level Accounts. Traditionally, the school has at various stages in the past offered economics/ political studies, economic history, business studies, commerce and accounts. In addition, at the end of year two, all classes are given a preliminary choice of subject before the major subject option in year three. The choice available in 1986 was one subject from art/craft/design technology/technical drawing/ German/economic awareness, and some 20 students (out of a total of 104) opted for the economic awareness option.

Economic awareness in the Careers Guidance programme

The writer's own subject of careers guidance and

Counselling has been a timetabled subject since September 1974. As a teacher with a background in teaching English language and literature, it was natural enough for me to turn to literature (poetry, stories and plays) as a source of inspiration for the guidance programme. However, as time wore on and the guidance programme developed, the real world of work appeared to be an important missing ingredient. In 1979 a 10-day work experience scheme for students in the lower sixth year was introduced. In the same year a programme was introduced for students in year four in which they were taken out of the school environment to study local people at work. Nevertheless the materials used remained patchy and the course lacked coherent themes which ran through the six-year programme.

In November 1985 the school was introduced to the Northern Ireland Council for Educational Development (NICED) initiative on economic literacy at an in-service course in Armagh Teachers Centre. The potential in the *Understanding Economics*[1] units for integration into careers guidance work was revealed and the decision to use a unit called 'Price of a Perm' in year four was quickly taken.

Year four pupils are divided into four forms of mixed ability and are timetabled for one period (35–40 minutes) per week of Careers guidance. In November 1985, fourth year pupils had begun a new range of option subjects and some had selected economics and home economics as options – factors that were to provide a healthy input into the guidance programme. The groups had been involved in the guidance programme since the second year and had been introduced to a short novel by Joan Tate called *Ginger Mick*. The book[2] is set in the two cities of Liverpool and Coventry and tells of the experience of a 16 year old who is attempting to make the transition from school to a world in which employment, unemployment, inner city decay, job mobility and employment changes are recurrent themes. Used in conjunction with the novel was another book, *How Britain Earns its Living*.[3] The intention here was to introduce the idea that work can be classified generally under the headings 'primary', 'secondary' and 'tertiary', and Ginger Mick's experiences provided useful examples of each sector.

'Price of a Perm' appeared to provide the opportunity to develop further the idea of secondary and tertiary industry which had been introduced in year two. Moreover, given that 1986 was Industry Year, it seemed appropriate to make efforts to bring industry closer to those students near enough to school leaving age to appreciate both its merits and shortcomings. Before carrying out the exercise, care was taken to check with the Economics Department that no duplication of work would result and to modify the contents of the unit to meet the school's aims and objectives.

It was decided to amend the unit to place the twins Jackie and John in a broader family unit and to extend their case histories. The career development of Jackie and John at St Patrick's Academy is traced. They are the youngest children in a family of four – their sister being an accountant, and their brother a glassblower in a local manufacturing company. The career paths of each member of the family is discussed.

Jackie and John dominate the first part of the exercise, deciding to leave school at 16 and go into training as hairdressers. The class is divided into pairs to play either the role of Jackie or John, and to consider two training options available for school leavers who wish to become hairdressers:

● going to an FE college for training
● seeking employment on a YTP scheme (YTS in Great Britain)

Fact sheets are produced for students to discuss FE courses and youth training programmes. Eventually their training is finished and both apply for work. Ironically the same firm of hairdressers in Belfast takes both young people on and so the pros and cons of a move from Dungannon to Belfast are

keenly debated. The decision is made and for some years both work contentedly in the city centre. Jackie has saved money and is contemplating venturing home to Dungannon to set up her own business. John wants to stay in the city. The attractions of city life are discussed. Jackie turns to her sister Ann, the accountant, for advice on 'going it alone', as a self-employed hairdresser. At this stage a video on self-employment, *Head for Business*,[4] is introduced and topics such as staying inside a large firm versus running a small shop and city trade versus small town demands are all vigorously debated.

Student attention is focused on Jackie for the next phase of the lesson. They are introduced to such terms as fixed and variable costs, cash flow and total revenue. Eventually, however, Jackie's business runs into troubled waters. By using a fact sheet and work cards the students are able to quickly appreciate how this has happened. The accountant is called in again to discuss how Jackie might best extricate herself from her difficulties. A role-playing activity is used – accountant and entrepreneur – to examine the pros and cons of the options available. Jackie also needs the expertise of a banker and an insurance broker, as well as an appointment to see an estate agent because the lease on the property has run into some difficulty. Before leaving Jackie's problem it is stressed that not all adventures into the world of self-employment are fraught with inevitable financial minefields, but that such manoeuvres require careful planning and help from the many agencies and business support services.

Attention then turns to the final member of the family, James, who is employed as a glassblower in one of the town's leading manufacturing firms. This provides an opportunity to investigate the secondary (manufacturing) sector. This part of the programme involves Form Tutors, who accompany their form to a local manufacturing firm. Prior to departure, however, the students agree that they would like to consider the following key areas:

1) the production process
2) marketing, advertising and selling
3) employment trends
4) the changes that have taken place over the past 10–15 years.

A questionnaire is devised by the class and copies made for each student. Letters are sent out to parents and each class spends a morning with the company. The manufacturing companies involved are Tyrone Brick Ltd, Tyrone Crystal Ltd, Blue Circle Cement and Unipork.

'A' level geography students accompany the fourth year students to the factories to take photographs for a project at the end of the visit. It was agreed that photographic descriptions of the activity are preferred to long essays. When the prints are developed students briefly describe features of the production process, different skilled workers, examples of advertising, old outdated/new computerized machinery, etc. The photographs are mounted in a folder which is made available as a very attractive but useful resource in the careers library.

In this way the programme deals with a family of four – one an accountant, who has gone through grammar school, university and professional examinations to become an accountant; two others, twins, who begin as hairdressers in the same firm, but who eventually go their separate ways; and finally, the practically minded James, who follows in his father's footsteps into the local manufacturing industry.

At the beginning of the programme a number of objectives had been outlined:

1) to develop the concept of secondary and tertiary sectors of industry which had been introduced in the second year
2) to examine some career options available at 16+ for school leavers
3) to consider some of the ramifications and consequences of decision-making
4) to introduce the idea of self-employment
5) to examine the advantages and disadvantages of being self-employed
6) to provide an opportunity to invite in local industrialists to talk on money matters, survival skills, and careers opportunities
7) to help students to be more aware of what goes on inside local manufacturing firms
8) to involve other members of staff/Form Tutors in the careers guidance programme
9) to produce a meaningful and resourceful piece of literature at the end of the industrial visits for use with other classes and as a stimulus to the classes following on for the next round of visits
10) to make a positive effort to do something challenging and meaningful in Industry Year.

The current position of economic awareness and future hopes

Economic awareness is to some extent still in the experimental stages. 'O' and 'A' level Economics remain popular options and it is certain that the existence of a thriving department has made, and will continue to make, curriculum innovation in economic awareness that much easier. Moreover, the fact that the Vice-Principal (a teacher of Economics), the Head of the Economics Department, and the writer are members of the school's Curriculum Review Committee is a major boost for the development of economic awareness throughout the entire curriculum. It is, therefore, not surprising that plans are presently being developed to introduce economic awareness into a non-examination sixth form course which is to begin in 1987.

It is difficult at this stage to evaluate the impact of the work that has begun. From the writer's viewpoint, the fact that his classroom contact time with individual classes is limited to one period in the week (35 or 40 minutes) makes it difficult for him to develop and maintain coherence and student motivation. In a normal academic subject a teacher can expect to see a class at least four times in a week, and this is unquestionably an advantage as far as ensuring coherence and progression in a teaching programme is concerned. However, the fact that it has become possible to introduce economic awareness in year three on a basis of a further two periods per week means that there are at least six teachers involved out of a total staff of 35 in the economic awareness programme who can be encouraged to take up some of the more practical options without overlapping with work in the careers guidance programme.

References

1   Economics Association, *Understanding Economics*, Longman, 1985.

2   Tate, J., *Ginger Mick*, Longman, 1983.

3   Birch. P. A., Sanday, A. P. and Wright, *How Britain Earns its Living*, Hodder and Stoughton, 1980.

4   Department of Trade and Industry, *Head for Business*, available from Central Film Library, Chalfont Grove, Gerards Cross.

Section 3 *The Scottish Experience*

14 Economics at 13 + in a Scottish secondary school

Irene Hewitt

Larbert High School, Stirlingshire

General background

The school has been established for over 100 years and is now a six-year comprehensive school with a student roll in the region of 1,300 pupils. There is a good academic record and the school is forward thinking in its attitude to courses and towards the role of technology in the curriculum. Pupils in S1 and S2 are given half-year taster courses in an attempt to help them to make more enlightened course choices in S3. (Note that secondary schooling in Scotland begins at 12 +. Symbols for year groupings are S1 (12 +), S2 (13 +), S3 (14 +) and S4 (15 +).)

The decision to run an economics course in S2 was made prior to the appointment of the present Principal Teacher (the writer). At the time greater emphasis was being placed on the social subjects and it was felt that this ought to be more fully reflected in the S2 curriculum. Moreover, not only had the new Principal Teacher the experience to introduce such a course, but there was also a surplus of staffing time in the Department of Business Studies and Economics which needed to be used constructively.

In the early stages, meetings were arranged between the Principal Teacher and the Rector. There were no Board of Management (Studies) problems as agreement in principle to the course had already been given. The fact that the school also wished to introduce computing into S2 allowed for a smoother introduction of both subjects into the curriculum. A few days of school-based INSET were provided when teachers could meet without teaching constraints. The Faculty Head attended the first of these, providing a channel of communication with the Board of Management. Consultation with Jordanhill College of Education, Glasgow, gave the basic outline for the final course structure, which was to be modular with three sections.

The course

The course is run in S2 (13–14 year olds) and is not linked with work in primary schools. There are also no plans at present to extend the course to S1 pupils. There is, however, a degree of unintended overlap with some areas of the geography course. The course content is designed to introduce pupils to simple aspects of the S3/S4 Ordinary Grade course and aims to give them an awareness and an understanding that economics is a wide-ranging subject which touches all aspects of their lives.

The course runs over a half year and shares its time allocation of one hour per week with computing. The departments agreed that blocks of time would be preferable to half-hour periods, and so a rota was devised in which classes change subjects three times during the year.

Each module has been designed as a separate entity to allow pupils to follow the course without referring to previous work. This allows for pupil absence which can be a problem in such a short course. Each module concludes with a progress test. The outcomes of these tests are used to build up pupil profiles which are used to assess capability in, and grasp of, the subject (see Appendix 1 for an example of a progress test).

Coursework is based on worksheets, the content of which is based either on a class lesson given by the teacher, on a film from the *Foundations of Wealth* series, or on a tape about barter which was produced by one of the teachers. The worksheets are devised to allow pupils of lower ability to follow the work and to participate in class discussion. Various techniques are used; for example, filling in blanks, drawing, wordsearch puzzles, crosswords, matching definitions, written answers and a minimal amount of copying out. The samples reproduced here in the Appendices are necessarily condensed.

The Production module (see Appendix 2)

The main economic concepts covered in this module are:

- choice
- factors of production
- resources
- making a surplus
- division of labour by product
- division of labour by process
- specialization
- mass production
- primary/extractive industry
- secondary/manufacturing industry
- tertiary/service industry

The module concludes by linking the production process to consumption, showing the distribution of finished goods to retail outlets.

The Consumption module (see Appendix 3)

The main economic concepts covered in this module are:

- choice
- goods and services
- durables
- non-durables
- opportunity cost
- scales of preference
- demand
- supply
- wealth
- scarcity
- advertising

The module concludes by linking the consumption process to exchange.

The Exchange module (see Appendix 4)

The main economic concepts and terms covered in this module are:

- barter
- markets
- goods used as money
- rates of exchange
- functions of money
- properties of money
- trade
- imports and exports
- chain of distribution
- retail outlets

Module workbooks are given out in the first lesson of each block of time. Each worksheet is written in simple language and attempts to draw the answers from the pupils.

Impressions from the course

The main aim of the course is to introduce economics to as many of the S2 pupils as possible with a view to both increasing their economic awareness and encouraging them to take the subject further at some later stage in their school career. The latter effect should be revealed in increased class sizes for economics. As yet this is difficult to assess. S3 numbers have been higher, but it will not be until 1987–8 that pupils who have studied economics in S2 will have the opportunity to take 'crash courses' in economics in S5.

The course appears to interest most pupils but may not be sufficiently demanding. This may be caused partially by the mixed-ability nature of the classes. The introduction of more topical material might help to bring the subject 'home' to pupils, but this could cause problems not only to less able pupils who might not follow the work but also to more able pupils who would require extra teacher time to go through the module. Diverting the attention of teachers to some groups of pupils might also lead to discipline problems. One possible solution to this problem could be larger modules and the use of team-teaching techniques.

The reaction of the school to the course is hard to evaluate as there are other aspects of course choices which the Board of Management appears to take into consideration. Staff running the course believe that some revisions are necessary, but it has not been decided just where the changes should be made. In ideal circumstances, it would be possible to slot in more video content based on present-day economic problems, but this presents difficulties as there are few programmes suitable without adaptation and fewer pre-prepared packages specific to economics.

In conclusion, the problems which appear to exist are:

- a lack of topical content
- an inherent lack of knowledge on the part of the pupils as to the subject economics
- a lack of information as to subject content at Board of Management level. (There has been a request from the Board that Departments prepare a description of their courses and possible career opportunities for distribution to pupils.)
- a lack of simple video and TV programmes for pupils
- a lack of preparation time for staff to take the course and restructure it in the light of their past experience.

Appendix 1: Example of progress text

Answer all the following questions in the spaces provided for you.

Question 1

a)   Match each of the phrases in column A below with the correct phrase in column B by drawing a line between each phrase.

Column A   *Column B*

i)   if the good   i)   he will catch more
     farmer spends   fish than he needs
     most of his
     time farming

ii) if the good   ii)   he will have more
     fisherman spends   meat and skins
     most of his time   than he needs
     fishing

iii) if the great hunter iii)   he will grow more
     hunts for most of   crops than he can
     his time   eat

b)   Now write them in the correct order beneath the sketch to which you think they belong:

c)   Complete the following sentence.

     The three sketches above show different kinds of S......................

d)   Suggest, in your own words, how division of labour might be used to produce more goods in the work being shown in sketch C.

Question 2
Tick the answer you think is correct in each of the following questions.

a)   With the use of specialization we obtain:
i)   more goods of a better quality
ii)   fewer goods but of a better quality
iii)   many more goods, but of a poorer quality

b)   When goods are mass-produced:
i)   a much smaller variety of goods is made
ii)   it takes longer for each good to be made
iii)   all goods must be checked and faulty goods rejected

c)   Transport is necessary in the production process because:
i)   otherwise consumers will not know about the products
ii)   unless goods are moved to where they are wanted, no trade will take place
iii)   if some consumers cannot get to the shops, the goods will not be bought

d)   The word 'manufacturer' describes a business which:
i)   stores large quantities of goods and sells smaller quantities to the retailer
ii)   makes goods
iii)   buys small quantities of goods then sells single goods

e)   The growing of fruit is an example of 'agriculture', which is one of the:
i)   manufacturing industries
ii)   tertiary industries
iii)   extractive industries

Question 3
State, against each of the following sentences, whether it is true or false.
a)   Resources are used to make things.
b)   A record studio is an example of a natural resource.
c)   Production can only take place in factories.
d)   Division of labour can only take place in factories.
e)   A teacher is a producer.

Question 4
Natural, human and man-made resources are needed to make school desks. The diagram shows the flow of these resources into the factory which makes these desks. In the space shown in each box, print an example of the kind of resource used.

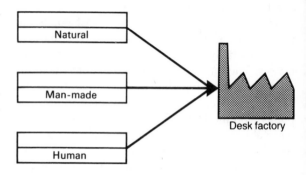

Desk factory

Question 5
How can the chopping down of trees help in the production of tinned pears? Explain in the space provided below.

....

Question 6
Column 1 below shows terms used in production, while column 2 gives explanations of these terms. In the table provided match column 2 to column 1.

Column 1
1   mass-production
2   business
3   labour
4   profit
5   income

Column 2
A   sales – cost of production
B   benefit of division of labour
C   money received for producing goods
D   doing manual work
E   making goods in large quantities
F   the human input to production
G   a retailer is one example of this

Term	1	2	3	4	5
Explanation	E				

Appendix 2: Sample activities from the Production module

Did you know?

A number of men in a single village might have been good hunters. They could have worked in a team and divided up the work of hunting. Some might have dug pits. Some might have driven the animals out into the open. Some might have wanted to make spears and others might have wanted to go hunting. This sharing out of specialized work is known as DIVISION OF LABOUR

Did you know?

Early man could exchange his goods in person. He could do this because trade in those days was carried out within a short distance from his home. Modern producers could be making goods for consumers in Inverness, Torquay or even Melbourne in Australia. So, unless goods are moved to where they can be traded, *no* trade will take place.

Did you know?

The earliest form of business activity was probably trading. Today many people buy and sell goods, hoping to earn profits. Although the specialization and division of labour that takes place today is more advanced than in early societies, it is not really *so* different.

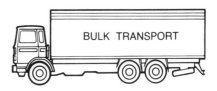

Did you know?

Production can mean the making of goods. Any worker paid to help in the making of these goods is a PRODUCER. The lorry driver moves goods from one place to another. He 'produces' a *service* for the maker of the goods.

Production

We cannot have everything we want. Why not?

....

When this happens we try to use what we do have as well as we can. Most people want more than they have. In *Economics* to explain this we say 'there are only limited resources to meet our unlimited wants'.

Resources used to make things are called the *factors of production*. These can be natural, man-made or human.

What do you think would be needed to produce the clothes peg?

1)_____   2)_____   3)_____

Which item is
a)   natural?   (LAND)
b)   man-made?   (CAPITAL)
c)   human?   (LABOUR)

The proper terms for these in economics are *Land,
Labour* and *Capital* – the factors of production.

LAND includes the free gifts of nature (e.g. a tree).
Can you fill in others in 2, 3 and 4?

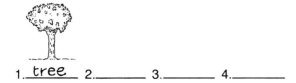

1.__tree__   2._____   3._____   4._____

LABOUR includes all jobs – unskilled, semi-skilled
and skilled. In the boxes draw a picture of each
type of worker and say what *your* worker does.

    unskilled   semi-skilled   skilled

CAPITAL includes all the things people have to
help them make other items. The most important is
to have a place to work. What else do you need?

Number 1 is drawn for you. Can you draw two
others and label all three?

1)_____   2)_____   3)_____

Production and distribution of goods

Industry can be divided into three groups for the
production of any finished article.

PRIMARY or EXTRACTIVE industries deal with
getting the raw materials by chopping down trees,
catching sardines, etc. (i.e. agriculture, fishing,
mining, etc.).

SECONDARY or MANUFACTURING industries
deal with making the raw materials into finished
goods (e.g. making furniture from the trees, clean-
ing the sardines and putting them into tins, etc.).

TERTIARY or SERVICE industries deal with getting the finished goods to the *consumers* (e.g.
delivering the furniture to the house where it is to
be used, transporting the tins of sardines from the
factory to the shop, etc.).

Exercise 1

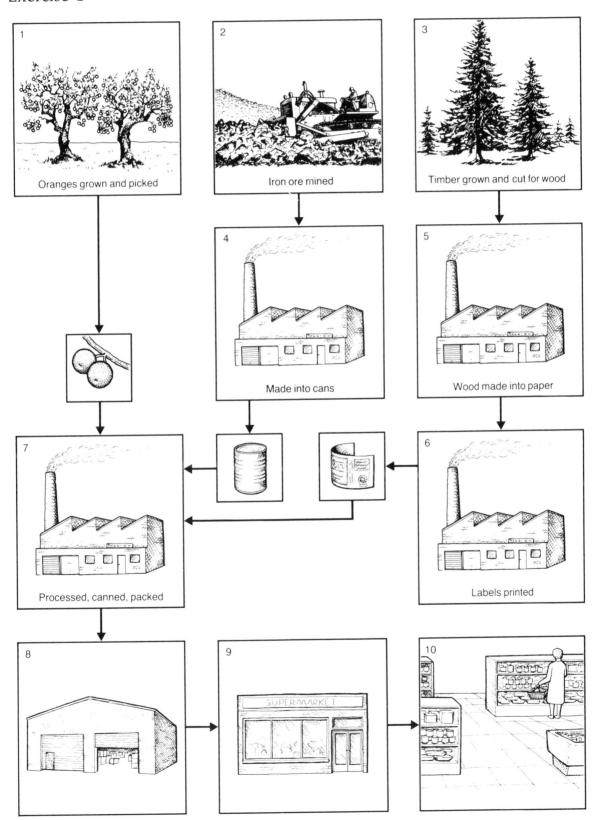

1. Oranges grown and picked
2. Iron ore mined
3. Timber grown and cut for wood
4. Made into cans
5. Wood made into paper
6. Labels printed
7. Processed, canned, packed
8.
9. SUPERMARKET
10.

The chart shows stages in the *production of tinned oranges*. Study this chart and then complete the following statements:

a) Transport would be needed to move parts at different stages of production. For example:

   i) ships might be needed between box.......... and box ....

   ii) railways might be needed between box.......... and box..........

   iii) road transport would be used between box.......... and box..........

b) Which box number shows a stage of production which could be called:

   i) agriculture ....

   ii) forestry ....

   iii) manufacture ....

   iv) distribution ....

Complete the following sentences by filling in the blanks with words chosen from this list: manufacturing; service; extractive; primary; agriculture; forestry.

a) Box 1 shows a branch of production known as.

b) Box 2 indicates the first stage in producing cans. This is an example of an.......... industry.

c) Box 3 shows an example of work in the ....industry

d) Boxes 4, 5, 6 and 7 all show examples of *secondary* industry, the most common type being the.. industry

e) Boxes 8 and 9 show the place of the *wholesaler* and the *retailer* in the production of tinned oranges. These are part of the.......... industry.

Exercise 2

WHY DO PEOPLE WORK? – The production of goods

People work, firstly, to look after themselves and their families. The type of work that they do depends on many things. Production is, therefore, not all the same. It can be divided into different sections:

Primary production
This form of production uses gifts of nature. Examples are:

These industries are called ..... because they use the gifts of nature which are found in the ground or the sea. These gifts of nature become the .... for the production of goods.

Secondary production
This branch of production can be separated into two main sections:

1) P---------: the making of goods from raw materials with the aid of tools and machinery.

2) C-----------: the name given to the production of houses, roads, bridges, etc. (all things that are built).

Tertiary
This is not involved with goods but with services given to the general public. For example:

a) ....gives advice about the law

b) .... gives advice about income tax payments

c) ....prepares food in a restaurant

d) ....helps you when you are ill

e) .... keeps law and order

f) ....helps you learn more about the scope of economics

Exercise 3

Put each of the following activities into the correct group (i.e. primary, secondary or tertiary):

coal mining	crop spraying
animal slaughtering	diamond cutting
photography	diamond mining
bacon curing	landscape gardening
biscuit manufacture	film processing
boat repairing	forestry
bricklaying	gamekeeping
fruit canning	glass blowing
fish farming	waste paper
carpet fitting	merchanting
cattle breeding	flour milling
central heating	egg packing
installation	pest control

Appendix 3: Sample activities from the Consumption module

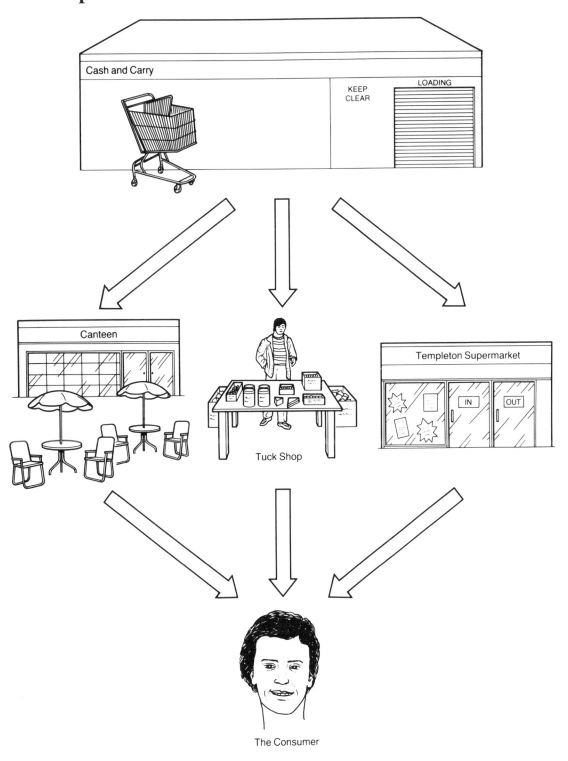

Consumption

What do *you* think consumption means? Answer in the space below.

....

When producers have made their goods, they try to sell them. If they are good at this, their goods are sent to different types of shops. Other businesses and people go to these shops and buy the things they want.

In Economics, these people and businesses are called *consumers*.

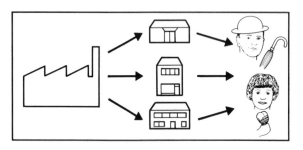

Consumers don't only go to shops to buy goods. Hotels do not sell new beds! They sell the *use* of a bed. Consumers buy this 'use'. When consumers buy this type of thing they are buying a SERVICE.

Look at the following list. Which of the items do you think are goods and which do you think are services?

eggs	cinema visit
a haircut	fridge
scissors	petrol
ice cream	hire of a car
bus journey	shoes

Every day people use up goods and services. Since you got up this morning, you have been consuming (using up) goods and services. Here are five things which you might have 'consumed' before you left the house this morning.

the use of your bed
today's use of your clothes
your breakfast
the use of the furniture
the use of plates and cups

Can you think of another 10 things you consumed before you got to your economics class? Write them down in the space below.

People all have wants. They use up goods and services to *satisfy* these wants. In economics, this is called *consumption.*

REMEMBER – ANYONE WHO USES UP GOODS AND SERVICES IS CALLED A CONSUMER.

An economic tale

Once upon a time, a little girl called Yellowhair walked out of her *tepee*, jumped on to her pony and rode away, eating *an apple*, to the big city. She realized when she got there that her clothes were not suitable and she sold her pony and went to the local shops. The *assistant* helped her to choose some new *clothes*. She went to the shop next door and bought a *stereo* and sat down in the park to listen to it. It was now getting quite late and she needed somewhere to stay. She left the park and *booked into a hotel* for the night.

The next day she went to the airport to *arrange a flight to London*. That evening, she boarded a jumbo jet and took off. During the flight, she *listened to the radio* and *watched a film*. When she arrived in London, she decided to go sight-seeing; she went to the *Art Gallery* and to *The Tower of London* to see *the jewels*. That evening, she stayed *at The Hilton*; the *food* was wonderful!

The next day, she *took the Underground* to the airport to start her journey home again.

Copy the words and phrases in italic in the passage, stating whether each one is a durable good, a non-durable good or a service.

Occupations

Look at the following list of occupations and make a note of the goods and/or services the people would provide you with.

dentist
bus driver
car salesman
check-out assistant in a supermarket
sales assistant in a dress shop

Consumers

Fill in the spaces below. Use last week's sheets to help you.

Producers supply g---- and s--- to c--------. These c--------- can be both b-------- and p-----. If you buy a g--- you buy an item. If you buy a s------ you buy the use of the item or a skill. Using up g---- and s------- is called c---------.

Producers make lots of things but not all consumers want the same things. Which *one* of the following consumers would buy *each* of the goods and services shown? Match them up using arrows.

Goods	*Consumer*
a bread oven	a school
cups and saucers	school children
a fishing net	crisp maker
a washing machine	fisherman
a bridge	a baker
potatoes	tea rooms
desks	the council
sweets	housewives

Not all g---- are used by only one c------- and many of the above g---- could be used by everybody. This means that there might be a large demand and this could change the price. If a g--- is s-----, like strawberries in winter, what happens to the price?

....

If nobody wants an item, like end-of-season fashion, what happens to the price?

....

Consumers can *buy* goods *for other people to use* (e.g. the bridge). The council (or the government) is a consumer.

Consumers can *buy* goods *to make other goods* (e.g. the bread oven to make loaves). People who make things are called producers. Producers then can also be consumers.

Can you think of three other consumers who buy goods to make other goods? Write down your answers.

Consumers can *buy* goods *to use them up themselves* (e.g. food to eat). YOU are this type of consumer.

Here are five things consumers might buy – food, soap, a washing machine, a house and a box of matches. Not all of these things last the same length of time.

In economics, goods that consumers like you buy are split up into two different types:

the ones that are used up in one go
the ones that can be used again and again!

Goods that don't last are called NON-DURABLE. Goods that do last are called DURABLE.

Make a list of 10 *durable* and 10 *non-durable* goods in your home. You may use the ones already given.

List the goods and services each of the following famous people would consume during their working day. State whether each good is durable or non-durable.

Felicity Kendal (actress)
Gemma Craven (actress and enthusiastic cook)
Margaret Thatcher (politician)

The list below contains several consumer goods. Identify those items which could be regarded as 'needs' if you see them as examples of the three basic needs of man. Place a tick against these items. 'Luxuries' are things which people can do without and still live a normal life. Place two ticks against those items you would be happy to live without. If any item is left without a tick, say why they are neither needs nor luxuries:

television set	shirt
milk	records
meat	books
sweets	car
house	

You can't have your cake and eat it!

Every day people have to choose. When you get up in the morning you choose what you will have for breakfast. If you have Rice Crispies today and finish them, you can't have the same ones tomorrow.

You have to choose how to spend any money you are given too. If you choose not to spend your money *now* then you cannot have the things that it would have bought *now*.

Let us suppose that you have 20p pocket money left. A bar of chocolate costs 20p. An ice cream costs 20p and your journey home on the train costs 20p. In the following list, tick those things that you could do, and put a cross against those things that you could not do:

buy an ice cream and a chocolate bar
buy only an ice cream
go home on a train and not have ice cream

buy chocolate and have change
buy chocolate and eat it on the train
buy only chocolate
keep your money and walk home

You must choose very carefully if you do not have a lot of money. If you had £5 to spend on *one thing only* what would you buy? What could you have bought but have decided not to have?

Money is only one resource that you have to use carefully. Time is another. If you watch a video, then you can't go outside with your friends. You cannot do everything at once. Doing one thing has cost you the chance or opportunity to do something else. In economics, we call the thing you cannot have the *opportunity cost*.

Economic wants
Look at the cartoon strip and then answer the questions that follow.

1) What things gave Harry satisfaction when he was out walking?

2) Name three things Harry wanted after the rain came on.

3) Name five things you would like to have.

4) Name five things you have bought in the last month.

5) List three services you have used in the last month.

6) If your list in exercise 3 is different from the items listed in 4 and 5, say why they are different.

7) Explain the meaning of the following words:
needs
scarcity
choice
resources

Appendix 4: Sample activities from the Exchange module

Exchange

In the films we saw last term we saw progress from a subsistence economy to an economy which was capable of production surpluses. This came about mainly by:

D------- of L----- and,
M-----------

What will happen to the 'extra' amount of goods that are produced? One way of dealing with them – as we saw in today's film – is to put them into a central store with someone in *command*. This means that ....
....

The success of this system depends on the absence of one basic human failing – GREED! In the film it was noticeable that some people saw nothing wrong with regularly taking out more than they put in.

On the other hand, when every family is allowed

to keep the surpluses they make, how do they get the other things they need?...
....

The name given to this system of exchange is *barter*. The advantages of this system include:

Swaps can be made just as soon as you agree with someone else
You will work harder to create more of a surplus in order to get more of the things you would like

But there are disadvantages to this system of barter too. Read the following story about Farmer McDonald and write down any three disadvantages that occur to you. Farmer McDonald is in desperate need of a new pair of shoes. He sets out to try to find someone willing to exchange shoes for his cow, Bessie.

After walking 2 miles

Farmer Fowl	Hello there! Can I interest you in some chickens for your cow?
Farmer McDonald	No, I'm looking for some shoes.
Farmer Fowl	Good luck then, cheerio.

3 miles further on

Mr Skinner	Please, please exchange your cow for this here hide.
Farmer McDonald	What! My cow is worth at least 5 of these hides.
Mr Skinner	Nonsense – feel the quality of this hide – look at the condition of your cow, 20 if she's a day.
Farmer McDonald	On your way man.

2 miles further on

Farmer McDonald	Boy am I weary and old Bessie can't go much further.
Mr Last	By jingo you look exhausted.
Farmer McDonald	Oh I am. Is that a pair of shoes you have there?
Mr Last	Aye, and that's an old beast you have there.
Farmer McDonald	This is Bessie – grand old girl. How about her for your shoes?
Mr Last	No way – I'm wanting some chickens for my shoes, not a cow.
Farmer McDonald	Looks like I'm stuck with you Bessie. Let's be for home then.

What are the disadvantages of barter?

As time goes on, the MARKET which develops out of this system of 'swapping' also creates another advantage. It becomes a place where people exchange not only goods but also exchange *information* with each other. This means that people get to know what each other want and so they can go home and make use of this knowledge. For example, think how pointless it would be for someone in a village to make fishing nets if there was no river nearby.

Using the information she picked up at the market, for example, Mrs Tailor might find that she is better to make bright red dresses instead of bright blue dresses because that is what people want and she can swap red dresses for more of the other things she needs.

Over a period of time, do you think that each family would keep making the same things or would they find other things to exchange?

Study the picture carefully, and, in your own words, tell the story of the events from 1 to 4.

The tale of a coat

Characters : Mr Potter, Mr Shepherd, Mr Taylor

Trade

The earliest form of business activity was barter. This was used before money was thought of and meant *trading goods that you didn't want* – perhaps a surplus – *for goods that you did want.*

Later on it was decided that barter was inconven-ient and trading came to mean exchanging money for goods.

Trade begins with the purchase of the original raw materials and ends with the sale of the finished product to the consumer. Not all the goods we need can be produced in this country, so some of our trade is done with countries overseas. The diagram shows the divisions of home and foreign trade.

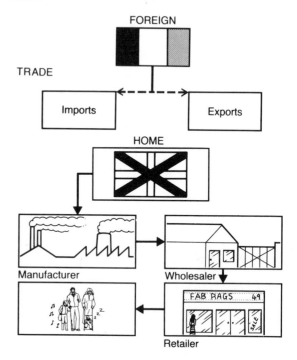

Let us look at home trade first of all. As we know, goods are produced by a m-----------. Sometimes he sells his goods direct to the public but more often he uses a *chain of distribution*.

See if you can fill in the blank spaces in the diagram.

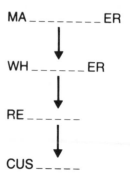

We all know what a manufacturer does (at least we should by now), but what do you think a wholesaler does? Well, if you look at the chain of distribution you can see that he is between the manufacturer and the retailer in the chain (i.e. he is in the middle). The function of a wholesaler is to be a *middleman* – the link between a manufacturer and a retailer.

Using modern production techniques most products are made in large quantities by the manufacturer. They are *mass-produced*. They are then sold in small quantities by the shopkeeper. A manufacturer finds it easier to sell his products to a few wholesalers who will buy in large quantities and who will re-sell in small quantities to retailers. The familiar sign 'Cash and -----' usually always indicates premises where there is a wholesaler.

15 Economics in S2

Mike Ryan

Jordanhill College School, Glasgow

The school

Jordanhill College School is a non-fee-paying, neighbourhood, comprehensive school drawing its pupils from a variety of socio-economic backgrounds. It is also an all-through school with pupils aged from 5 to 18 years. The infant/primary and secondary departments are run separately, although the Headteacher is head of the whole school. In the infant/primary department there are about 460 pupils, while there are about 570 in the secondary.

Social subjects in the school

There are three separate social-subjects departments in the school: Economics/Modern Studies, History, and Geography. In the first year (S1), all pupils study modern studies, history and geography. In the second year (S2) all pupils study economics, history and geography. At the end of year two all pupils choose whether to study economics or history or geography in years three and four, leading up to the SCE 'O' Grade at the end of the fourth year. In the session 1986–7, 16 pupils are studying economics in year three and seven in year four. Pupils in years five and six study for the SCE Higher Grade examination.

Economics in S1/S2

Economics was introduced into S1/S2 as a consequence of the school becoming a pilot school for draft guidelines in the teaching of social subjects in S1/S2. The guidelines were prepared for the Consultative Committee on the Curriculum. This, first established in 1965, is the main advisory body to the Secretary of State for Scotland. The CCC is responsible for a number of curriculum committees and the curriculum development service centres.

Before piloting began there was a pre-pilot year. This took place in 1983–4. During this year S1 was given about 14 periods of economics (a period lasted for 35 minutes). Full piloting began in 1984–5. In this session S1 only were given economics. In 1985–6, economics/modern studies was extended to S2 but, for reasons to do with the transition from S1, both years were taught modern studies and no economics. In session 1986–7, S1 are being taught modern studies and S2 are being taught economics.

There is one full-time teacher of economics in the school, although he also teaches modern studies for part of the time.

In S2 there are four classes. Each class completes 10 subject-based modules and one multi-subject module. Because of staffing (and perhaps other) factors, each class completes four modules in both history and geography but only two modules in economics.

The broad aims of the economics modules are:

1) to give pupils some idea of the nature of economics so as to encourage them to choose economics in S3
2) to give pupils some understanding of certain basic economic concepts and terms
3) to develop skills which will be useful in studying economics at 'O' Grade.

The two economics modules are called 'Production and Consumption' and 'Business Organization and Finance'. The multi-subject module is called 'The West Highland Line'. Each module lasts for 14 lessons of 40 minutes each.

The Production and Consumption module

Appendix 1 lists the aims of the module. It consists of five units of work, unit one providing opportunities for whole-class activities, units two, three and five for both whole-class and individual activities, and unit four for group work. Appendix 1 also describes the characteristics of each unit.

Resources used are both school-produced and from published sources. Books produced by industrial companies are used (for example, a book on oil production from BP plc). Two computer programs involve pupils in manipulating production variables. The first program is about working out the total cost of production. Pupils feed in information, and are told if they are correct. The correct response together with the working out is displayed. The second program looks at the way methods of production might change in response to changes in the wage levels of workers. Pupils estimate the level of wages at which machines might replace workers and are told when they are correct or incorrect.

Assessment is both diagnostic and summative. The fields assessed are mainly 'knowledge and understanding' and 'critical thinking'. Exercises have to be completed during the module. These are marked and further work is then based on the level of competence of the pupil. Pupils sit a test at the end of the module.

The Business Organization and Finance module

Appendix 2 sets out the aims of the module and describes the six units. Prospectuses from Britoil, British Telecom and British Gas are used in units three and four to help groups write their own prospectuses. Appendix 3 gives an example of an activity used in unit five.

The West Highland Line module

This module is taught as a multi-subject module with the Economics, Geography and History Departments cooperating in the preparation and teaching. The History Department deals with the building of the line in the 1890s and the Geography Department deals with the physical environment of the line. The Economics Department deals with the economics of the line and the advantages and disadvantages of keeping the line open. The aims of the module are listed in Appendix 4.

When this module was first taught in 1984–5 it lasted for about 30 periods. The Economics Department saw each class for a total of six periods. The allocation of time for 1986–7 was not decided at the time of writing.

The module provides scope for whole-class teaching, group work and individual work. Individual work could be used for the calculation of costs, revenue, profits and losses, in the mapwork and in the writing of a decision-making report at the end. Group work could be used when pupils discuss the advantages and disadvantages of keeping the line open and whether or not to close it.

Assessment could be of the individual work produced by pupils during the module and of the report produced at the end to indicate whether they support keeping the line open or closing it. The assessment would be predominantly of knowledge and understanding, and critical thinking, but there is also scope for assessing enquiry skills and communication.

During work on the module, pupils are taken on a trip to the West Highland Line. In 1984–5 one group was taken to Tyndrum Lower and studied the area before reboarding the train at Tyndrum Upper. The main group continued on to Bridge of Orchy and walked back to Tyndrum station. The main benefits of the visit were obviously geographical, but there was some scope for reinforcing elements of economics. For example, the small size of towns and villages on the route helped to reinforce the lack of demand for passenger travel.

Problems of course construction

A number of problems in course construction have emerged. For example, in selecting concepts suitable for S2, they need to be such that they can be put into a fairly concrete form. At the S2 stage pupils have limited ability to think in abstract terms.

Putting concepts into a form which is both meaningful and interesting is not easy. In history and geography there is plenty of material which is both concrete and personal: what people did in the past, how people live in different parts of the world. The concepts in economics have to be presented in a similar way to appeal to pupils in S2.

Working out the level to which the material can be taught is another problem. It should not be too difficult for pupils to master, but neither should it be pitched at a level which is so low that it does not stretch the more-able pupils.

Finally, there is a lack of suitable textbooks for this level. Unlike history and geography, where there is a wealth of attractively produced textbooks geared to the learning needs of pupils in S2, the Economics Department has to produce most of its own material. Such material suffers from two drawbacks: first, it takes an enormous amount of time to prepare; and second, materials prepared in school cannot usually be as attractive as those prepared commercially. If there is somebody with the time and ability to produce some good drawings, this is a help, but otherwise the material is somewhat unattractive, especially to the less-able pupils. The preparation time is therefore considerably greater than it is for other subjects and the end-product often less attractive.

Available materials tend to be for older pupils and would need to be considerably adapted to be of use to pupils in S2.

Appendix 1: The Production and Consumption module

Aims: cognitive

The pupils should

1) understand that economics is concerned with the way we satisfy our wants
2) understand that resources are required to produce goods and services
3) understand the difference between materials, people and equipment
4) understand that people, materials and equipment have to be combined in order to produce goods and services
5) understand that people and equipment can be combined in different proportions to produce the same output
6) understand why the combination may change
7) uderstand that specialization aids production
8) know and understand the factors which affect the demand for a product
9) know and understand the factors which affect the price of a product.

Aims: skills

The pupils should be able to:

1) work out the total revenue made by a firm, given the price and the quantity sold
2) work out the quantity sold by a firm, given the total revenue and the price
3) work out the total cost of production, given the inputs and the prices of the inputs
4) work out the profit made by the firm
5) work out the most profitable output/price given a range of situations
6) draw and read a range of diagrams showing such things as a demand curve
7) identify some consequences of economic changes.

Outline of units

Unit One

Pupils are asked to write down 10 things that they would like to have. These are then discussed.

Points to notice: some things cannot be bought; some things are goods, some are services.

Pupils then note that economics is concerned with the ways that we get the things that we want.

They are taught the distinction between goods and services.

They are taken through a number of sheets that demonstrate that to produce goods and services we have to use resources, and that these resources are materials, equipment and people. They are shown how the finished product in one production flow may become part of the production flow for another finished product.

Pupils are then given a finished product of their own and they have to fill in the same set of sheets for that finished product.

Unit Two

Pupils are taught the connection between price and quantity sold. This is done by reference to the school tuck-shop.

Referring to the tuck-shop, a local shop and a large superstore, the pupils learn some other factors that can influence the demand for a product.

They learn how to calculate the total revenue a firm earns. This involves both statistical material and graphical material.

Pupils are made to realize that the highest price does not necessarily give the highest revenue.

Unit Three

The pupils learn what determines the costs of production, and how to calculate these costs. They learn how to calculate the cost of producing an article.

They learn how to calculate the profit a firm makes.

An extension of the unit is to work out the price which gives the best profit.

Unit Four

Simulation on methods of production: specialization. Pupils are given a task to do in a certain period of time. Each pupil makes a complete product. The total number of products made is ascertained. The class is then divided into groups of five and each member of the group is given one part of the product to make. The same time is allocated to production and the total number produced is ascertained. A comparison of the

results of the two methods is then made and the reasons for the difference are discussed.

Pupils then apply this understanding to other situations (e.g. making cars).

Unit Five

Pupils are taught the difference between labour-intensive methods and capital-intensive methods of production. They learn why one method may give way to a different method. They do exercises on distinguishing the methods and working out which would be the better method.

Appendix 2: The Business Organization and Finance module

Aims: cognitive

The broad aims of the module are to teach the pupils the importance of investment in the economy and where the money comes from to pay for it. The pupil should:

1) understand the concept of investment
2) know and understand some of the factors affecting investment
3) know some of the sources of money available to firms for investment
4) know and understand some of the consequences of investment
5) know and understand some of the consequences of a lack of investment
6) know some of the factors affecting the success of investment
7) know and understand what happens to the profits which firms make
8) know and understand the following terms: shares, shareholders and directors
9) know something about the way that shares are issued
10) understand the link between saving and investment
11) understand why a firm has to get money before it can start up in business
12) understand the difference between the costs of setting up a business and the costs of running the business.

Aims: skills

1) enquiry: extracting information from a prospectus
2) critical thinking:
   - identifying consequences of investment/lack of investment
   - assessing the advantages and disadvantages of reinvesting profits or handing them out to shareholders
   - identifying the links between profit and investment
   - drawing conclusions about the level of investment/profit from data
   - giving reasons for choosing to invest/not to invest
   - evaluating different investment opportunities
3) communication: production of a prospectus
4) personal and social development:
   - ability to work in a group
   - ability to organize own work.

Outline of units

Unit One

Discusses why we save money.

Classification skills: identify reason from a number of statements.

Pupils given information on variety of ways of saving money: explanation given; exercises involving enquiry skills.

Extension work: calculate the returns from a variety of ways of saving money – assess the advantages and disadvantages of each.

Unit Two

Discusses why businesses need money *before* they can start.

Makes distinction between those expenses that are necessary before production can start and those that can be met after production starts.

This is applied to a number of situations (e.g. a firm making clothes, a firm printing magazines, a hairdressing firm, a taxi-driver, a firm making sweets or crisps, a firm providing take-away meals).

Unit Three

Establishes the link between people wanting to save money and people needing money to set up in business.

Outlines how people wanting to set up in business can get money from their own savings and from banks.

Outlines how such people could also get the money by issuing shares.

Discusses the reasons why people might buy shares – the desire to get some of the profits.

Terms to be learnt: shares, shareholders, directors.

Unit Four

Pupils produce a prospectus and, working in groups, set up a company. This involves deciding the product the firm is producing, the name of the company, the board of directors. They then produce a prospectus for their company, giving details of the nature of the business, the recent performance of the company, what the money is to be used for and an application form.

Unit Five

Pupils investigate the meaning and importance of investment; and the idea that investment involves a sacrifice.

The story 'Desert Island Tricks' is used to look at the difference between capital goods and consumer goods.

Unit Six

Pupils learn the factors which influence the success of investment and apply this knowledge to a variety of situations.

The class as a whole or in groups discusses the chances of the investment succeeding. The discussion is rounded off by drawing general conclusions about the factors which influence success. Pupils are then given some new situations and are asked to indicate which are likely to succeed and which are likely to fail, giving reasons in each case.

Appendix 3: Desert Island Tricks – resource exemplar

Jim Smith and Bobby Brown were the only survivors of a cruise ship that sank in a fierce storm.

They both managed to reach an island but did not know that the other person had also arrived there.

When Jim had recovered from his ordeal he looked around and examined his situation. The only things that he had were the clothes that he was wearing and a penknife in his pocket. As it was several hours since he had eaten he was feeling very hungry and so he looked around to see if he could find something to eat. After looking for quite some time he eventually found a number of palm trees. These trees were very high and the coconuts were at the very top. It took Jim a long time to climb to the top and he spent four hours climbing up and down trees before he had enough coconuts to keep him going for one day. The rest of the day he spent either sleeping or building himself a shelter.

Meanwhile, Bobby had also woken up to find that he too had only his clothes and a penknife. Like Jim he started looking for some food and eventually found some palm trees. It also took Bobby four hours to collect enough coconuts to feed himself for one day. The rest of the day he too spent sleeping or building himself a shelter.

The next day, Jim went back to the palm trees and spent four hours climbing up and down them to get his day's food. After that he was too exhausted to do anything else. Bobby, however, decided that he must find a better way of getting the coconuts so he took his knife and began to make a ladder. He cut down some branches from a nearby tree and using roots he bound the branches together to make his ladder. This took him two hours to do and by the time he was finished he was so tired that he was only able to spend one hour collecting coconuts. However, because he had the use of the ladder he was able to collect a half day's supply of coconuts.

Two weeks later, Bobby arrived at the mainland in a boat he had built himself. It had taken him three days to get from the island to the mainland. Jim, however, was still climbing up and down the palm trees every day.

1) how many hours did it take Jim to collect a day's supply of coconuts on the first day?
2) how many hours did it take Bobby to collect a day's supply of coconuts on the first day?
3) how many hours did it take Jim to collect a day's supply of coconuts on the third day?
4) how many hours did it take Bobby to collect a day's supply of coconuts on the third day?
5) compare how Bobby and Jim got on during the first day they were on the island
6) compare how Bobby and Jim got on during the second day they were on the island
7) which boy had the better meal on the second day? why was this?
8) how much longer did Jim have to spend on the third day to get the same amount of coconuts as Bobby?
9) how many hours did Bobby save each day as a result of having a ladder?
10) what does this story tell you about investment?

Appendix 4: The West Highland Line module

Aims: cognitive

Pupils should:

1) understand that there are costs involved in operating the line
2) know what costs are involved in operating the line
3) understand the term 'total costs of production'
4) understand that British Rail received revenues from operating the line
5) know that the line is used by both goods and passenger trains
6) understand that the revenue received depends on the amount of goods carried and the number of passengers carried
7) understand the term 'total revenue'
8) understand the terms 'profit' and 'loss'
9) understand the term 'subsidy'
10) understand the term 'efficiency'
11) know where the money can come from to pay for a subsidy.

Aims: skills

1) enquiry:
    recording and classifying statistical information
    extraction of information from a map
2) critical thinking: pupils can:
    give reasons why the line is making a loss
    give reasons why it is difficult to increase the revenue
    give advatages and disadvantages for particular people of closing the line
    come to a decision about keeping the line open and provide reasons for his/her choice.

Section 4 *Economic Awareness as a Focus for Change*

16 *Economic awareness as a focus for change*

Paul Clarke and Steve Lepper

Great Cornard Upper School, Suffolk

Introduction

This paper reviews the progress made during the period 1985–7 in the introduction of 'economic and political awareness' to an upper-school 13–16 curriculum. The school is a 13–18 comprehensive opened in 1973. It currently has 1,100 students on roll, half from housing estates within the immediate area and the remainder from a rural catchment area extending up to 15 miles.

Economics within the traditional school curriculum

Economics is currently the most popular 'A' level choice for students and, in addition, in 1986–7 some 18 students were studying for CEE Economics as a by-product of their CPVE course. In the 13–16 curriculum, economics has been taught only to those students studying a CSE Mode 3 in World Studies (just under half of the year group). This was a non-examination economic literacy course developed over the previous three years. The course ended with the start of GCSE in 1986–7. Courses are staffed by the Department Head and Coordinator, the Head of fifth year (who was Industry Year coordinator) and a Deputy Headteacher (who was acting Headteacher for one and a half terms until Spring 1987). Regular help on the economic literacy course had been given by a geographer and a supply teacher, an historian.

The changing curriculum scene

Since 1976–7, senior management has discussed a more pupil-centred approach to the curriculum. This had led to the notion of certain perspectives permeating through traditional department work. Discussion of cross-curricular approaches has centred on a DES paper[1] and an HMI paper.[2] In addition a local initiative, *The Suffolk Curriculum*, reinforced this approach and gave further support to the place of economic and political awareness.

Economic and political awareness became one aspect of the cross-curricular curriculum development within the school and was to be developed through the creation of a Coordinator for Economic and Political Awareness (CEPA) in 1985–6. This post was one of a team of six who were to form the school's central coordinating team. The other coordinators were for information technology, health education, mathematics education, tutorial work and year three.

The responsibilities of the CEPA were described as being to:

1) identify in all curriculum areas opportunities for developing economic and political awareness in students
2) supply the relevant supplementary teaching and learning materials to staff
3) offer guidance and assistance to staff through INSET
4) work as a member of a team, both with the other coordinators and with subject area representatives.

Implementation

At the outset each member of the coordinating team identified a formal process whereby he or she hoped to achieve the aims of coordination. Resource requirements were identified and formed the basis of a TVEI-related in-service training (TRIST) submission which it was hoped would give supply cover time to free key staff for planning and development meetings. Time was spent studying workschemes and syllabuses. Resources were produced and INSET activities carried out to establish joint aims and objectives. Classroom work was to be either 'stand alone' (taught by other subject staff) or to involve 'team teaching'. Working in several different subject areas also implied attention to sequencing and continuity.

Phase 1: September–October half term 1985

The Year Three Coordinator organized meetings with heads of department (initially geography, chemistry, physics and biology) to identify possible links between subjects, or alternatively where help from one area might benefit another. The geographers readily identified opportunities for linking work, but it was felt that the CEPA might better spend time helping those areas of the curriculum where economic concepts might be less familiar.

From the outset it was clear that, even with extra help, the time requirements on colleagues would be enormous. The additional constraint of teachers' industrial action severely curtailed the possibilities of meetings outside the school day. For coordinators the problem was even more acute. It was agreed that

1) the original aim of examining year three in its totality was unrealistic
2) the starting rationale (that economic awareness was a good thing and that a cross-curricular approach was the way forward) was too general
3) written schemes of work were best discussed in conjunction with, not separately from, negotiations with staff.

On the positive side, the initial work was necessary to clarify aims and methodology. The flurry of activity also helped create general interest, and a large amount of informal work and contact was taking place.

Phase 2: Spring and Summer terms 1986

The ideas were further clarified by the publication of a number of articles, including the Economics Association's statement on economic awareness.[3] This gave formal expression to economic awareness aims. General concern over the 'relevance' to the 'real world' of the curriculum (however defined) strengthened the view that economic awareness was a good 'link' between subjects and helped to place subject material in a 'life skills context'. Two terms of development work are best illustrated by a detailed description of links with mathematics and a summary description of contacts with other 'departments'.

Economics and mathematics

The Coordinator for Mathematics had been appointed a year earlier and had been able to do more preliminary work. The Cockcroft Report on Mathematics had also formed part of a general trend towards a 'life skills' approach. Part of the third year mathematics course involved work on statistics, and it seemed an ideal opportunity for the CEPA to work with mathematics on 'real numbers' – with a wider context given to their 'handling'.

An initial aim for mathematics might be to use 'real data' rather than imaginary examples. In economics, data are often used without taking the opportunity to reinforce mathematical skills. Indeed, an exercise may 'fall down' because of a false assumption about the students' mathematical ability. Both the mathematician and economist working in his or her own subject may be unaware of the points the other would wish to make!

Working on these premises two lessons took place early in the Spring term.

The first used a case study 'Price of a Perm' (*Understanding Economics*)[4] to investigate budget decisions in the world of small business. Students used visual, written and numerical resources to clarify costs and to question the viability of the business. The future of the enterprise could be interpreted to include social, political and moral as well as economic dimensions.

An introductory lesson was led by the CEPA with the mathematics teacher, but it was the latter who supervised the follow-up work.

With a third year group, the aims were to

- illustrate different uses and presentation of data through a variety of examples
- give students experience in the collection, selection and display of data within a specific context

From the point of view of economics, students were introduced to the different types of costs incurred in production.

The second set of lessons took a similar mathematics theme but involved a group of 'below average' ability. A survey completed by the students provided a bank of data to introduce the idea of income distribution and to investigate the relationship between levels of income and spending ('Paying', *Understanding Economics*).

From an economics point of view it was intended to highlight scarcity and choice facing individuals. This work was less successful, mainly because the students' experience of handling money had been overestimated. Few students had part-time jobs and most relied on small sums of pocket money; and so, while this information in itself could have been used, it needed to be collected and collated in a form different from that suggested by the published resource.

From this early work a pattern of cooperation emerged which was subsequently used to develop work involving mathematics, health education and economics. This is illustrated in Figure 2. *Informal negotiations* established the lesson context, identified resources and how they might be used to put over various aims. *Resource development* involved raw materials (in this case provided by economics and health education) being put into a formal lesson context by the Mathematics Department. The resources were then re-examined by the coordinators and formal aims were established for the materials' wider context.

It seemed that no matter how careful the preparation there was always the unexpected to deal with. From the mathematician's point of view problems arise from the use of 'real data' rather than carefully constructed examples. With broader aims to a lesson, there are more avenues for students to pursue; this is not necessarily a bad thing, but when these are points about economics or health education the mathematician might not always feel competent to deal with them.

However, it was hoped that there would be benefits all round in that students would improve their understanding in all these areas, and thereby find the mathematics more relevant and the lessons more enjoyable.

Figure 2 The scheme used to develop cooperative work

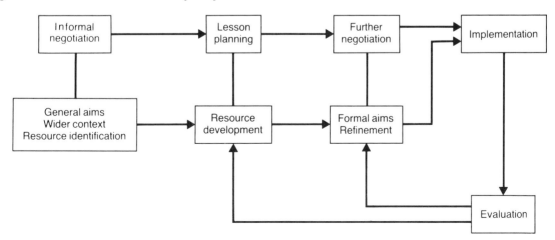

Further work in mathematics

National No Smoking Day

During the week of National No Smoking Day, third year mathematics work was based on statistics from ASH (Action on Smoking and Health). Interesting discussions took place in class. What was particularly pleasing was how the idea of 'opportunity costs' was used by students without prompting. Despite the earlier time-consuming briefings the Coordinator for Mathematics still felt that the work would have benefited from a class input by a specialist, particularly to respond to discussion points as they arose in the class. For the next piece of work a team-taught 'discussion lesson' was built into the programme.

Road safety

The next block of work took similar aims but this time using the theme of road safety. In addition to economics and health education, the work also involved the Active Tutorial Programme. The mathematics work had less structure, with statistics being there as a stimulus to project work. During a team-taught discussion lesson points were raised concerning public transport, the cost of safety features, and how to allocate a monetary cost to such things as 'pain and suffering'.

'Economaths'

On two days in July 1986, the third year timetable was suspended for what were called 'Maths Days'. Students were asked to choose three from a list of activities with a mathematics theme, each to last 80 minutes. The Coordinator for Economics was asked to provide an input to be called 'Economaths'. After consultation with the Coordinator for Mathematics, a lesson was developed using a computer-assisted learning unit called *Break Even*[5] (see Appendix 1).

Over two days, six mixed-ability groups went through the exercise with encouraging results. Unsolicited responses from the students included 'why can't we do economics until the sixth form?' and 'it's better than just using ordinary numbers in boring problems.' Some students involved in this had earlier been working on 'Price of a Perm'. These were the only students who positively identified themselves as having made 'Economaths' a first choice. They also showed during the work

that they had retained a good understanding of the distinction between fixed and variable costs. While such evaluations are subjective, one acid test of students' interest was to offer a follow-up activity in the form of a competition running *Teddytronic*[5] over three lunchtimes in the last week of term. More than 20 students volunteered and, while a prize of £5 may explain some of the attendance, nearly all had attended one of the 'Economaths' sessions. Eventually six teams participated, along with a Mathematics Department team who were sufficiently encouraged to suggest it as an annual event. Students were motivated and obviously had put considerable thought into decisions outside the formal sessions.

Conclusions

By the end of the 1985–6 school year the majority of third year students had been involved in some form of cross-curriculum work involving mathematics and economic awareness, and the majority of mathematics teachers had been involved in the delivery of some form of work. Cooperation had extended to the delivery of mathematics aims by economists within the school. The motivation and interest shown by both students and teachers was high.

The work was largely experimental and therefore lacked an overall context and structure as far as economic awareness was concerned. Further developments within the school curriculum, such as GCSE, Foundation Programme for Pre-vocational Studies (FPPVS) and CPVE, alongside changes in the management structure (described later), will all help to increase the possibilities for cross-curricular work.

Links with other departments

In addition to work with mathematics, consultations also took place with home economics, music and history.

Economics and home economics

Cooperative work led to a formal project where students were asked to compare various household gadgets for efficiency and price. They then used gadgets to produce various foods from raw ingredients, to be compared with fast-food substitutes. This provided a context in which students recognized the need to make choices, that such choices involve forgoing alternatives, and that the basis for making such choices includes costs (for example, money, opportunity costs, externalities) and utility (for example, satisfaction, time).

Students tended to dwell on the use of additives or the need for a particular gadget, but motivation was again high, as evidenced in the quality of most reports. Also, the cooperation and involvement of particular students was seen as especially encouraging by the class teacher.

A longer block of work was due to be introduced into the fourth year course in 1986–7 using various TV programmes on diet and health, alongside programme 1 of a BBC radio series *Economics in Social Education*[6]. In addition, cooperation was extended to year three. Students are to work on an assignment involving the steps taken to establish a restaurant/cafe. This includes costings, aspects of law affecting the preparation and cooking of food, along with menu design, pricing and marketing policies.

Economics and music

Economics, geography and music have combined within the creative arts team to plan a 10-week course on the music industry. The intention is to broaden out beyond the listening, composing and performing of music to look at the pop industry as a business, including fashions, promotion, publishing, electronics and new technology. Session musicians, pop managers and orchestra organizers have views to explore on music as a creator of wealth. There is scope for practical activities, including compositions based on local industrial 'sounds'.

An assignment-based course was developed for 1986–7. Starting with an analysis of a chart music programme as a wealth creator, and reflecting the music business as experienced by most teenagers, the course provides an opportunity for students, working in small groups, to develop a promotional folder for an imaginary group. This includes careful planning on costs, style of music, alongside the group's image and audience. In addition to an analysis of images provided by music styles, the

work provides an opportunity to develop word processing skills alongside design skills with careful preparation of support materials for the folder. The final lesson in the block of work includes a comparison of 60s and 80s music styles as a reflection of changing society. This is done by combining visual and audio images with economic history and student perceptions of life in an empathy exercise.

The folder exercise generates tremendous enthusiasm from students, with one unexpected outcome being a greater appreciation of the costs of musical equipment. One student commented that it would make them more careful when handling equipment. A bank loan simulation, adapted from *Bank Loan*[7] and based on promotional folders, has been devised to follow this up.

The joint delivery and development of this work by a non-specialist has served to illustrate the flexibility of cross-curricular approaches to increasing economic awareness.

Economics and history

Within the GCSE World History course, and in previous GCE and CSE courses on the same theme, many economic issues arise, ranging from different economic systems to the causes and effects of inflation. These have often been only obliquely dealt with in the past, but lessons are being planned with the CEPA to tackle the economics questions more directly.

Future developments

The pace of development has a momentum of its own, reflecting a generally favourable response to the work. This response has been influenced by three main factors:

1) the impact of Industry Year, and particularly the efforts of the school's Industry Year Coordinator, in encouraging departments to look to industry links
2) the school's participation in a DES scheme run by the Cambridge Institute of Education to examine strategies for managing curriculum change in schools

3)   the school's involvement as a pilot school for the Foundation Programme for Pre-Vocational Studies (FPPVS).

The introduction of FPPVS (from January 1987) in particular gave a clearer focus for cross-curricular work. The school has chosen to deliver FPPVS initially to a trial group of 60 students from across the ability range. They will continue to study mainstream GCSE courses which, as part of the school's cross-curricular work, will include assignment and case study work. The assignments will form the basis of the FPPVS profiles for the 60 students.

If FPPVS criteria are to be successfully delivered, consultation and cooperation is necessary between departments, the FPPVS coordinator and all other coordinators, to ensure that assignments fully reflect the areas of experience set out in FPPVS guidelines.

Conclusions

At the outset, while strategic reasons for developing economic awareness through cross-curricular work were understood, it was not clear whether permeation was preferable to a separate 'subject' status. Experience of the past year has shown that, within the specific circumstances of Great Cornard Upper School, economic awareness as a timetabled subject would be a retrograde step. The perceived benefits of cross-curricular work reflect the experience of colleagues in practice, with an overall impression of improved student motivation. Structural changes, such as GCSE, FPPVS, a changed management structure and the experience of colleagues with CPVE, all go to reinforce cross-curricular work as part of the daily reality of the school curriculum.

While such work is clearly only in its early stages, the developments outlined above, alongside the possible introduction of a modular timetable, lead to questions about continuity and public examinations as well as staffing. Could cross-curricular delivery of economic and political awareness enable entry of students into GCSE without the need for formal timetabling of economics? While considerable progress has been made within the first two years, a considerable amount of work remains, particularly in sequencing, before such a notion can become reality. However, such an idea may not seem quite so unrealistic now after the experience of the previous 12 months. The coordinator's role has become more clearly defined within an altered school management structure. However, there must be a limit on the amount of work a coordinator can successfully combine with the more traditional role of Head of Department.

Attainment of GCSE is not the only measure of improved economic awareness, and considerable progress can be made by using the opportunities already presented across the curriculum in economic awareness. This is a much more straightforward task and more attainable within a general school context. In this sense cross-curricular economic awareness aids colleagues in other areas rather than adding to their burden.

The cost has been considerable in terms of staff time and resources. With the introduction of FPPVS a definite ceiling appears to have been reached. Limiting the coordinator's direct responsibility within economics to 14–16 cross-curricular work is one way forward. This would involve the creation of a separate post with responsibility for 16 +. Also, traditional timetable structures, where teacher time is allocated to specific classes at a specific time, are proving prohibitive. Enhanced non-contact time would help, but current staffing allocations according to a strict pupil/teacher ratio make this difficult to achieve, and usually only at the cost of something else.

Clearly, therefore, the commitment to change needs matching with concrete backing from senior management and with local authority support. The implications of this work are that, when successful, demands on staff time are equivalent to those generated by separate subject status. However, in the final analysis it may be a more cost-effective way of introducing economic awareness into the core. Coordination may be achieved by one full-time member of staff, whereas the teaching of a core subject in a specific timetabled slot may require more staff while adding to curriculum clutter. It does, however, require an initial investment which may be beyond that possible in many schools given existing arrangements.

References

1   DES, *A Framework for the School Curriculum*, HMSO, 1980.
2   Her Majesty's Inspectorate, *Curriculum Matters*, HMSO, 1985.
3   Economics Association, 'Economic awareness in the school curriculum', *Economics*, Autumn 1985.
4   Economics Association, *Understanding Economics*, Longman, 1985.
5   *Computers in the Curriculum*/Economics Education 14–16 Project, 'Break-Even' and 'Teddytronic', *Understanding Economics*, Longman 1985.
6   *Economics in Social Education*, British Broadcasting Corporation, 1986.
7   *Bank Loan*, Banking Information Service, 1984.

Appendix 1: 'Economaths' lesson using Break-Even program

Introduction (20–30 minutes)

What is 'economics'? Brainstorming to bring out the problems of scarcity and choice. In a business context, how are scarce resources combined to satisfy wants? Involves costs, especially money costs in production. Division into 'fixed' and 'variable' costs. Explanation of other terms necessary for 'break-even'.

Students are divided into two groups on advice from maths colleagues.

Group A: 'Sounds Good Disco'

Students enter their own estimates for appropriate price to charge, or for number of customers required to 'break-even', to cover the fixed and variable costs involved in a mobile disco.

Students given exercise to define terms, to try some examples of calculations involving costs, revenue, profits. Functional notation used (i.e. $TVC = Q \times VC$; for break-even, $AR = ATC$).

Students use program with data provided. They finish in discussion groups considering issues (should the business expand? what are the risks?).

Bar charts with accurate scales and notation used to present costs/revenue for one disco and for several.

Group B: 'County Bus Co.'

Variables in program include cost in pence per kilometre, passengers carried, price charged, and subsidy available from local council.

Students used combination of data to calculate total costs, average cost per km, fare necessary to break-even given number of customers.

Effectively manipulating equations to make different variables the subject of the equation.

Students asked to discuss the idea of subsidy and the choices facing a loss-making bus company.

Extension exercise

Students form teams to take part in *Teddytronic*. This is a computer-managed business simulation in which groups run a soft toy firm. Orders depend on the time of year, and decisions are based on production, sales cost, cash-flow data and random events arising from 'real world' incidents. Students can present their results in terms of cost-analysis, sales graphs, group cooperation. . . . Run as lunchtime competition.

17 Economics as an agent of change

Peter Leech and Ken Hall

King James's High School, Knaresborough

King James's School is an 11–18 comprehensive in a market town. The school services the whole of the town and has an intake of about 1,300 pupils. It has its own sixth form and a high reputation for academic success as well as a growing reputation for curriculum development across a wide front.

By 1982, economics as a subject was well established at sixth form level and with excellent results. GCE and CSE courses also existed with consistently good results. At the end of 1982, the Head of Economics was appointed Sixth Form Head, and replaced as Head of Economics by a teacher with experience of work in a curriculum development project (the Economics Education 14–16). By Easter 1983, the latter had been appointed Head of Middle School (responsible for years 3–5) and much of the development of the work of the department was left in the hands of the deputy. There was also one other full-time member of the department (later to be appointed Deputy Head of Year Five) and several others who took occasional lessons.

Prior to 1983 the school had been involved in the school trials for the Economics Education 14–16 Project's exemplar materials, and the ideas encapsulated in the materials became established in the thinking of the staff of the department.

The initial position

At the start of the period of change economics was offered in the pre-sixth form curriculum in various forms:

1) as an option for the top-ability band in year three
2) as a CSE Mode-3 option course in years four and five
3) as a GCE 'O' level subject in years four and five, with pupils allowed to opt for the economics section of the Joint Matriculation Board's Government, Economics and Commerce syllabus.

A high proportion of pupils in years 3–5 therefore experienced some form of economics education under the title of Economics.

The third year course reviewed

In the light of discussions, the third year syllabus underwent a thorough review. It became a more practical course, involving pupils in a range of active learning situations. The intention was to provide a self-contained course rather than one which was seen simply as a preparation for examination courses. Emphasis was also shifted away from the transmission of theory, a central pillar of the fourth and fifth year 'O' level course. (The syllabus for the third year course is included in Appendix 1.)

The CSE course reviewed

The next course to be scrutinized was the CSE Economics course, which had previously been modelled closely on the GCE syllabus, but with a much reduced theoretical content. A number of important decisions that were to have a great bearing on its later development were taken early on in the review of this course. Amongst the most important of these decisions were the following:

1) emphasis would be on social economics
2) the approach in the course would build on the obvious success of the practical, activity-oriented third year course
3) there would be considerable involvement in the local community
4) the course would be seen as a preparation for 'life after school' and be organized around units related to the roles that pupils play on leaving school
5) the balance of assessment for the course would shift away from a great emphasis on terminal examinations and towards a greater bias in favour of short profiles related to the units in the syllabus, combined with school-based testing
6) a compulsory work experience component would be included.

The syllabus for this course is given in Appendix 2, together with a description of the assessment scheme.

Economics as part of the core for some pupils

The response to the changes to the two courses outlined above (and the consequent changes in the teaching strategies employed in the GCE course) was such that a policy decision was made by the Headteacher. From the following year social economics would become one of the core subjects (along with English, mathematics and a science subject) for the two groups of pupils who were expected to take a majority of CSE courses. This affected 40 of the 160 pupils entered for GCE/CSE. The majority of the rest of the 160 pupils also opted to take economics even though it was not compulsory, either in years four and five, or as part of third year studies.

Economics as part of the core for non-exam pupils

The next stage in the development of the school's provision of economic awareness was to involve the 35–40 pupils not entered for GCE/CSE examinations but who were taught in two vocationally oriented City and Guilds Foundation course groups. Social economics was made one of the core subjects for these pupils. Although it was already a very practical course, the added economics dimension was seen as being extremely beneficial to these pupils.

By this stage economics was compulsory for 80 out of just under 200 pupils and was taken as an option subject by a large majority of the rest.

The course tutor concept

A system of course tutor support had existed for the city and guilds groups. Each group had a course tutor who not only took a greater interest in an individual pupil's welfare than was normally expected, but also took responsibility for coordinating the various components of the course. Whenever possible the course tutor also taught the pupils for more than one subject.

The success of the course tutor concept led it to be applied to the CSE groups. (By this stage the groups were identified for timetabling purposes as 4SA and 4SB, the 'S' standing for social economics.) The social economics teacher became the course tutor to these groups and the Economics Department took on the coordinating role for mathematics, English, science, and vocational preparation for these pupils. This decision was reached because the social economics course was seen to be most significant in providing these pupils with an identity and in setting the pace for others in terms of the approach being taken to the pupils' general education. An important aspect of the course tutor's role was to coordinate the programme of visits into the community, which were seen as an important element in the course.

The in-service function

By this time the provision of economics in the school had become such that the department did not have the staffing to cover all of the work being asked of it. Other members of staff were attached to the department, though usually for a minority of their time. This step had as much to do with putting out messages to the staff about the methodology involved in the teaching of economics as it had to do with filling in staff shortages. It also allowed course tutors to teach groups for more than one subject.

Thus by 1986 staff teaching economics included the following:

- Head of Sixth Form (and Head of Economics until mid-1986)
- Deputy Head (Curriculum)
- Head of Middle School
- second in department (Head of Department from 1986)
- Deputy Head of Year Five
- an economics/mathematics teacher
- an economics/history teacher (later Head of Year three).

Conclusions

The developments described could only have occurred with a great deal of high-quality, dedicated teaching. However, such developments may not automatically follow from good teaching in a department. Some other factors that appear to have enhanced development in this case are summarized below.

An approach to teaching had been developed in the department which involved a balance of abstract ideas set in a practical context and related to the world likely to be met by pupils when they leave school. The work of the department was concentrated on learning strategies, which involved pupils in doing things and studying real-life situations, where possible at first hand (there was, for example, no course text).

The department had kept a close eye on the work of other departments in the school and was prepared to offer to enrich rather than to merely duplicate the rest of the curriculum.

The school was already susceptible to curricular change. Initiatives like the course tutor concept had already been developed. The Economics Department was prepared to join these changes, even in situations where members of the department may have taken on less favourable teaching situations to do so.

The Economics Department had made a conscious effort not to allow its own schemes of work to become fossilized. Extensive reviews had been undertaken, including the contribution it made to the curriculum as a whole. The members of the department also saw that the provision of economic awareness to so many pupils could not be done within the department. Their reaction to this was not to fight for a bigger empire, but instead to see their role as coordinators of a team of staff, some of whom had no training in the subject and were in need of support.

The members of the department shared a view that the division of a school into pastoral and curricular was at best false and at worst destructive. Their teaching represented an amalgam of their best didactic approaches and a commitment to the overall welfare of the individual pupil.

The factors outlined above do not minimize the undoubted difficulties faced by many teachers of economics hoping to make a fuller provision for their school. Problems clearly exist and it should not be assumed that all was plain sailing at King James's. Moreover, the particular combination of talents and interests present are not found often in a single department. However, some of the factors which led to the developments outlined above might serve as a stimulus for thought for other teachers nearer the start of their mission to provide 'economic awareness for all'.

Appendix 1: Third year economics course

Aims

To develop:

1) an understanding of economics and basic economic concepts
2) an understanding of the inter-relationship between economic units at local, national, and international levels
3) a recognition that economics is a dynamic subject
4) an appreciation of the relevance of economics both in an explanation of the past and in current events today.

Objectives

By the end of the course students should be able to:

1) understand and apply basic economic concepts
2) develop skills for life through the study of institutions such as banks, insurance companies, building societies, etc.
3) develop personal skills such as reading, verbal and written discussion, use of mathematics and statistics in an economic context
4) show a knowledge of current affairs
5) make a contribution in the discussion of current economic issues, particularly those affecting the individual directly.

Methods

This will vary across teachers and classes but the following techniques might be usefully employed:

1) traditional teacher-directed activities
2) use of simulations and games
3) inquiry, by the use of statistics and information
4) use of drama
5) pupil initiative (e.g. project work, surveys)
6) imaginative written work
7) pupil experience (e.g. part-time work, factory visits).

Scheme of work (four periods a week)

Autumn term

1) Introduction to economics
   a) Basic economic problems: unlimited wants, limited resources, scarcity and choice; factors of production; personal economic problem (lack of pocket money); family economic problem – typical family expenditure
   b) growing richer: importance of investment in capital goods; opportunity costs
2) Standards of living:
   a) production – what it is, classification (primary, secondary, tertiary)
   b) specialization – different types, division of labour
   c) wealth and standard of living – what is meant by the two terms
   d) Third World – what it is, problems and solutions
3) Transport:
   a) different types – advantages and disadvantages of different forms
   b) cost of transport – public and private cost of running a car
4) Project work: Ideas include job surveys – types and location of work; spending patterns – different ages; Third World countries; factories in Knaresborough (parents, etc.); imports – family cars, etc.; how we used to live in Britain; economics on a tropical island

Spring term

1) Working and earning:
   a) occupational distribution of labour
   b) why wages vary: differentials; methods of payment – piece-rate, time-rate, salary, etc.
   c) receiving your pay: cheque or cash; gross pay, net pay, deductions; where deductions go (importance of government spending)
2) Money management:
   a) barter and the history of money
   b) the development of commercial banking; banks – their function and service; bank accounts
   c) building societies and housing

3) Protecting yourself:
   a) insurance – what it is, how it works, types of insurance
   b) life assurance – different types
   c) Lloyd's of London – brief history and description

Summer term

1) Spending your money:
   a) Retailing: what it is; advantages and disadvantages of different retailers; trends in retailing; shopping in Knaresborough
   b) buying goods on credit
   c) importance of spending – demand, unemployment and inflation
2) Advertising:
   a) What it is: its different forms; advantages and disadvantages
   b) advertising campaigns: agencies; examples; effects
   c) consumer protection: main legislation; institutions

Assessment

Assessment is based on a final examination carrying a 70% weighting and a coursework element. The coursework element will be graded in the following way:

excellent	25%
good	20%
satisfactory	15%
poor	10%

Appendix 2: CSE Mode 3(S) – Social Economics

Aims

1) to prepare the pupils to cope with the economic aspect of a number of roles they will encounter when they leave school; these roles are specified in the syllabus content
2) to develop a range of practical and academic skills at a level necessary to cope with common socio-economic roles
3) to encourage the pupils to be confident and adaptable in the pursuit of these roles
4) to promote 'economic literacy' which requires an understanding of the wider context of the system into which these roles might fit (e.g. money and banking)
5) to provide pupils with experience of industry and commerce by the use of visits, speakers, projects and, where apprpriate, work experience
6) to develop wider, cross curricular skills such as numeracy, literacy, comprehension and expression.

Objectives

By the end of the course candidates should be able to:

1) identify and distinguish the economic roles a young person may encounter
2) perform simple calculations related to these economic roles
3) define and discuss the main economic institutions and concepts described in the syllabus content
4) convert figures into graphical form and translate graphs into figures, recognizing their significance
5) interpret information, both written and numerical, showing the ability to appraise and compare this information
6) collect and categorize (organize and express) information by the use of reference books, surveys, visits and interviews, and organize and express this in both written and oral forms

Assessment

Pupils will submit three 'economic profiles' on topics of a differing nature, each carrying 10% of the final mark. Examples may be 'worker profiles', 'business profiles', 'market research'. Objectives 1–5 will collectively account for 60% of these marks, objective 6 the remaining 40%. Pupils will be set three interim and one final examination, collectively carrying 70% of the final mark. Objectives 1 and 3 will carry a weighting of 70% objectives 2, 4 and 5 will carry a 30% weighting.

3) Consumer protection: legislation to protect the consumer; guarantees, codes of practice and Kitemarks; channels of complaint

Summer term

Unemployment: the pattern of unemployment; causes and effects of unemployment; youth unemployment; what can be done about employment.

Scheme of work for year four

Autumn term

1) The young person as a consumer: the basic and sophisticated wants of mankind; how these wants are satisfied – consumption; what is a consumer?; the importance of the consumer; introduce concepts of demand, production, unemployment
2) Obtaining the resources to satisfy wants: specialization; earning a wage; wage differences – why they exist, examples; methods of payment – time, piece, salary payments; advantages/disadvantages of the employer/employee; receiving your pay – wage slips, deductions; taxation, national insurance – how it works, what it pays for; voluntary deductions

Spring term

11) Retailing: definition of retailing; different classifications of retail outlets; shopping survey of Knaresborough; advantages and disadvantages of different retail outlets; changes in retail outlets, including the introduction of new technology; different methods of paying for goods (e.g. credit cards, hire purchase)
2) Advertising: types of advertising; advertising media, their advantages and disadvantages; case study of an advertising campaign

Scheme of work for year five

Autumn term

1) Money and finance: the nature and functions of money; methods of payment; banks and the services they provide; the young person as a saver – alternatives and savings institutions; the young person as a debtor – alternative forms of credit; inflation and its effects
2) The young person as a job seeker: the pattern of employment in the UK; finding a job – sources of information; applying for a job; the job interview
3) The young person as an employee: types of employers; the advantages/disadvantages of different forms of business organization; business and worker profiles; trades unions – advantages/disadvantages of membership; industrial relations

Spring term

Mock examination.

1) The young person as a taxpayer: revision – main types of taxation; principles of taxation; government expenditure – its structure and desirability
2) The structure and role of government: local and central government; the individual's role – elections, candidates and voters; the role of the government in the economy – direct and indirect intervention

3) Britain in the world economy; terminology of international trade; the pattern of UK trade; the advantages of international trade; the EEC – its structure, advantages and disadvantages

Summer term

Revision.

Final examination.

End of course.

Section 5 *A School's History and a School's Thinking*

18 A course biography: the changing face of economic awareness in a core course, 1974–86

Peter Thomas

Ashington High School, Northumberland

Ashington is a 13–18 comprehensive school with between 1,000 and 1,050 pupils, of whom 120 are in the sixth form. It is one of two high schools in a large town situated about three miles from the coast and 20 miles from Newcastle upon Tyne in a declining coal mining area. It is surrounded by a rural community and yet is one of the most densely populated areas in Northumberland. The type and nature of employment is changing from extractive and engineering towards processing, small manufactures and tertiary. Unemployment stands at about 19%. The pupils come from a good mixture of socio-economic groups, but, overall, they tend to lack ambition and belief in their own abilities, and parental pressure is not excessive.

The course

A glance at the school's timetable reveals mysterious letters appearing for both fourth and fifth year pupils – PDC. This case study poses three questions:

1) what is meant by PDC?
2) how did it become part of the curriculum?
3) what is the relevance of economic awareness to PDC?

Responses to these questions attempt to trace the historical development of the course and to indicate the current provision of economic awareness within it.

Stage 1 (c. 1974): liberal studies

Liberal studies was introduced into the curriculum when the school was changing from grammar to comprehensive. Initially both fourth and fifth year pupils were to receive their 'dose' in mixed-ability form groups, lasting a double lesson of 70 minutes. The course was devised by a working party which was then dissolved, leaving a single teacher (also Head of Economics) in charge and, as its major resource, the Schools Council Humanities Pack. A number of teachers (mainly volunteers, and several of them probationers) was found from the science, arts and humanities to teach the course. Some resources were produced centrally or recommended by the teacher in charge, but each teacher more or less followed his or her own interests and routes. There was no rotation of staff, but a lot of team-teaching evolved. There was some experiential learning, but it was largely a diet of passive, information giving. Economic awareness elements are difficult to discern in the course structure, which is outlined below:

The individual	Development of personality
	Problems of age groups
Close	Family and functions
relationships	Families abroad
	Changed role of sexes

Group	Tribe, gang, club, etc.
relationships	Deviant behaviour
	Class and status
	Race/problems of immigrants
Ideas	Mass media
and attitudes	World religions
	Polls and surveys
Education	Types of schools
	Curriculum
	Organization
Work	Choice of careers
	Changes in working conditions
	Discontent
	Automation
Local	Local government
community	Urban/rural problems
National	Central government
society	Law and order
	Welfare state
	Housing and poverty
The world	Population
	Commonwealth/EEC/world
	World organizations
	World trade
	Developing countries

Stage 2 (1975–9): CSE Mode-3 Social Studies

After discussions at various levels, it was decided to give greater status (from both pupil and staff viewpoints) to liberal studies by turning it into an externally examined course. The following five topics were chosen:

The Family
Politics
Mass Media
Work and Careers
Immigration/Housing/Poverty/Education

Each teacher taught one set throughout the course, the setting being determined by performance in mathematics and English. Teaching materials for each topic were centrally produced by two or three staff and included a suggested teaching order,

methods and examinable content. The content was largely sociological, but aspects of economic awareness were to be found in the areas of 'Politics' and 'Work and Careers'. Pupils were still seen as passive receivers of information – for example, 'these are the main forms of taxation' and 'this is what is happening in primary/secondary/tertiary job sectors'.

Stage 3 (1980–1): Personal Development course (PDC), Mark 1

In 1980 the letters PDC were created to replace the course name Social Studies. 'Expert' teachers were to be introduced, specializing and rotating so that a wider number of modules/topics could be taught. Another eight topics were added:

Decision-making
Me and my Planet
Body Maintenance
Health/Moral Education
Consumer Society
Societies
Industrial Society
Housing and Finance

Pupils now covered any nine of the thirteen 'modules' over the five terms, depending on staff availability and the rotation sequence employed. A definite place for economic awareness (though it was not called that at the time) was found in the 'Consumer Society' and 'Industrial Society' modules (see Appendix 1).

The time allowed for each module was 70 minutes per week for seven weeks. The modules were like mini-commerce and mini-economics subject courses and the emphasis was on giving information considered by the teachers to be of use to pupils in their preparation for life. However, a flexible examination course and the use of specialist teachers did begin to affect teaching styles, and some role-playing was attempted in the consumer module and case studies were used in both.

Stage 4 (1981–2): PDC, Mark 2

A curriculum review was undertaken in 1981. One of the few resultant changes was the introduction to PDC of 'O' Level Integrated Humanities (Joint Matriculation Board) to stretch and motivate the most-able pupils (the top three English sets). Link courses with the local technical college for mixed-ability groups going on 'Motor Vehicle Maintenance' and 'Beauty and Grooming' courses were also introduced.

Integrated Humanities proved to be of use in a number of ways. It mirrored the topics in the CSE Social Studies course and an interesting mix of topics was possible to suit the specialisms of the staff involved. The assessment system allowed a wider variety of teaching approaches to be employed, with increasing use of case studies and decision-making exercises. In addition to the topics of 'Mass Media' and 'The Family', three others included elements of economic awareness. 'People and Work' dealt with the need to work and the effects of work, spheres of work, organization of work and the government and work. 'Consumer Affairs' included shopping, sales promotion and consumer protection. The 'Poverty' topic raised issues like the problems of defining poverty, poverty in Britain, poverty in the third world, and human reactions to poverty.

Also, in May 1982, the Headteacher drew up a list of general aims for PDC. These were that pupils should:

1) understand the workings of the British political system at national and local level
2) understand the structure of the economy and the ways in which Britain makes and spends money
3) leave school equipped with certain basic social and life skills, vocational skills, personal skills
4) make contact with the local community, understanding its resources and the way of life and make regular contact with its people
5) develop leisure experiences and interests
6) understand and appreciate the various roles of the adult (e.g. family, consumers, etc.)
7) learn about their physical and emotional development as a means to self understanding and responsibility
8) consider moral issues as a basis to decision-making and character development
9) develop some understanding of the world of work and unemployment.

These, along with the further aim of providing pupils (where appropriate and possible) with opportunities to sample semi-vocational courses and to gain experience outside the school community, formed the basis for the next development.

Stage 5 (1982–3): PDC, Mark 3

In 1982, one half of the fourth year was moved on to a non-examination, modular Personal and Social Education (PSE) course:

Modules (6/7/8/9-week duration)
Personal Relations (sex education)
Health Education (drugs, alcohol, etc.)
Computer Appreciation
Law and Order
Moral Education (RE, family matters, etc.)
Mass Media
Current Affairs/Politics
Consumer Literacy (wants, needs, scarcity, budgeting, pay and deductions, consumer protection)
People and Work/Industrial Relations (see Appendix 2 for details)

Pupils were to receive a 'dose' from most of these modules over a two-year period. The other half of the fourth year continued to take either CSE Social Studies or 'O' level Integrated Humanities.

Stage 6 (1983–4): PDC, Mark 4

A decision taken late in June 1983 led to the introduction of a completely non-assessed modular PSE course for all fourth year pupils. The modules came from those listed above and operated over a six to nine week rotation. At this time one half of the fifth year pupils were following examination courses and the other half had a one-term leisure course and a one-term technical college link course of work experience.

Stage 7 (1984–5): PDC, Mark 5A

All pupils in the fourth year followed a PSE modular course, while all those in the fifth year followed a Leisure course and/or link courses and/or work experience.

The leisure courses included an option run jointly by the two economics and business studies teachers. This had started as an extension of the fourth year modular course to fill in the gaps for some pupils, but for various reasons it ended up as a giant, experimental, experiential learning module. Many games, role-plays and simulations were carried out, including units like *Bank Loan*,[1] 'Community Expenditure', 'Public Spending',[2] *Grain Drain*[3] and the *Poverty Game*.[4]

Stage 8 (1985–6): PDC, Mark 5B

This stage consisted of a repeat of the previous year's work, with minor modifications to the range of modules and courses available; and with the extension of work experience to some 55 pupils out of 320 in the fifth year.

Stage 9 (1986–7): PDC, Mark 6

The fourth year is continuing as it has done in the two previous years. Timetabling problems have prevented a rearrangement of teaching groups by tutor groups instead of English/maths sets. The fifth year course appears to be 'almost accidentally'

turning into a mixture of 'recreational courses' and 'pre-vocational courses':

Recreation	*Pre-vocational*
Health and Related Fitness	Motor Vehicle Maintenance
Youth Leadership	Construction Trades
Outdoor Pursuits	Instant Fashion
Healthy Eating	Hair Care
Photography/Video	Beauty Care
Music	Pre-nursery Nursing
	Young Enterprise
	Work Experience

Stage 10 (1987 onwards): PDC, Mark 7?

At some time in the near or distant future, Ashington High will join the TVEI scheme which already operates in five of Northumberland's 16 high schools. Indeed, in time all 16 schools will be involved. At present, TVEI provision in those five schools affects a relatively small proportion of the pupil population. One question which has to be faced is whether the school adopts this same system or whether it creates a scheme which will affect the whole school population. Current thinking in the school seems to favour the latter and first plans indicate the following possible changes:

1) change a five-option block system into a six-option block system with consequent changes in the number of periods per subject, etc.
2) create courses or linked subjects that will be taught across two option blocks (e.g. the Hampshire Business and Information Studies scheme)
3) arrange some form of rotation so that pupils in one half of the year group 'taste' more than one course, with perhaps some narrowing of choice in the fifth year
4) link 3 above in with the existing PDC course; or perhaps undertake a more radical change of PDC to integrate with and enrich these new courses.

Whatever plan is finally adopted, PDC will change,

However, much of it will be easily adapted to meet the needs of TVEI. For example, work experience is an important element in any TVEI scheme; and links for pre-vocational tasters at the technical college and contacts with local industry and commerce are extensive. (In October 1986, 91 out of 333 pupils from across the ability range in the fifth year were on permanent work experience, one afternoon per week, for two terms.)

The Young Enterprise scheme is also well established in the school. In 1986–7, for example, a group of 28 pupils opted to take part in Young Enterprise for two terms. The scheme is being run by three advisers from the nearby Alcan UK smelter plant.

What is more speculative is the future structure and role of the fourth year PDC course. Where and how will 'economic awareness' fit into the model? What 'economic awareness' ought to be taught to all of our pupils? For example, the module illustrated in Appendix 2 has been used for the past three years. This has never failed to stimulate the pupils, not least because of the extensive experiential learning techniques employed. However, will it become redundant under a TVEI scheme since it may simply repeat part of some other courses? Or, will it become a mandatory module for all pupils in some gigantic unit-accreditation scheme of assessment?

Conclusions

PDC has, then, a long and evolving history at Ashington High School and further change seems inevitable.

Initially, the introduction of liberal studies into the curriculum was undertaken by the school's curriculum development committee. Subsequent developments have been initiated almost exclusively by a small group of staff, including the present and former Heads of Economics/PDC, the former Careers teacher, and the present Headteacher. This group has now been augmented by a team of committed volunteer teachers who, in most cases, have developed their own specialist modules.

General comments about the teaching styles adopted over the years have already been made.

What needs stressing is that since 1983 a major shift in teaching styles has taken place. The impetus for this came from the then Head of English who was sitting in on the first PDC review meeting. He had listened as each of the teachers involved had briefly explained what they did and taught in their modules. He agreed that much of the information was useful and probably interesting in its own right, but asked 'what do the pupils *do* in their lessons?' A fair summary of the responses would be, 'not a lot!' This challenge, together with the introduction of non-examinable courses for all, radically changed teaching styles and strategies used. Role-plays, simulations, case studies, visits, visiting speakers, group decision, marketing exercises and even meditation are now commonplace. In fact it has created one problem: what can be set when a teacher is absent on a PDC afternoon, and can the substitute teacher cope with the nature of the work?

The status given to the course has also altered over the years. The arrival of the present Headteacher in 1979 boosted the status of the course. He encouraged the building up of staff teams and gave it some priority on the timetable. Those 'on the team' are volunteers and are fully committed to the course, but many staff still steer well clear.

Staff development has been left almost entirely to the individual teacher. Three teachers shared attendance at a DES regional course entitled 'Life and Social Skills'; but apart from the INSET run in conjunction with the dissemination phase of the Economics Education 14–16 Project, no other courses have been available. It is hoped that Northumberland's plans under the new national INSET provisions to be introduced in April 1987 will give schools the opportunity to organize their own staff development programmes.

References

1 *Bank Loan*, Banking Information Service, 1984.
2 Economics Association, *Understanding Economics*, Longman, 1985.
3 *Grain Drain*. Available from Christian Aid, PO Box 1, London SW9 8BH.
4 *Poverty Game*. Available from Christian Aid, PO Box 1, London SW9 8BH.

Appendix 1: Economic awareness in the PDC course, 1980–1

10 Consumer Society

a) consumer protection and guidance: legislation; agencies; organization; government departments
b) shopping wisely: responsibilities of consumers; types of shop; sales psychology
c) advertising: types; media; psychology
d) credit buying: credit sales; hire purchase; credit cards; loans; budget accounts
e) budgeting: necessity for it; construction and breakdown of budgets

12 Industrial Society

a) organization of industry: primary, secondary, tertiary; private and public
b) location of industry: factors affecting; government influence; local examples
c) employees: types; trades unions; wages; taxes and other deductions
d) operation and management of a firm: departments; planning; production; distribution
e) current issues

Appendix 2: The People and Work/Industrial Relations module

1) why work? – the changing nature of work
(discussion; exercise; quiz)

2) internal organization of firms
(filmstrip; follow-up exercise)

3) structure of local firm
(visit to a firm; questionnaire)

4) the language of the world of work
(filmstrip; follow-up exercise)

5) wage negotiation
(role-play – 'Wages' from the 14–16 Economics Project)

6) role of unions
(discussion; case studies; speaker)

7) issues; procedure at work
(examples; quiz)

8) the work of the shop steward
(video; follow-up exercise, Q/A).

19 Economic awareness at Southgate School, Enfield

Sarah Wilkinson and Sara Wall

This case study is written in two parts and from two different perspectives. Part 1 is written by the Head of Economics, responsible for encouraging the school to introduce economic awareness into its curriculum. She has now moved to another teaching post in another LEA. Part 2 is written by the new Head of Economics who joined the staff of the school after a gap of one term. She describes her reactions to a change in which she was not involved.

Part 1

Ideas

I was keen to introduce economics into the lower school curriculum at Southgate School for several reasons.

First, I have a strong belief that everyone should be economically literate; indeed, DES documents since 1977 have advocated economic literacy for all. Very few students leaving Southgate School were economically literate. In the autumn of 1984, 'British Industrial Society' was offered as an option in years four and five and some 20 students per year were choosing the course. In the sixth form approximately 20 students per year were studying CSE/'O' level Economics and a further 20 were studying 'A' level Economics. The school was eight form entry with a sixth form of 200–250 students. That so few students were introduced to economics during their time at Southgate School concerned me greatly.

Second, I was concerned about the fact that students were opting for courses to follow in the upper school about which they knew nothing. An economics course in their first three years would

have put them in a better position to decide whether or not to study the subject further.

Third, economics was perceived as a 'male' subject with very few girls opting for it. It was my feeling that a core economics course in the first three years might help to destroy this stereotyped image – particularly if it was taught by both female and male members of staff. (I had been teaching a third year Integrated Social Science course at my previous school, along with a male colleague; and we had fairly equal numbers of boys and girls for economics in years 4–7.) At Southgate School economics was taught solely by male members of staff from 1977 to 1984.

Finally, having taught third year economics in the past, I felt able to counter the possible argument that 'economics is too difficult for younger students'.

I therefore decided to put the case forward that economics should form part of the lower school core course.

Innovation

The core course at the school is organized as a carousel. When it was first established the format was as follows:

Years 1–3
1 period per week
9-week modules
4 modules per year

Years 4–6
2 periods per week
6-week modules
6 modules per year

The core philosophy can be summarized as follows. First, it should contain areas of study to which all students should be introduced before leaving school. Second, it should be committed to mixed-ability teaching and learning situations. Third, it should emphasize student-centred and active learning approaches whereby the development of skills can be encouraged.

The process of incorporating economics into the lower school core involved discussions with the core coordinator, the Deputy Headteachers and the Headteacher. It was necessary to convince them that an economics course was compatible with the core philosophy. I circulated a document stating the case and enclosed material which I considered to be supportive (see Appendix 1).

The core coordinator was in favour of including economics in the core but did not want to drop any of the existing modules. He also wished to introduce other new modules in years one, two and three. We decided between us to push for a change in the lower school core programme so that it had the same format as in years four, five and six.

The Deputy Headteachers and the Headteacher considered in detail the proposed changes to the lower school core programme over a period of four or five months. They needed little persuasion that the course would probably be valuable; and seemed more concerned with the practical problems associated with its implementation. However, the format of the lower school core was changed and economics was included as an addition to the 'World of Work' modules in each of years one, two and three.

Teaching/learning/ assessment

The aim was to develop active learning situations which would allow and encourage the students to develop an economics perspective on issues. Students would be learning the skill of applying the concept of opportunity cost to a variety of issues. It was also hoped that the use of role-plays, simulations, group work and a variety of stimulus materials would encourage the development of broader educational skills such as numeracy, communication and cooperation.

The structure of the course is explained in Appendix 2. Ten units of work were devised. Since all students were starting economics for the first time it was decided that all would begin with the same experience. After that it was suggested that units of work be chosen depending on the interests of the staff and students; no unit should last for more than two weeks; and homework, if set, should be skills-based (e.g. investigative work). The idea was that staff teaching the course would have clear guidelines but could be flexible within that broad framework.

Details of the assessment for the course were not finalized by July 1985. A key idea of the core was that students should be responsible, at least in part, for assessing their own progress in all their modules. The core coordinator was to develop a student self-assessment sheet for completion during the lesson, and this would cover the broad educational skills. This would be supplemented by teacher assessment based not only on written work but also on observation of students during the lessons. The limitations of this were recognized but it was felt important to move away from more formal and traditional methods of assessment, given the informal nature of the course.

Part 2

It was inevitable that, when I arrived as the new Head of Economics, someone would ask me what I thought of the lower school economics course. Whilst I had thoughts about it, it was something I had not studied carefully for a number of reasons. As Head of Economics in a department whose existence depends upon examination courses, my timetable is restricted to fourth, fifth and sixth year classes. The school is split, with the first, second and third years being taught 'down the road', where I have no reason to visit regularly because of my upper school teaching commitment. The day-to-day running of economics in the core curriculum comes under the core coordinator's umbrella rather than mine. The person who teaches the economics component is not in the economics department and so does not participate in departmental discussion.

I started to think about the course under the following heads:

1) the course as a set of materials
2) teaching and learning methods
3) pupil assessment
4) staffing and staff support
5) the place of economics in the core curriculum
6) the extent to which the course achieves its aims.

Consequently, in an attempt to address these issues, information was gathered from the following people who have had varying degrees of involvement in the course:

- the Head of Lower School (in charge of curriculum) – an economics specialist
- the core coordinator – a non-specialist
- the teacher of the course – a non-specialist pupil
- an Enfield economics teacher seconded for a year as an LEA Associate to the University of London Institute of Education

The course as a set of materials

Given that the units in the course are mainly taken from *Understanding Economics*,[1] the course seems to encounter some of the problems associated with these resources. The pupil materials are not intended to be prescriptive, but aim to provide teachers with a base from which to develop their own ideas for lesson structure, both context and organization. In this it is presumed that the instructions and explanation of terminology are sufficient to take the teacher inside the ethos of the materials, and enable him or her to run the activities in the implicitly desired way. However, in practice this is more difficult since, as the seconded teacher commented, 'there is a minimum of information on *how* to debrief pupils'.

Another problem may be that the materials become the course. Whilst there are links between the *Understanding Economics* units, the materials cannot become an adequate course 'as there is no discernible theme running through them'. Of course the materials were designed as a resource pack to allow the teachers to pursue their own and the pupils' interests. However, this presupposes

that teachers have a notion of economic literacy and can select material appropriately. Insights into the ways in which the units are used in the classroom do, therefore, appear to be crucial if the stated aims of the course are to be examined.

Teaching and learning methods

One of the purposes of the core programme is to give space for 'active learning'. More accurately, this means non-didactic teaching, since the Head of Lower School sees teachers as being entrenched in traditional methods in the mainstream curriculum because of the pressure of time, pupil expectations, syllabus constraints, etc. Core lessons therefore provide staff with the opportunity to experiment in the classroom without having to offer up their subject discipline as a sacrifice. Of course this opportunity may not always be taken up given the range of courses and multitude of staff in the core programme.

In the economics lessons the allocation of time (used as a loose reflection of teaching style) during a 70-minute lesson, as identified by the teacher, was typically:

instructions	5–10 minutes
teacher talk	5 + minutes
questions and answers	5–10 minutes
group work	35 + minutes (half the lesson)
written work	10–15 minutes

These crude divisions are not necessarily mutually exclusive, but the teacher sees lessons as being dominated by group work. This might well be because 'group work' is an all-embracing term for different types of activity and simple physical grouping of pupils. When pupils were involved in these groups he 'flitted from group to group – showing interest and encouragement', indicating that they were involved in some specified task. What about the pupils? Did they perceive the organization of the lesson in this way?

The writers devised a questionnaire which was given by the Head of Careers (who teaches the economics component) to 25 second year and 50 third year pupils. Appendix 3 shows the questionnaire and reproduces the response of one third year girl. This particular pupil is quite evidently receptive to working with other pupils rather than receiving information from the teacher. She verifies this in her response to the question about the connection with what happens in other lessons: 'It was connected by working in groups'.

Pupil responses generally indicated that a variety of non-didactic teaching styles, possibly pupil-centred activities, were occurring in the classroom. Pupils also felt that the variety within lessons made them more enjoyable and the subject easier to learn, although some did not see teacher talk as contributing to this: one third year boy commented that 'the teachers do go on a bit', and one third year girl did not like the teacher 'spending 10 minutes on one aspect'.

These comments might have implications for the debriefing of pupils, since pupils might be more prepared to listen to the teacher when they are receiving instructions before embarking on activities than when the outcomes of activities are being discussed. There is, moreover, no clear indication from the pupils' responses or from the teacher that debriefing takes place in the classroom, and indeed sometimes written homework had to be used to complete work started in class.

The responses indicate some agreement that combinations of different styles are used in core lessons, but little is said about what is being learnt (although some pupils say they are enjoying lessons).

Pupil assessment

The core course is non-examinable. Whilst this has caused problems of motivation in the fourth and fifth years, this has not been the case in the lower school. In general pupil assessment is by means of written homework tasks. In addition, during the lesson the teacher checks to see if things are 'going well' and whether or not pupils are 'doing work'. But whilst this describes a lesson in isolation, can it highlight its purpose? Can it also provide a means for either teacher or pupil to assess attainment over time? Since both teacher and pupils identify the greater part of the lesson revolving around group work, does there not need to be some pre-determined and specific purpose in the teacher visiting

each group, and, if not, might pupils either use the teacher as a means of resolving problems rather than handling them themselves, or seek to avoid pursuing the task by not requesting help or bringing their presence to the attention of the teacher?

One third year boy enjoyed 'core' because 'it wasted time'. However, the same boy said he disliked the core because it was 'boring', as there was 'not enough to do'. Perhaps this response comes from a lack of understanding of the purpose of the lessons and might point to the need for a means of assessment during group activities which could help provide the pupil with a structure to understand the work. His comment also has implications for the debriefing of pupils, and its importance as an integral part of the course.

When pupils were asked to reflect upon one of the lessons from the economics component of 'core', some second and third year pupils chose the 'Survival Game' (see Appendix 2). They were asked to consider what they though they had learnt from the lesson:

'I learnt that in the real world, you need to group up to be able to survive.'

'How to make fish and igloos and ponchos out of cardboard. I don't think it was worth it because they did not fit me.'

'How to cooperate.'

'I have learnt a lot from these lessons because I had never heard of this subject before I came to this school.'

'I learnt that people can't make things all come at once.'

'How to tackle the real world.'

These responses refer to the activity both in a descriptive manner and in terms of the interpretation and application of ideas. This may in part be due to differing interpretations of the question, but it may also be a further indication of the need for debriefing – knowing *what* happened is only of use as an illustration of *why* the activities were being run.

Another reason for clearly defined monitoring during lesson time is to prevent assessment being based only on written work done in the teacher's absence. Whilst a teacher cannot totally control the dynamic environment which exists within the classroom, he or she might have an opportunity to use the experiences brought into the classroom and dovetail them into the new experiences which are being provided. Once a pupil leaves the classroom such potential scope is considerably diminished.

There may, therefore, be a strong case for introducing structured internal assessment into the 'core' programme, not to increase motivation, but to ensure that pupils and teacher have the kind of information necessary to make judgements about the quality of the activities, individual inputs to them and to consider outcomes.

The core coordinator would like to have staff who are enthusiastic about and committed to their contribution to the core programme. However, it is unlikely that a 'team' of core programme teachers could be created in the present situation of staffing constraint and the low priority given to the staffing of the core which leads to teachers coming to it because they have slack in their timetables. In this situation, compensating factors like staff development time for teaching and learning strategies, classroom management and assessment, and a firm view on the meaning of economic awareness, might reasonably be expected. However, in practice the following situation has arisen:

1)   the class teacher goes in and 'teaches' the economics module, concerning him/herself with the day-to day running of the course
2)   the co-ordinator has the authority to adapt the course, but is receiving little feedback about the economics component.

Economic awareness has, therefore, achieved its slot in the lower school curriculum with a minimum of staff interaction. Its validity will not be challenged until another module is proposed in its stead. But will it be possible for staff to defend economic awareness if they do not meet together to formulate a common and coherent rationale for its existence and operation?

Economics in the core within the curriculum

The Head of Lower School was reluctant to talk about a rationale, since this might imply 'control of the curriculum'. Instead he described the school's curriculum as a set of 'historical compromises'. Amongst other factors, parental pressures had ensured the continuation of a mainly traditional subject-based curriculum. The core therefore existed as an attempt to patch up some of the holes. He also viewed 'core' positively – as a way of *extending* the curriculum to allow pupils to sample the 'surplus knowledge' on offer. The limitations in examining the curriculum as a range of subject disciplines meant, in his view, emphasis on the need to concentrate upon the quality of experiences which pupils encounter. Changes are therefore difficult to implement and compromises have been made.

In 1983 the timetable was changed from a 35 to a 40 period week to allow for the introduction of the core programme. This shows some commitment to the principle of core.

The Head of Lower School justified the inclusion of economic awareness in the 'core' programme in the following terms:

1)   little is known about wealth creation
2)   problems of allocation are interesting
3)   there is a mistaken belief that economics and commerce are synonymous, and this needs to be rectified.

However, he also accepted that the place of economics as a mainstream examination option subject gives it claims to be offered to a wider audience of pupils – the historical compromise again. Whilst this might appear to be arguing for an extension of a subject-based curriculum, he also saw a need to reduce the number of subject labels and to examine the curriculum for areas of duplication.

This seems to imply that the debate about economic awareness may be of more use than the reasons for establishing a timetable slot for economics. He also emphasized the need 'to devise appropriate teaching methods and strategies' for mixed-ability classes and stressed the importance of assessment and evaluation, making clear that as teachers 'we make qualitative as well as quantitative judgements'. Economic awareness could, therefore, act as a vehicle for much of the debate which will be required if these issues are to be tackled.

Does the course achieve its aim?

The course has involved the use of non-didactic teaching. This does not necessarily imply that active learning has occurred, but pupils enjoyed lessons and the teacher found the different organization easier to manage as the course progressed. The teacher felt that pupils were sometimes overwhelmed by the activities. Possible reasons for this might include:

- there was too much for pupils to do
- pupils were not adequately debriefed
- the teacher was not happy with the classroom organization
- the activity was inappropriate

Whether or not the different style of teaching has facilitated the development of an economic perspective is impossible to judge, because of the lack of assessment and a clear description of what an economics perspective is. Whilst the stated key concepts and key ideas can be interpreted, both the specialist and non-specialist economics teachers require a working definition. The use of jargon leaves greater scope for interpretation and misinterpretation by the practitioner. This is of particular significance as the economics component of the core forms half of the unit called 'World of Work'; the other half of the unit is careers education, with the entire unit being taught by the Head of Careers. He feels the aim of 'World of Work' is to create an awareness of the implications of work, and that the function of economics is to relate to work. This could be interpreted as a financial view involving some decision-making, rather than the application of opportunity cost analysis to specific issues to try to make sense of them.

Pupils were asked what the term world of work meant to them (see Appendix 3, Question 5). Here are some representative responses:

> 'what kinds of jobs there are and how to live in the real world'
> 'means thinking about things that are happening outside school'
> 'the preparation of the life ahead of me'
> 'learning how to manage when we leave school'
> 'what goes on after school'
> 'it means jobs for people'

These responses seem to imply that pupils have picked up a message about jobs, with the emphasis being that what they do in lessons will be important to them when they leave school, rather than relevant to understanding the system which they are part of now.

Where next?

Already one step has been taken, because from September 1986 all fourth and fifth year pupils have a module of economic and political literacy which uses 'Land Use Planning' (*Understanding Economics*) as its starting point. This means that all pupils receive some economics education in every year of their compulsory schooling. However, this gives no indication of the outcome of the course for pupils. When examining the materials the seconded teacher commented that 'teachers might be running the activities and relying on the course being designed so well that economic awareness evolves'. His suggestion was that particular focus should be on coherence, continuity and progression.

Any attempt to do this will depend on staff cooperation being made available to guarantee a professional approach.

Another important step may be to identify issues about which staff should be conscious. These will then need to be examined to promote a greater understanding of the important questions which exist so that possible strategies to deal with them can be formulated. Whilst the following is not a comprehensive list these are questions which seem applicable to Southgate School.

1) What is economic awareness and can we provide a working definition which will be useful to *all* staff?
2) Who is responsible for economic awareness?
3) How can a coherent course be developed which can be followed by non-specialists and specialists, without being prescriptive?
4) How can duplication be avoided and continuity between years ensured?
5) What is active learning? Is it appropriate for mixed-ability groups? How can classrooms be organized and managed to facilitate active learning within mixed-ability groups?

6) What assessment techniques will give data as to whether or not pupils are acquiring an economics perspective?

The introduction of an economic awareness course at Southgate School happened because of an individual's commitment to economic literacy and her teaching experience in another school. This in itself was an achievement. Whilst it is impossible to make any generalizations from our experience at Southgate, the need for staff development must be emphasized. The success of such a curriculum development depends on teachers making sense of what is happening, and then being actively involved in implementation, evaluation and further development at all levels.

Reference

1 Economics Association, *Understanding Economics*, Longman, 1985.

Appendix 1: Documents given to the Headteacher in support of the case for economic awareness

Document 1: paper written by Head of Economics, S. K. Wilkinson, October 1984
Document 2: background outline paper on economic literacy – a statement from the Economics Research and Curriculum Unit at the Institute of Education, August 1984
Document 3: Example of lower school economics input
Document 4: example of economic analysis – taken from *The Guardian*, 24 September 1984

Document 1

Economics below the fourth year

1) The third years have the option of studying British Industrial Society in years four and five

and have no idea at all of what the course will be like. Some economics in the third year would give them an idea of the subject and they would be in a better position to make the choice.

2) The majority of pupils at Southgate School leave, never having studied any economics. I believe that since we all play a part in the economic system, we should all be given a chance to try to understand it.

3) I do not wish to teach third years complicated economic theories, but I do want to give them an 'economic perspective' which I think is possible (having taught economics to third years at my last school).

It is often argued that the content of a subject is less important than the discipline itself – it is the chance to study the subject discipline that allows pupils to acquire and develop certain skills which may be useful and beneficial for the pupil.

In history, for example, is it important which periods are studied? Surely it is more important for students to be allowed to develop an historical perspective which can be applied to any issue which is presented to them throughout their lives?

An economics perspective can only serve to enhance the gains from studying subjects such as history and geography; and would allow a fuller understanding of contemporary issues.

Practical problems

1) Timetable
I would ideally like to teach all the third year classes for a double lesson every week, but I can see that the problems with this would be very difficult to overcome.

I suggest teaching economics as part of the core so that each class is taught for a double lesson over a 6-week period.

Is this a possibility bearing in mind the current content of the core?

2) Staffing
Ideally the course would be taught by the two economics specialists on the staff. Three possible lines of thought come to mind:

a) Lower sixth one-year 'O' level. This is currently taught in six 35-minute lessons per week. An alternative would be to organize this course on a 'self-teaching' basis in as little as two 35-minute lessons per week.

   Pupils would receive a textbook plus handouts and worksheets; and would receive clear guidance on the work to be completed each week. The lessons would be used to clear up any difficulties, return and discuss pupils' work and set work for the following weeks.

b) Both upper sixth 'A' level classes are taught in six lessons per week instead of eight. The Economics Department is therefore 'owed' four lessons per week. In addition, I have seven non-contact lessons per week when apparently I am entitled to eight. If there is support for teaching economics below the fourth year, then perhaps the school should be looking for a part-time economics teacher.

c) I know that there are members of staff who have economics qualifications. Would any of them like to teach economics? Do any of them have slack on their timetables? Does anyone have slack on their timetable which might allow some flexibility?

Document 2

What content area should/could legitimately be included in core programmes designed to promote economic literacy in the 14–18 curriculum? – A response from Linda Thomas and Steve Hodkinson

1)   The purpose of economics education

1.1) The content of school courses in economics gives the impression that the subject is sometimes viewed as a means of describing economic activity. Since the contexts in which economic activity occurs are limitless, school courses are often engaged in frantic effort to 'cover the ground' and it is difficult to determine exactly what is achieved.

Other courses (e.g. BIS) abandon the attempt. They concentrate, instead, on the provision of detailed information in one context. Once again the outcomes are not clear but it is doubtful if any of these courses encourage creative or critical responses. They are more likely to be concerned to transmit a 'received' view of the economic system.

1.2) We prefer to view economics as the kind of analytical and evaluative tool which provides the means objectively to investigate the meaning and function of economic activity. We believe that students should be encouraged to use a general theoretical framework to organize information and reflect on experience. The procedural framework which is derived from economic theory is the key to a true understanding of economic activity because its use encourages the development of the intellectual, procedural and practical skills which are necessary to handle information, coordinate data, explore relationships, form concepts, etc. These skills allow students to make sense, in their own terms, of the concepts (e.g. scarcity and choice, supply, demand and productivity) used by economists to define those relationships in the economic system which are of interest to them (e.g. the difference between income, value added and wealth, the effect of government, the links between money incomes, changing prices and living standards, the relationship of the parts to the whole, the consequence of changing technology for firms, industries and employment). These skills also allow students to generate an objective and dynamic base of information concerning the meaning of terms in common usage in economics (e.g. production, balance of payments, exports, credit, income, savings), the function and characteristics of institutions (e.g. trade unions, banks, local authorities) and of particular aspects of the economic system which bear on their lives (e.g. how prices are arrived at, how wages and other factor prices are determined, the role of money).

1.3) We believe that school courses should not transmit a received view. Rather, young people should be provided with access to an economic perspective through which they will gain appropriate knowledge and know-how that will empower them to act confidently in the complex world in an informed and competent way.

2) Apropriate contexts

2.1) Students can gain access to an economics perspective – the means for objective analysis – by applying the procedural framework in contexts which are within the range of their present experience.

It would be legitimate, within our argument, to expect students to be able to cope with and operate in such content areas as: advertising, budgeting, insurance, saving, the markets for motor bikes, football players, petrol, cigarettes, drink, leisure goods, fashion goods, LPs and the casual labour market.

2.2) It would be legitimate to prepare students for areas which they will experience in future by introducing them to such contexts as: work and wages; housing; leisure; the community; transport.

2.3) It would be legitimate to help students to cope with areas which will influence and affect their lives by introducing them to: the corporate activities of institutions – for example, banks, building societies, firms, trades unions, etc.; state activity, especially in such areas as education, health, revenue raising, etc.; the international dimension – for example, multinational companies, the EEC etc.; the dynamic forces in the economic system – for example, technological change.

Document 3

Third year social studies syllabus

Aims
To provide an introduction to basic economic ideas and problems; to introduce sociology and politics.

Objectives
1) to give a basic economic education to pupils who will not study economics at a higher level
2) to outline the nature of the social sciences to allow an informed choice of options at a higher level
3) to examine current economic problems and policies.

Syllabus
The economic problem: diagram, scarcity and choice; markets, comparison of auctions and shops

Demand and supply: use of lemonade computer game and radio programmes; demand and supply of labour

Unemployment: causes (e.g. demand for labour); effects on families and young people; policies to cure or ameliorate (e.g. youth training); rates of unemployment and social security benefit

Work: determination of wages, poverty trap; low pay, poverty trap, women's pay; teenagers' jobs and local position; rights at work, tribunals

Wealth: income compared with wealth; distribution

Class (sociology): determinants of class (e.g. income, wealth); the politics of the class structure; class links of the parties, effects of the distribution of seats (boundary changes); economic policies of the parties

Overview: examination of recent events in politics and economics (e.g. trade problems, inflation – use of a 'shopping basket' of goods; calculation of RPI

Time allocation
One lesson per week for half the academic year.

Document 4

An example of economic analysis taken from *The Guardian*, September 1984 – 'Economists offer new formula to end deadlock on pit closures'

'A new compromise has been submitted to bridge the gap between the National Coal Board and the National Union of Mineworkers over the definition of uneconomic pits.

The formula, prepared by two independent economists, rejects both the NCB and NUM criteria and suggests that pits should be closed only when their "real value" to the whole economy, in net output and social terms, is no longer positive.

The economists, Mr Gavyn Davies of the City

stockbrokers Simon and Coates and Professor David Metcalf, of the University of Kent, say that in general this would point to closure for most pits at a date somewhere between the loss of financial viability and the point of exhaustion.

The report, prepared for London Weekend TV's Weekend World, argues that the "real resource" criterion is capable of putting the word economic back into the issue of uneconomic pits.

The economists say it is insufficient to use NCB finance and accounting conventions to define uneconomic pits, because they take no account of the social costs or the true cost of labour in an underemployed economy. Equally, they argue, it is impossible to support the NUM criteria, which have no grounding in economics or welfare theory.

They insist that on resource grounds there may be a case for leaving loss-making pits open, or phasing them out more slowly, because even in these miners are contributing to national output.

"All recent governments have subsidised loss-making pits, implicitly recognising that resource gains are worth paying for," they say. "But now there are suspicions that a push is on towards a target of eventual break-even for the industry, a target which would mean substantial closures on top of the 4 million tonnes of capacity which was the immediate trigger for the dispute."

Mr Davies and Professor Metcalf say that simply halving NCB losses could involve the closure of 50 to 60 pits and the loss of 40,000 jobs. On narrow financial grounds, the pair say there is a strong case for early closure, but the financial return to the Treasury, after adjusting to redundancy and unemployment payments, would be between 3 and 5 per cent. This is "on the margin of desirability as a public investment."

The report suggests that on social and real resource grounds the worst pits should perhaps be closed at a rate of five or six a year over the next decade. This would be less than is needed for the coal board to break-even and much more than required under the mineworkers' exhaustion principle.

"Some pits in this group should almost certainly be closed immediately, others left open for 10 years or more." They also say that immediate closure of all "uneconomic" pits for financial reasons would involve significant losses of resources in the early years.'

Appendix 2: Lower school economics course

Key concepts

1) Opportunity cost: resources are scarce relative to wants, therefore choices must be made regarding:
    what to produce
    how to produce
    how much to produce
    how to distribute among members of the economy
2) Marginality: decisions made (see above) are at the margin
3) Efficiency: regarding the allocation of resources

Points 2 and 3 are really incorporated into the idea of opportunity cost.

Key ideas

The application of opportunity cost analysis to issues brings out other key ideas:

1) Inequality (e.g. of resources, income, wealth, race, education, health, sex, etc.)
2) Social + private costs; money + non-money costs – who pays?

Framework

Costs are incurred whenever a decision is made (at the margin) regarding the use of our scarce resources:
    who makes these decisions?
    what are the costs/benefits involved?
    who pays these costs?
    does it represent the best use of our resources?

Course outline

1) Survival simulation*: The simulation introduces: economic resources of land, labour and capital; scarcity of resources, choice and opportunity cost; specialization; interdependence

* Whitehead, D. J. ed. *Handbook for Economics Teachers*, Heinemann Educational, 1979.

2) Auction†: Simulation of an auction: shows that prices can allocate resources; income can be unequally distributed

3) Megatronics‡: Case study/role-play shows: labour as an economic resource; costs of unemployment (opportunity costs); decisions made regarding use of resources; who makes the decisions? who pays the costs?

4) Whose health is it anyway?§: This unit puts over the following ideas: a healthy population is a valuable economic resource; private/public sector – government intervention to provide basic health care for all; to what extent should the government legislate to improve the health of the population? actions by individuals which could damage their own health impose costs on others

5) Public transport: 'At the Bus Stop' §: Short script/play introduces: reasons for public transport + idea of subsidies; costs + benefits of decisions made regarding public transport (use of resources); who pays?

6) Wanting §: Exercise deals with advertising: advantages + disadvantages; decisions made regarding use of resources to advertise – opportunity costs; costs + benefits – who pays?

7) Vandalism ‖: Effect on resources; costs; who pays?

8) The Accident §: Costs incurred as a result of a road accident; who pays?

9) Hairdressers §: Case study drawing attention to costs and benefits of various courses of action that could be taken by a small business to try to get out of financial difficulty

10) Prisons: Exercise/role-play to consider the economics of prisons: costs/benefits; effectiveness; who pays?

Appendix 3: Pupil questionnaire about the core programme

Would you please answer these questions, which are about your core lessons.

This is not a test!

There are spaces for you to write your answers on the paper. If you want to write any more, there is a blank piece of paper at the end of the questionnaire.

1) What did you enjoy about 'core'? (List as many things as you want to.)

2) *Why* did you enjoy these things?

3) What did you not enjoy about 'core'? (List as many things as you want to.)

4) *Why* did you not enjoy these things?

5) Now try to remember the part of the core called WORLD OF WORK – they were the lessons taken by Mr Vernon. Choose something that you did in these lessons and then answer these questions.

   a) Explain what happened in the lesson.

   b) Do you think it was connected with anything you do in other lessons?

   c) Do you think it was connected with anything that happens outside school?

   d) What do you think you learnt from the lesson?

   e) What do the words 'world of work' mean to you?

THANK YOU VERY MUCH FOR YOUR HELP

---

† Whitehead, D. J. *ed. Economics Education: A Second Handbook for Economics Teachers*, Heinemann Educational, 1986.
‡ Riley, C. *Megatronics*, Longman, 1987.
§ Economics Association, *Understanding Economics*, Longman, 1985.
‖ This was one of the pilot units for the Economics Education 14–16 Project, parts of which are incorporated into the unit 'Costs and Benefits' from *Understanding Economics*.

A third year girl's response to the questionnaire

What did you enjoy about core?
   '. . . listening to tapes, games, doing worksheets, working in groups, auctions.'

Why did you enjoy these things?
  'Because it was not all writing, and we did a lot
  of practical work.'
What did you not enjoy about core?
  'Too much writing, working by yourself.'
Why did you not enjoy these things?

  'Because when you work by yourself you do not
  have so many ideas as if you work in a group.'
*Do you think it was connected with anything you do in
other lessons?*
  'It was connected by working in groups.'

Details of organizations involved in the seminar

Banking Information Service

Banking Information Service is sponsored by 11 banks and seeks to form working partnerships between those banks and secondary education throughout England, Scotland and Wales. It seeks to do that through each of four inter-related areas of activity:

- Careers service: working with the network of careers officers and teachers
- speaker service: some 230 bankers around England and Wales are attached to BIS and provide a local professional resource for schools either to give talks, or to be involved in activities or projects
- teaching materials: a number of print-based, video and computer disk learning materials are developed with teachers and made available to schools at greatly reduced cost
- projects: these include INSET work with a number of LEAs, teacher attachments, particular curriculum development projects

BIS also acts as a specialist unit providing information to the banks on developments in education. For further information, contact: Brian Stevens, Manager, Banking Information Service, 10 Lombard Street, London EC3V 9AT (tel: 01 626 9386).

BP Educational Relations

This branch of British Petroleum's Government and Public Affairs Department is responsible for coordinating the company's relations with the education system. The aim is to promote a working partnership between industry and education based on mutual understanding and benefit. At the secondary level activities include a School Link Scheme based on major BP sites, a support programme for educational development projects (e.g. the Economic Awareness Teacher Training Pro-gramme) and the production of a wide range of educational resource materials. Enquiries to: Mr. C. L. Marsden, Manager, Educational Relations, British Petroleum Company plc, Britannic House, Moor Lane, London EC2Y 9BU.

The Centre for the Study of Comprehensive Schools

The CSCS is a national organization for all those who have an interest in the quality of education received by 94% of our children who attend comprehensive schools. It exists to promote good educational practice, to encourage research and to build a national network for disseminating information to all those concerned with comprehensive schools.

CSCS promotes good educational practice through:

- the CSCS databank – of interesting developments and practice taking place in schools
- regional networks – 20 regional groups act as centres for sharing experiences and exchange of ideas
- publications – CSCS produces broadsheets on topics of current interest to meet the needs of teachers, parents, industrialists and others for brief, clear guides on topics of current concern
- research – CSCS promotes research by practising teachers seconded by their LEA as Centre Fellows (the outcomes of their research are published by CSCS)
- industrial links – CSCS maintains strong links with industry and obtains funding from industry and commerce
- small-scale curriculum development projects – pump priming money to fund practical curriculum development work in schools (this has been provided by BP and more recently by British Telecom, Esso, IBM and J. Sainsbury)

Enquiries to: Centre for the Study of Comprehensive Schools, Wentworth College, University of York, Heslington, York YO1 5DD (tel: 0904 414137).

Economic Awareness Teacher Training Programme (EcATT)

EcATT is a partnership between industry and commerce, LEAs, central government and higher education. It aims to meet the long-term training needs of teachers, Local Authority coordinators, advisory teachers and others involved in the implementation of economic awareness programmes in schools and colleges.

EcATT's training and development role is designed:

- to help LEAs and schools/colleges to identify their training needs in such areas as the management of change related to economic awareness/business studies, the management of student-centred learning, the development of curriculum units/modules for teaching purposes and student assessment
- to help LEAs and schools/colleges to plan and implement INSET activities (school based/teacher centre based/university based) designed to meet needs and to utilize and develop existing expertise within LEAs
- to help LEAs and schools/colleges to evaluate the outcomes of INSET
- to inform LEAs and schools/colleges of developments in a growing network of curriculum development activities in economic awareness

EcATT is funded by contributions from the Banking Information Service, British Petroleum plc, Department of Trade and Industry, Department of Education and Science, Manpower Services Commission and Unilever plc.

EcATT has offices at the University of London Institute of Education and the Department of Education, University of Manchester:
University of London, Institute of Education, 20 Bedford Way, London WC1H 0AL (tel: 01 636 1500 Ext. 308 or 403) (TTNS No. TCD 100233)

Department of Education, University of Manchester, Oxford Road, Manchester M13 9PL, (tel: 061 273 4452) (TTNS No. TCD 100175).

The Economics Association

The Economics Association represents teachers of Economics and related subjects in schools and colleges throughout the UK and provides its members with the professional support and backup they need in the classroom. It aims to encourage and promote the teaching and study of economics and related subjects within a broadly based curriculum.

The association has 16 local branches and numerous activity centres and is governed by an elected council. A full-time officer coordinates the association's administration.

Members look to the association for the practical help and advice it provides through branches and national activities and the quarterly journal *Economics*. Branches run their own programmes of local events. The association publishes, both by itself and in conjunction with commercial publishers, a number of titles, many of which are available to members at special prices.

The association is also actively involved in curriculum development and maintains close links with the DES, HMI, SEC, SCDC, examining boards and commercial publishers. Its annual three-day residential conference is a forum for the discussion of important issues, enabling members to exchange views with colleagues in the educational world at large.

Further details about the association and its activities can be obtained from: Economics Association, Maxwelton House, 41–43 Boltro Road, Haywards Heath, West Sussex RH16 1BJ (tel: 0444 455084).

Economics Education 14–16 Project

The project is sponsored by the Economics Association and was established in 1976. Its central purpose is to contribute to the extension of economics education within the general education of all pupils in secondary schools, and to this end it has:

- developed and published exemplar curriculum materials, incorporating guidance to teachers and pupil materials
- incorporated these materials into a dissemination programme in cooperation with institutions, LEAs and other bodies, and evaluated the outcome
- initiated a programme to increase public awareness of the needs to expand economics education within general education

The project's materials, *Understanding Economics*, published in 1985 by Longman, have already had a far-reaching effect on classroom practice in UK schools. Further details can be obtained from: The Economics Education 14–16 Project, Department of Education, University of Manchester, Manchester M13 9PL (tel: 061 273 4494).

The Geography, Schools and Industry Project

The GSIP was established by the Georgraphical Association in 1984. It currently involves geography teachers in many schools in LEA-based groups. The project's main aims are to identify the contributions of geography teachers in helping pupils aged 11–16 to increase their economic understanding, and to involve geography teachers, together with other adults, in the development, evaluation and dissemination of activities designed to increase such understanding. Teachers are supported in their work in changing their curriculum to meet the needs of their own pupils in their local school context by the project's central team and by a broad network of coordinators, advisers, industrialists and others. A series of six Project Papers is available and a Teachers' Handbook containing guidelines for curriculum planning, sample schemes of work and pupil writing will be published in 1988. Enquiries to: Geography, Schools and Industry Project, University of Oxford Department of Educational Studies, 15 Norham Gardens, Oxford OX2 6PY (tel: 0865 274024).

The Industry/Education Unit, Department of Trade and Industry

The IEU is responsible for encouraging links between industry and education at all levels, including schools and further and higher education. It also works to encourage the take-up of new technology in the education system, and to promote enterprise, understanding of wealth creation activities, and economic awareness. Enquiries to: Stephen Colville, Industry/Education Unit, Department of Trade and Industry, Bridge Place, 89 Eccleston Square, London SW1V 1PT (tel: 01 212 0681).

The Northern Ireland Council for Educational Development

NICED is the main advisory body on the curriculum and educational technology in Northern Ireland. NICED carries out development work, and on the basis of conclusions reached from that work provides advice to the Department of Education for Northern Ireland, schools and institutions of further education. Enquiries to: Northern Ireland Council for Educational Development, NICED Centre, Stranmillis College, Belfast BT9 5DY (tel: 0232 682414).

The School Curriculum Development Committee

SCDC's role is to 'promote education by supporting curriculum development relevant to the needs of schools in England and Wales'. Its main tasks are:

- to inform itself of curriculum development work being undertaken by other persons or bodies
- to review and evaluate such work with particular reference to the likely future needs of the

school education system, and thereby to identify what further curriculum development work
is, in the committee's judgement, essential

- to undertake, and to assist others to undertake,
such essential curriculum development work
- to disseminate, and to promote the dissemination of, the results of curriculum development
work whether undertaken by itself or others

Enquiries to: 'Educating for Economic Awareness'
Project, SCDC, Newcombe House, 45 Notting Hill
Gate, London W11 3JB (tel: 01 229 1234).

Economic awareness bibliography

Atkinson, G.B.J. *ed. Teaching Economics*, 3rd edn., Heinemann Educational, 1985.

DES, *Economic Understanding in the School Curriculum – Report by HM Inspectorate*, 1987.

DES, *The Curriculum from 5–16*, HMSO, 1985.

Economic Awareness for All Across the Curriculum, TRIST Paper of National Interest, MSC, 1987.

Economic Literacy: An Approach for Schools, Northern Ireland Council for Educational Development, 1985.

Economics: A Question of Choice, BBC, 1985.

Economics Association, 'Economic awareness in the school curriculum' , in *Economics*, Autumn 1985.

Economics Association, *Understanding Economics*, Longman, 1985.

HMI, *Curriculum 11–16*, HMSO, 1977.

Hodkinson, S.R. and Thomas, L.M. *Economic Literacy in the General Curriculum 14–18*, University of London Institute of Education, 1984.

Hodkinson, S.R. and Whitehead, D.J. *eds. Economics Education Research and Development Issues*, Longman, 1986.

Hurd, S.J. *ed. Computers in Economics and Business Education*, Heinemann Educational, 1987.

Kirby, K. 'Economic awareness – the state of the art', in *Education*, 9 May 1986.

Lawton, D. *School Curriculum Planning*, Routledge & Kegan Paul, 1986.

Robinson, T. K. and Wilson, R. D. *eds. Extending Economics within the Curriculum*, Routledge & Kegan Paul, 1974.

Scottish Industry/Education Committee, *Guidelines on Economic Awareness*, Consultative Committee on the Curriculum, March 1987.

Social Education: Understanding Economics, BBC, 1986.

Whitehead, D. J. *ed. Economics Education: A Second Handbook for Economics Teachers*, Heinemann Educational, 1986.

Index

OLCHFA SCHOOL
SKETTY
SWANSEA